A GARDEN ENCLOSED

A HISTORICAL STUDY AND EVALUATION OF THE
FORM OF CHURCH GOVERNMENT PRACTISED BY THE
PARTICULAR BAPTISTS IN THE 17TH AND 18TH
CENTURIES

About the author

Boon-Sing Poh was born in Malaysia in 1954. Brought up in a pagan background, he was saved by God's grace through faith in Jesus Christ while studying in the United Kingdom. He returned to Malaysia to become a lecturer in a university for six years, founded the first Reformed Baptist Church in the country in 1983, and was imprisoned for his faith from 1987 to 1988 for a period of 325 days. He is pastor emeritus of Damansara Reformed Baptist Church (DRBC) in Kuala Lumpur, a contented husband, a thankful father of four sons, and a happy grandfather. He earned the PhD degree in Electronics Engineering from the University of Liverpool, UK, the Diploma in Religious Study from Cambridge University, UK, and the PhD degree in Theology from North-West University, SA.

A GARDEN ENCLOSED

A HISTORICAL STUDY AND EVALUATION OF THE
FORM OF CHURCH GOVERNMENT PRACTISED BY THE
PARTICULAR BAPTISTS IN THE 17TH AND 18TH
CENTURIES[1]

B S POH

PUBLISHED BY GOOD NEWS ENTERPRISE

[1]Thesis submitted for the degree Doctor of Philosophy in Church and Dogma History at the Potchefstroom Campus of the North-West University SA, in co-operation with Greenwich School of Theology UK. 2012

A GARDEN ENCLOSED:
A historical study and evaluation of the form of church government practised by the Particular Baptists in the 17th and 18th centuries

Copyright ©Boon-Sing Poh, 2013

ISBN: 978-983-9180-20-6

First published: 2013
Second imprint: March 2014 (A sharper font was used, leading to slight changes in pagination.)
Third imprint: August 2016 ([from 1663] added on p. 220.)
This imprint: September 2025 (Additions in square brackets [ ] on pp. 161, 199, 206)

Published by:

GOOD NEWS ENTERPRISE, 52 Jalan SS 21/2,
Damansara Utama, 47400 Petaling Jaya, Malaysia.
www.DamansaraRBC.com; www.gospelhighway.net

Printed by:
Kindle Direct Publishing, an Amazon company, United States of America.
Typeset by the author using TeXworks, the memoir class.

Dedicated to my dear wife,

Goody,

who has stood by me

through thick and thin.

"Many daughters have done well, but you excel them all."

(Prov. 31:29)

Contents

Abstract

This thesis is a historical study and evaluation of the form of church government practised by the Particular Baptists of the 17th and 18th centuries, from the years 1650 to 1750. This study is based on confessional statements, the ecclesiological literature, and the extant church books of the Particular Baptists. It is shown that the Particular Baptists practised a definitive form of church government known traditionally as Independency, similar to that expounded by John Owen, minus infant baptism.

Under the principle of the autonomy of the church the Particular Baptists practised believer's baptism, an explicit church membership, and upheld covenant theology. Under the principle of the headship of Christ, they practised the separation of church and state, upheld the divine right of the magistrate, and also believed in the liberty of conscience. Under the principle of rule by elders the majority of the Particular Baptists practised a plurality of elders in which there was a distinction made between the roles of the pastor or minister and the ruling elders, although they occupy the same basic office of rule. However, deviation from a plural eldership took place, leading to the single-pastor-and-multiple-deacons situation, accompanied by the disappearance of ruling elders and the practice of congregational democracy in governance. This arrangement is characteristic of modern Congregationalism. Under the principle of the communion of churches the regional associations of churches accomplished much good, while a number of issues remained unresolved, including open and closed communion, congregational hymn singing, and the training of ministers. In the final chapter, the study attempts to resolve some ecclesiological issues controverted among Reformed Baptists today by applying the lessons learned from the Particular Baptists.

To the Particular Baptists, Independency was the *jus divinum* (divinely ordained) form of church government used by God as the vehicle to carry out the Great Commission with a view to establishing biblically ordered churches, which upheld the 1689 Baptist Confession of Faith. These three components of church life – mission-mindedness, biblical church order, and the 1689 Confession of Faith – arose from the thorough biblicism of the Particular Baptists.

Key words: Keys of the kingdom, church government, polity, Reformed, Particular Baptist, 1689 Baptist Confession, *jus divinum*, Independency, Congregationalism, elders

Preface

10pts In 1995 the present writer's book "The Keys of the Kingdom: A Study on the Biblical Form of Church Government" was published. The book puts forward the Independency propounded by John Owen, infant baptism excepted, as the *jus divinum* (divinely ordained) form of church government. This writer does not claim to have perfectly understood nor expressed everything correctly, for, as with all truths, there is always room for improvement as more light comes from the study of the Bible. The true significance of the book needs to be appreciated. To the knowledge of this writer, no one has written a comprehensive book expounding Independency since John Owen's book "The True Nature of a Gospel Church and Its Government", published in 1689. Ralph Wardlaw published a comprehensive book entitled "Congregational Independency" in 1864 but his view did not exactly coincide with that of Owen. A number of smaller books focusing on church discipline or church order have been published, which are not the same as a comprehensive treatment of the Independent form of church government.

The book "The Keys of the Kingdom" was essentially a biblical study on the form of church government, supported by reference to John Owen's writings and the 1689 Baptist Confession of Faith. The author interacted with the Presbyterian writers of the 19th and 20th centuries, whose books were heavily relied upon by those Reformed Baptists who have been advocating a system of eldership which might be called the "Absolute Equality view". A number of those Reformed Baptists reacted to the book strongly, but have not been able to convince the author of the correctness of their view and the wrongness of his. With great reluctance, he has responded to their criticism in a book, "Against Parity" (Poh, 2006). He regarded the matter closed at that time, preferring to focus more on the positive work of preaching and planting churches. He was made aware of an academic attempt to interact with his book, but chose to ignore it, believing that his book, "The Keys of the Kingdom" would speak for itself. That work, of course, was the PhD thesis of James Renihan. In recent days, Renihan's thesis has been quoted quite widely by others. It recently has been published as a book, making it more easily available.

This writer has had the opportunity to teach in a number of seminaries and Bible colleges in Indonesia, Myanmar and Nepal. Some of these institutions are government-accredited, and require that the teachers be those who have a post-graduate degree in theology. In order to facilitate teaching in these institutions, he finally decided to embark on earning a second PhD, this time in theology. This, providentially, provides him the opportunity to follow up his study on the church government of the Particular Baptists, and to interact with Renihan on an academic level. The present thesis will supplement his book "The Keys of the Kingdom" by providing strong historical support from primary sources. Most pastors, seminarians, and serious Christians would find the reading of "The Keys of the Kingdom" sufficient to give a clear idea of that form of church government called Independency. However, those who follow through with a reading of this thesis will be considerably helped towards forming a personal conviction of the *jus divinum* form of church government. Needless to say, this thesis may be read with profit without the prior reading of "The Keys of the Kingdom".

The writer takes this opportunity to thank the following:

(i)   The Greenwich School of Theology, which facilitated this PhD programme with the North-West University. Mrs. Peg Evans has been the indefatigable administrator, monitoring his progress and liaising between him and the promoters.

(ii) The staff of North-West University (Potchefstroom Campus) for their roles in this programme, including Mrs. H. Dreyer, Ms. Tienie Buys, Professor A le R Du Plooy, Professor B. Zuiddam, and Professor J. Smit. Professors Zuiddam and Smit supervised this project.

(iii) Ms. Emily Burgoyne of Regent's Park College, University of Oxford, for help in procuring manuscript materials from the

Angus Library.

(iv) Ms. Sue Hourigan of the Berkshire Record Office, Reading, for making available photographed pages of certain church books.

(v) The archivists of the London Metropolitan Archives for providing copies of pages from certain church record books.

(vi) Dr. Richard Smart of the Bedfordshire Historical Record Society for providing "Some Early Nonconformist Church Books" edited by H. G. Tibbutt.

(vii) Dr. Roger Hayden of the Baptist Historical Society for books and copies of the Association Records of the Particular Baptists.

(viii) The brethren of the Grace Reformed Evangelical Church, Hong Kong, for their encouragement at the beginning of this project. Brother Daniel Lo provided broadband internet facility while Brother Joseph Chan loaned books.

(ix) The members of the Damansara Reformed Baptist Church and the Subang Jaya Reformed Baptist Church for their support in various ways.

(x) Various other individuals who have contributed in one way or another towards making this project possible and enjoyable.

(xi) Thomas Nelson, Inc. for quotations from the New King James version of the Bible. Unless otherwise indicated, all quotations are from this version.

The writer's wife, Goody, and their four sons and daughter-in-law have played their roles in helping and encouraging their "old man" in this project. Yeh Tze and Yeh Chuin, based in the United Kingdom and the United States of America, respectively, were able to procure copies of critical manuscripts and books for him.

The present writer, alone, is to be held responsible for this work and the views expressed. In his book "The Keys of the Kingdom" he focused on issues, and not on personalities. In the present work, his interactions with those with whom he disagrees are done solely with the aim of extricating truth from error, and are not meant as personal attacks. It is his prayer that the Triune God would bless this work to many who harbour a charitable spirit towards this undeserving sinner.

B.S. Poh
2012

One

INTRODUCTION

1.1   BACKGROUND

Any ecclesial grouping may be characterized by its distinctive doctrine, practice, history and/or confession of faith. The Particular Baptists of the 17th and 18th centuries in England and Wales (and extending into Ireland, Scotland, and North America) have long been recognized as a distinct ecclesial grouping different from the mainstream churches of the time, namely, the Anglican Church, the Presbyterian Church, and the Independent Nonconformist congregations. They were also distinct from the sizable grouping known as the General Baptists, and from the sects such as the Quakers and Seekers. One way of identifying an ecclesial grouping is to determine its form of church government. Were the Particular Baptists prelatical, presbyterial, or congregational in their form of church government? Was there an identifiable form of church government which they practised? Strangely, this aspect of Particular Baptist characterization has not been studied.

The purpose of this chapter is to provide the necessary historical background for an appreciation of the ecclesiology of the Particular Baptists, and thereby to identify the problem that will be studied in this thesis. The aim and associated objectives of this study are specified, followed by the central theoretical argument and the methodology that will be used.

1.2   THE 1689 CONFESSION

There are three views of Baptist origins – those of successionism, Anabaptist root, and Puritan-Separatist descent (Haykin, 1996). The first view argues for an organic succession of Baptist churches extending all the way back to John the Baptist (see, for example, Cramp, 1868; Carroll, 1931). The major weakness of this view is that it lacks strong evidential support (McGoldrick, 1994; Patterson, 1969). The second view argues that Baptist origins may be traced back to the sixteenth-century Anabaptist movement in Europe and its offshoots in England (see, for example, Payne, 1956 and Estep, 1993). Because of the political tyranny of Philip II of the Netherlands, as many as 30,000 Dutch Anabaptists were known to have settled in England as religious immigrants in the 1550s (Campbell, 1892: 1: 488-489; Troeltsch, 1931: 706). The Baptists of the seventeenth century, however, clearly distanced themselves from the Anabaptists, as seen in their confessions of faith. Furthermore, they baptised by immersion while the Anabaptists baptised by affusion. The third view maintains that the Baptists emerged from the English Puritan and Separatist movements of the late sixteenth to the mid-seventeenth centuries (see, for example, Whitley, 1924; White, 1971: 162-169; Manley, 1987). The third view appears to enjoy wide acceptance currently, although some degree of contact with the Anabaptists before the adoption of believer's baptism by the Particular Baptists has been acknowledged (Stassen, 1962; White, 1967; Haykin, 1996: 29-30; Cross, 2010: 15).

While the relation to the Anabaptists has been a matter of debate, the immediate origins of the first General Baptist and Particular Baptist churches are not in dispute. General Baptists were so-called because of their belief in a general atonement, in keeping with their Arminian soteriology. Their beginning may be traced to Thomas Helwys (c. 1575-1616), who founded the first Baptist church in England in 1612, after breaking away from the English Separatist congregation of John Smyth (c. 1570-1612) in Amsterdam (White, 1982-84: 76-77, 186-187). Smyth had moved successively from being an ordained minister of the Church of England to starting a separatist congregation in the town of Gainsborough, to adopting believer's baptism while in Amsterdam, to abandoning Calvinism in favour of Arminianism, and to seeking union with the Waterlander Mennonite church (Haykin, 1996: 21-25). The Particular Baptists, on the other hand, derived their name from the belief in the doctrine of particular redemption, consistent with the Calvinism which they held in common with the Reformed and Puritan churches of the day. Their historical origin may be traced to the semi-separatist church founded in 1616 by Henry Jacob (1563-1624), which became known as the Jacob-Lathrop-Jessey (J-L-J) church, after its successive pastors (White, 1966: 31-32). This church refused to completely repudiate the Church of England as a false church, although certain rigorist tendencies began to manifest themselves among some members about 1630 (White, 1968b: 572, 590). The first Particular Baptist churches evolved from the J-L-J Church between 1633 and 1638, while continuing to have links with various Independent congregations (White, 1968b: 572; Belyea, 2007: 40-67).

As the Baptist congregations grew in number and prominence it was perhaps inevitable that numerous false accusations were leveled at them, one of which was that they were Anabaptists. The reason for this was to insinuate quite deliberately that these English dissenters were extremists just like the fanatical Anabaptists of Münster who were put down by government forces in 1533-36 (Baylor, 1991). It implied, too, that they were Arminian in doctrine and anti-establishment in their attitude to the state. The consequence was that the Particular Baptists found it necessary to defend themselves against such false accusations and to distance themselves from the beliefs of the General Baptists. In 1644 seven existing congregations in London issued a confession of faith signed by fifteen men. On the title page of the Confession were these words:

> The CONFESSION OF FAITH Of those CHURCHES which are commonly (though falsly [sic]) called ANABAPTISTS; Presented to the view of all that feare [sic] God, to examine by the touchstone of the Word of Truth: As likewise for the taking off those aspersions which are frequently both in Pulpit and Print, (although unjustly) cast upon them.

The Confession of Faith was republished a number of times. This went a long way in clearing misrepresentation of the Particular Baptists and allaying distrust against them. Kiffin, et al. (1692) attested to the beneficial effects of this Confession when they corrected Benjamin Keach, who had claimed erroneously that the Particular Baptists of the 1640s were opposed to churches supporting their ministers:

> Which Confession of Faith was five times printed in the year 1644, and from that, to the year 1651, without the least alteration of any one Article of what was printed: which Confession gave such general satisfaction to most Christians of all sorts of differing Perswasions [sic] from us, that it took off from many that Prejudice and Offence that was formerly taken by them against our Profession.

The Particular Baptists thus showed themselves to be standing in the orthodoxy of the Reformed tradition. The Confession became known as the *First London Baptist Confession*, or simply the *1644 Confession*.

Back-tracking a little, it is to be noted that the Reformation had come to England during the reign of Henry VIII (r. 1509-1547). This was followed by the reign of his son Edward VI (r. 1509-1547), and then that of his daughter Elizabeth I (r. 1559-1603). By the time of Elizabeth, the church was "Calvinistic in theology, Erastian in Church order and government, and largely mediaeval in liturgy" (Walton, 1946: 59). Eventually, some radical Puritans, despairing of reformation within the Church of England, began to separate from the state church and organise their own Separatist congregations. The most influential of the Separatists was Robert Browne (c. 1550-1633), who published "A Treatise of Reformation without Tarrying for Anie [sic]" in 1582. During the reign of James I (r. 1603-1625), a series of church decrees was issued, requiring complete conformity of all Church of England ministers to the Thirty-Nine Articles, the Book of Common Prayer, and acceptance of the Episcopal form of church government. It was then that John Smyth fled to Amsterdam.

The English Civil War began in 1642, and lasted until 1646. Charles I was eventually beheaded. England and Scotland bound themselves to each other in a civil and religious bond called "the Solemn League and Covenant", and the Commonwealth was established under the guidance of Oliver Cromwell (1599-1658). The Westminster Assembly met in 1643 to draw up a confession of faith for the nation. The divines who met at this assembly came from all over Scotland and England. They were mostly Presbyterians. Some were Anglicans, while a few were Independents (Reid, 1983). The strict Presbyterians, especially those from Scotland, wanted the Presbyterian model of government to be imposed on every parish in the nation, with no toleration allowed to those with other convictions about church government. The Westminster Confession, drawn up and finally published in 1647, was essentially a Presbyterian document. The attempt to establish a Presbyterian-type national church, however, did not materialise (Heatherington, 1853: 135-199).

Although the Independents in the Westminster Assembly were few in number, they included some of the most able and respected men of the time. Moreover, they represented a considerable body of opinion existing beyond the assembly, and particularly in the parliamentary army. The nucleus was a group of five men who became known as "the Dissenting Brethren". All had been exiles in Holland, including Thomas Goodwin, Philip Nye, Sidrach Simpson, Jeremiah Burroughs and William Bridge (Neal, 1822: 255-256). In January 1644 they produced "An Apologeticall [sic] Narration" (Goodwin, *et al.* 1643). This was in effect an appeal to Parliament in defence of their dissenting position.

From about 1645 to 1653 the Presbyterians were in the ascendant (Wright, 2006). However, from about 1653 to the end of the Commonwealth period the Independents gained control. Parliament was abolished and Cromwell was officially installed as Protector on 16 December 1653 (Firth, 1934: 334), with the title "His Highness, Lord Protector of the Commonwealth of England, Scotland, and Ireland, and of the dominions thereunto belonging" (Ivimey, 1811, Vol. I: 220). Cromwell himself was nominally an Independent (Firth, 1934: 145-146), who soon realized that the "the new presbyter was but old priest writ large" (Firth, 1934: 140; Blauvelt, 1937: 113), a maxim borrowed from Milton (1823: 194). Firth (1934: 362) said of Cromwell: "Thanks to him, Nonconformity had time to take root and to grow so strong in England that the storm which followed the Restoration had no power to root it up." Out of political expediency, Cromwell reorganised the national church and appointed local commissioners, called Triers, in every county to remove scandalous and inefficient ministers and schoolmasters within its limits (Firth, 1934: 351-352). The Triers were drawn from the Presbyterians, the Independents and the Baptists. This was to be a cause of contention among the Particular Baptists, for some of them had no scruples about being appointed a Trier while many were against it, including those who held to Fifth Monarchy views. The Fifth Monarchy men were hostile to anything that resembled a monarchy or an established church (Firth, 1934: 337). Cromwell's Secretary for State and head of intelligence, Thurloe (Birch, 1742: 620-629) reported that "the Anabaptisticall [sic.] ministers preach constantly with very great bitternes [sic] against the present government, but especially against his excellency, calling him the man of sin, the old dragon, and many other scripture ill names".

During the period of Independent ascendancy in England, various extreme and heretical sects flourished especially in the army. Quite properly, the orthodox Independents were anxious to distinguish themselves from all such. In 1658, ministers of Independent persuasion throughout the land were summoned to a synod at the Savoy Palace in London. A committee of distinguished divines, including Thomas Goodwin, John Owen, Philip Nye, William Bridge, Joseph Caryl and William Greenhill, was appointed to draw up a confession. All except John Owen (1616-1683) had been present at the Westminster Assembly. Apart from being one of the chief draftsmen, Owen was also assigned to write the preface to the Declaration (Toon, 1971: 103-122).

In the 1640s, John Cotton, a leading Independent in New England, had expounded and defended Independency in two books, "The Keys of the Kingdom of Heaven" (Cotton, 1644) and "The Way Of The Churches Of Christ In New England" (Cotton, 1645). Cotton's book, "The Keys", appeared in London a few months before the publication of the 1644 Confession by the seven Particular Baptist congregations. The appearance of Cotton's "The Keys", with its clear and strong emphasis on inter-church fellowship, confirmed the thinking of the Particular Baptists, and spurred them to develop the regional associations peculiar to them (White, 1968b: 587-588). Cotton's book, together with "An Apologeticall Narration", published by the dissenting brethren within the Westminster Assembly, was instrumental in changing John Owen from Presbyterianism to Independency (Toon, 1971: 18-19, 27).

In 1643 Owen published a short book entitled "The Duty Of Pastors And People Distinguished" (Owen, 1976, Vol. 13) to vindicate the Presbyterian view of church polity against Episcopacy on the one hand, and extreme Congregationalism on the other. From 1646 (Toon, 1971: 28) he began to write a number of tracts and books in defence of Independency (Owen, 1976, Vols. 13, 15 and 16). In 1667 he published "A Brief Introduction To The Worship Of God And Discipline Of The Churches Of The New Testament" (Owen, 1976, Vol. 15). At the time many dissenting congregations were springing up, and this book, which came to be known as "The Independents' Catechism", was a great help to their cause (Owen, 1976, Vol. 15: 44). Finally, Owen wrote "The True Nature Of The Gospel Church", which was published posthumously in 1689 (Owen, 1976, Vol. 16). This was for many years regarded as the definitive exposition of Independency (Toon, 1971: 164). Although John Owen did not set foot on American shores, his ideas on Independency were to exert tremendous influence there as well (Bearman, 2005). Describing the relationship between the English government and the New England colonies when the Commonwealth began, Firth (1934: 384) stated that "the intellectual sympathy of the two was never stronger". Owen's influence on both sides of the Atlantic was enhanced by the fact that he was appointed the Vice-Chancellor of Oxford University by Cromwell in 1651 (Firth, 1934: 348). Anthony Wood, the noted eighteenth century historian of Oxford, declared John Owen "the prince, the oracle, the metropolitan of Independency" (Wood, 4: 15).

The confession of the Savoy Assembly of which Owen was a chief architect, called "the Savoy Declaration of Faith and Order", was in most respects identical to the Westminster Confession (Heatherington, 1853: 271). The really original part of the Savoy Declaration was the "Platform of Church Polity". Here, the distinctive views of the Independents were set forth, which Murray (1965: 275) summarizes under three points:

(i) Full spiritual power and authority resides in a particular local congregation.

(ii) The essence of the call of a minister is his election by the congregation. Formal ordination is a ratification of this, and is normally to be performed by the eldership of the local congregation.

(iii) Synods are expedient for the discussion and resolution of difficulties, but they have no power over churches and individuals. The system of standing synods subordinate to one another is rejected.

After the death of Oliver Cromwell in 1658, his son Richard took over as Lord Protector. His incompetence as a ruler resulted in the restoration of Charles II to the throne in 1660. The Anglican system was re-established. The "Clarendon Code" came into effect between the years 1661 and 1665. This included four parliamentary acts bringing extreme pressures upon non-Anglicans. In 1662 the first Act of Uniformity was ratified by the sovereign. This required everybody to conform as worshipping adherents of the established church. Among other matters, ministers were required to be ordained in the episcopal manner, while the Prayer Book was the standard for public worship. Many of the Puritans refused to conform, with the result that two thousand ministers were ejected from the Anglican Church. Many of these men attached themselves to the Baptists and the Independents, thus strengthening greatly the cause of Nonconformity (Neal, 1755: 293-322).

The Particular Baptists felt the need to identity themselves with the large body of Calvinistic non-Anglicans. The 1644 Confession was by then a document not well-known. The *Second London Baptist Confession of Faith* was, therefore, issued in 1677. In the preface of the Confession were found these words made in reference to the 1644 Confession (Underhill, 1854: 173):

> And forasmuch as that Confession is not now commonly to be had, and also that many others have since embraced the same truth which is owned therein, it was judged necessary by us to join together in giving a testimony to the world of our firm adhering to those wholesome principles, by the publication of this which is now in your hand.

This confession was based largely on the Westminster Confession and the Savoy Declaration, "to convince all that we have no itch to clog religion with new words, but do readily acquiesce in that form of sound words, which hath been in consent with the holy scriptures, used by others before us". The second edition of the Confession appeared in 1688.

Upon the death of Charles II, his brother the Roman Catholic James II (r. 1685-1688), succeeded to the throne. However, there were those who regarded the Duke of Monmouth, a professing Protestant and an illegitimate son of Charles II, as the rightful heir. A rebellion in support of the Duke was crushed by James with much bloodshed. A groundswell of rebellion followed, leading to the exile of James II to the continent as his regime crumbled. The Glorious Revolution of 1688 put William of Orange on the throne as William III.

In 1689 William III authorized the passing of the Act of Toleration, which gave Dissenters freedom of worship and immunity from persecution, although certain civil restrictions against them remained in force (Grell, Israel & Tyacke, 1991). This was when the Particular Baptists in London called for a General Assembly, in which the Confession of Faith of 1677 was subscribed by thirty-seven leading ministers, representing more than one hundred churches all over England and Wales (Narrative, 1689). This document became known widely as *the Second London Baptist Confession of Faith of 1689*, or simply *the 1689 Confession*, despite the fact that it was first produced in 1677.

1.3 JOHN OWEN'S INDEPENDENCY

Chapter 26 of the 1677/89 Confession, entitled "Of The Church", deviated considerably from the Westminster Confession, relying almost wholly on the "Savoy Platform of Church Polity". This had been appended to the 1658 Savoy Declaration. By adopting the Savoy Platform, with minor amendments, the Particular Baptists were not departing from their commitment to the Independent form of church government expressed in the earlier 1644 Confession. An essential agreement with this confession was asserted in the preface of the 1677/89 documents: "forasmuch as our method and manner of expressing our sentiments in this doth vary from the former (although the substance of the matter is the same)". Being far more complete and better ordered than the earlier confession, that of 1677/89 may be considered as a definitive exposition of the beliefs of the Particular Baptists.

The questions that arise at this point are: "What was the degree of subscription of the Particular Baptists to their Confession of Faith?" and, "What was the extent of their subscription – did it encompass the stated principles of church government?" The answer to the first question is not difficult to find. The preface of the Confession ended with these words, "We shall conclude with our earnest prayer, that the God of all grace will pour out those measures of his Holy Spirit upon us, **that the profession of truth may be accompanied with the sound belief and diligent practice of it by us;** that his name may in all things be glorified, through Jesus Christ our Lord. *Amen.*" [Italics original. Emphasis in bold added]. The notice prefixed to the Confession, and signed by the men representing the churches read as follows (Underhill, 1854: 171):

> We, the ministers and messengers of, and concerned for,
> upwards of one hundred baptized congregations in Eng-
> land and Wales (denying Arminianism), being met to-
> gether in London, from the third of the seventh month
> to the eleventh of the same, 1689, to consider of some
> things that might be for the glory of God, and the good
> of these congregations; have thought meet (for the sat-
> isfaction of all other Christians that differ from us in the
> point of baptism) to recommend to their perusal the Con-
> fession of our Faith, printed for and sold by *Mr. John Har-*
> *ris*, at the *Harrow* in the *Poultry*. **Which Confession we**
> **own, as containing the doctrine of our faith and prac-**
> **tice; and do desire that the members of our churches**
> **respectively do furnish themselves therewith.** [Italics
> original. Emphasis in bold added.]

The words speak for themselves. The subscribing churches had every
intention to hold to the Confession of Faith. It will be shown in the
subsequent chapters of this thesis that the Confession of Faith was
constantly appealed to with regard to the doctrine and practice of
the churches.

What of the second question – did subscription encompass the
articles on church government? The above quotation also provides
the answer. The Confession they owned contained the doctrine of
their "faith and practice", the latter of which would include largely
their church polity. Since the chapter on church polity had been
borrowed, with slight amendments, from the Savoy Platform, one
would expect that the Particular Baptists and the paedobaptist Independents shared virtually the same form of church government,
baptism excepted. A lengthy Appendix on baptism was appended
to the Confession of Faith (Appendix, 1677). Unlike the Westminster Confession and the Savoy Declaration, which encompassed only
doctrine, with the articles on church order placed in separate documents, the 1689 Confession places the fifteen articles on church
order in Chapter 26 of the thirty-two chapters. To the Particular
Baptists, church polity was as much the teaching of the Bible as was
church doctrine. It will be shown in Chapter 7 of this thesis that the
Particular Baptists believed in a *jus divinum* form of church govern-

ment, which they attempted to establish from Scripture, consistent with their belief in the Reformation principle of *sola scriptura*.

While the Independents, especially John Owen, wrote extensively on church government (notably, Owen, 1976, Vols. 13, 15 & 16), the Particular Baptists were kept busy planting churches in the midst of much opposition. Unlike the Independents, who were persecuted together with the Baptists for part of the time, the latter were persecuted most of the time. The pastors were constantly in and out of prison. Relief came only with the Act of Toleration of 1689, which allowed Nonconformists their own places of worship and their own teachers and preachers, subject to acceptance of certain oaths of allegiance. The Baptists were constantly debating with the Episcopalians and Presbyterians over the validity of a national church and of infant baptism. They had also to contend among themselves over a host of issues, including whether communion should be "closed" or "open" to unbaptised believers, whether ministers should accept government support, and whether the government of Cromwell should be supported when he dissolved parliament and was declared Protector. Apart from a treatise by Benjamin Keach (1697), and a few similar ones across the Atlantic, no significant work espousing the form of church government practised by the Particular Baptists appeared until that of Ralph Wardlaw (1864). The Particular Baptists seemed content to allow John Owen to speak for them as far as church government was concerned. All they needed to do was to strengthen the area where they thought Owen's Independency weak, namely the baptism of believers by immersion, and its concomitants – a task which they accomplished through their writings and in public debates (see, for example, Tombes, 1641, 1645, 1652 & 1659; Knollys, 1645 & 1646; Richardson, 1645; King, 1656; Spilsbury, 1652). These two characteristics of the Particular Baptists of the time had been noted by the eminent scholar, Joseph Angus (1895: 183-190): "Two peculiarities distinguish the Baptist history of the seventeenth century. It was the age of public disputation; and ministers devoted a large amount of time to evangelistic work."

That the Particular Baptists were practising an Independency essentially the same as that of the Savoy Platform may be seen in the observation of Isaac Watts (1674-1748). Watts was a hymn-writer, preacher and educationist of the Independent persuasion. He was also a paedobaptist. As a well-respected minister during the period immediately after the death of John Owen, and the re-affirmation of the 1677 Confession by the Particular Baptists in 1689, he must be considered to have been a competent judge of the church situation of his day. In 1700 he wrote to his brother, Enoch, outlining the difference between the various opinions held at that time. Concerning the "Anabaptists", which was a reference to the Particular Baptists, he wrote (Milner, 1845: 193):

> They differ not from Calvinists in their doctrine, unless in the article of infant baptism. They generally deny any children to be in the covenant of grace, and so deny the seal of the covenant to them. They deny baptism by sprinkling to be real and true baptism. In church government [they were] generally Independents.

According to Isaac Watts, "the generalities of Independents follow rather Dr. Owen's notions ..." (Milner, 1845: 197). It has been noted above that Owen was the doyen of Independency in his days and for a long while after that. If it is asked, "Which version of Independency did the Particular Baptists practise?" one would have to say it was John Owen's version, minus the practice of infant baptism. This conclusion is based on the facts that:

i The church government of the 1689 Confession of Faith of the Particular Baptists was based on the Platform of Church Polity of the Savoy Declaration of the paedobaptist Independents, of which John Owen was a chief framer.

ii Isaac Watts, a highly esteemed and competent judge of the ecclesiastical situation of his days (Watts, 1700; Fountain, 1974), had testified that the "Anabaptists" were Independents.

iii It is known that the Particular Baptists continued to have close interactions with the paedobaptist Independents from the time of their emergence between 1633 and 1638 (White, 1968b: 572). In tracing the origins of the Baptists, Manley (1987: 41) noted that the Separatists were already practising a form of church government that was close to the believers' church ideal, a reference to Independency.

Owen's view of Independency, however, was not necessarily complete or consistent. This was on account of his retention of infant

baptism – a conclusion drawn from the federal theology of the Presbyterians (Owen, 1976, Vol. 16: 22-23). The Particular Baptists
were driven to their views of baptism and church polity because of
their commitment to the Reformation principle of *sola scriptura*. In
the Appendix of the 1677/89 Confession they said:

> Let it not therefore be judged of us (because much hath
> been written on this subject, and yet we continue this our
> practise different from others) that it is out of obstinacy,
> but rather as the truth is, that we do herein according
> to the best of our understandings worship God, out of
> a pure mind yielding obedience to his precept, in that
> method which we take to be most agreeable to the Scrip-
> tures of truth, and primitive practise.

Therefore, for a more complete understanding of the Independency
of the Particular Baptists, one would need to consult their extant
writings and the church records of the 17th and 18th centuries.
Given the limitations necessary to this work, it would not be possible
to investigate all the available material nor to investigate every nu-
ance in belief or practice. Nevertheless, sufficient pertinent material
can be garnered to establish a case, covering the period concerned.

In summary, the sources for an appreciation of Independency,
in descending order of importance, are: Scripture, the 1644 and
1677/89 Confessions of Faith in conjunction with John Owen's writings, and the extant writings and church records of the Particular
Baptists.

1.4 PROBLEM STATEMENT

Many Reformed Baptist churches have sprung up all over the world
in these recent years. Largely, they hold to the 1689 Baptist Confession of Faith and align themselves doctrinally and historically with
the Particular Baptists of the 17th century. They are to be distinguished from the General Baptists, who are Arminian in soteriology
and who practise congregational democracy (Hiscox, 1978: 144-
145; Poh, 2000: 16-17). The Reformed Baptists have been grappling
over a number of issues regarding their ecclesiology. The uninformed
observer might be pardoned for drawing the conclusion that these issues are due simply to the fact that they do not have an ecclesiology

to speak of. A more generous and accurate assessment of the situation is that Reformed Baptists, like their Particular Baptist forebears, are concerned to bring all their belief and practice under the searchlight of Scripture. They are not content to accept traditions that do not bear up under the touchstone of God's word. They are ever restless to pursue a closer conformity to the teaching of their Master, believing with John Robinson (1575-1625) that "the Lord hath more truth yet to break forth out of His Holy word" (Broadbent, 1981: 245).

Broadly speaking, the Reformed Baptists of today claim to be practising an Independency that encompasses certain common characteristics, namely (Poh, 2000): (i) the autonomy of the local church: (ii) the headship of Christ; (ii) rule by elders; (iv) the gathered church; and (v) the communion of churches. Disagreements and uncertainty lie in the areas of: (a) the roles, and nature of the office, of elders relative to those of the minister; (b) the manner of governance relative to the role of the congregation; and (c) the nature and practice of the communion of churches. That these are issues still unresolved may be seen in the recent publications.

Waldron *et al.* (1997) have challenged the view the present writer propounded (Poh, 2000), based on John Owen, that there is a distinction between teaching elders and ruling elders within the same basic office of rule – an office in which "all pastors are elders, but not all elders are pastors". The view of Waldron *et al.* is that there should be a plurality and parity of elders, with no distinction made between the officers, apart from the functions that they perform. Based on a poorly argued case, Renihan (1998: 200, 238) claims that among the Particular Baptists, "The majority of the writers and churches did not recognize a distinct office of ruling elders", while there were "a few churches that made a distinction between ruling and teaching elders". This misleading claim has been picked up by at least one other writer (Newton, 2005: 26). As in Newton (2005), Dever and Alexander (2004, 2005) encourage the recovery of a plurality of elders while remaining ambiguous about the nature of the pastoral ministry *vis-à-vis* the roles of the other elders.

Renihan (1997: 137, 158) also alleges that the present writer claims a rule by elders that is "extensive", instead of being limited by the Word of God. He further claims that in church governance, the Particular Baptists resembled more the Congregationalism of the Brownists than the Independency of Owen, in which the elders "attempt to maintain the rights of the people while carrying out the appointed tasks of the eldership" (Renihan, 1998: 174, 176). In the process of arguing for his case, he confuses the extent over which rule is exercised by the elders with the extent of the elders' power, and the manner by which rule is exercised in the church with the manner by which decisions are arrived at in the church. These matters will be examined in Chapters 4, 5 and 7 of this thesis. That church polity continues to be a hotly debated issue is indicated by a recent publication edited by Brand and Norman (2004).

The necessity and value of churches associating together have been debated among the Reformed Baptists since the 1990s (e.g., Kingdon, 1993). Attempts have been made by Reformed Baptist churches in various parts of the world to form associations, with differing degrees of success. Other churches have shunned explicit association, preferring a looser form of fellowship between churches. Members and friends of the Association of Reformed Baptist Churches of America have argued strongly for their position on association, while many other churches stand wary of their heavily structured form (Renihan, 2001).

Believing that the Reformed Baptists would be helped in resolving outstanding ecclesiological issues by learning from their spiritual forebears, the present work attempts to answer the question, "What was the form and character of church government practised by the Particular Baptists in the 17th and 18th centuries?"

Other questions that arise from this central one are:

i How did the Particular Baptists work out and uphold the principle of *the autonomy of the local church* in the historical and ecclesiological climate of the time?

ii How did the Particular Baptists work out and uphold the principle of *the headship of Christ* in the historical and ecclesiological climate of the time?

iii Was a plurality of elders in each church upheld and practised by the Particular Baptists, and if so, what was the nature of that plurality *vis-à-vis* the minister and the ruling elders?

iv Did the Particular Baptists continue to uphold the principle of plural elders all through the 17th and 18th centuries, and if not, how did deviation take place and what were the consequences in the subsequent generations?

15

   v How did the Particular Baptists express the communion of churches, and what were the issues dealt with, their achievements and shortfalls?

  vi In what ways do Reformed Baptists today differ from the Particular Baptists in church polity, and what lessons are there to be learned from the Particular Baptists?

1.5   THE AIM AND OBJECTIVES

The aim of this thesis is to describe and evaluate the form of church government practised by the Particular Baptists of the 17th and 18th centuries. It intends to show that this form of government has a firm foundation in Scripture and contains valuable solutions for issues presently faced in Reformed Baptist circles.

In order to achieve the aim, the following objectives will be pursued:

   i to show that the Particular Baptists of the 17th and 18th centuries in England and Wales practised believer's baptism and explicit church membership, and upheld a covenant theology, consistent with their understanding of the autonomy of the local church.

  ii to show that the Particular Baptists of the 17th and 18th centuries in England and Wales practised the separation of church and state, and upheld the divine right of the magistrate and the liberty of conscience, arising from their understanding of the headship of Christ.

 iii to show that a sizable number, if not the majority, of the Particular Baptists whose views were represented in the 1689 Confession, practised a plurality of elders in which there was a distinction made between the roles of the pastor or minister and the ruling elders, although these occupy the same basic office of rule.

 iv to show how deviation from a plural eldership took place leading to the "single-pastor-and-multiple-deacons" situation, accompanied by the disappearance of ruling elders and the practice of congregational democracy in governance, which are actually characteristics of modern Congregationalism.

v to show how the communion of churches was expressed in the regional associations of churches of the Particular Baptists which accomplished much good, while some important issues remained unresolved.

vi to compare the practices of the Reformed Baptists today with those of the historical Particular Baptists, in order to recommend what the Reformed Baptists would do well to consider and apply.

1.6 CENTRAL THEORETICAL ARGUMENT

The central theoretical argument of this study is that despite differences in views and nuances in practice among the Particular Baptists of the 17th and 18th centuries, covering the period 1650-1750, in England and Wales, they practised a form of church government which is traditionally known as Independency.

The rationale for choosing the period covering 1650-1750 is that round about the year 1650, the Particular Baptists were in the process of crystallizing their thoughts on ecclesiology after publishing the 1644 Confession and John Owen was actively writing on the subject, while in the year 1750, Isaac Watts (1674-1748) had recently died and John Gill (1697-1771) was actively writing. As has been noted, Isaac Watts was a paedobaptist Independent who had made some perceptive observations on the differences of church polity that existed in his time. John Gill was a leading Particular Baptist whose prolific writing influenced the theology and ecclesiology of many in his days and subsequently.

The Particular Baptists practised a church connectionalism which consisted of church representatives, known as "messengers", meeting in regional associations from about 1650, to consider matters relating to church issues and missions. The Confession (1689: 26: 15) states that "these messengers assembled are not entrusted with any Church-power properly so called; or with any jurisdiction over the Churches themselves, to exercise any censures either over any Churches, or Persons: to impose their determination on the Churches, or Officers". The messengers also met in annual General Assemblies, the first of which was held in 1689. The well-known historian on the Baptists, B. R. White (1968a: 256), had noted that:

As the result of the problems of faith and conduct brought

before the messengers for their joint solution a body of decisions on various matters, with scripture reasons annexed, was built up for the guidance of the churches. It must be realised that these men were trying to think all the old questions out afresh in the light of their understanding of the Bible and in the attempt to provide virtually a new framework of Baptist casuistical divinity. By trial and error they were seeking to build up a pattern of inter-church relations, of the duties of members to each other and to their churches.

The extant proceedings of the General Assemblies (Narrative, 1689, 1690, 1691 & 1692) and association meetings (White, 1971-74; Copson, 1991) shed much light on the ecclesiology of the Particular Baptists. The extant church records (Reading, 1656-1894; Broughton, 1657-1684 and 1699-1730; Bampton, 1690-1825; Maze Pond, 1691-1708; Tottlebank, 1669-1854; Bag-nio/Cripplegate, 1695-1723; Underhill, 1847; Bunyan Meeting, 1928; Tibbutt, 1972), reveal the practical outworking of the beliefs of the Particular Baptists. Aspects of the ecclesiology of the Particular Baptists have been studied in a general way with regard to their identity as a distinct body amidst the Reformed and Puritan ecclesiastical communities of the 17th century (White, 1966 & 1968b; Renihan, 1998). However, no scholarly study has been made to identify and delineate the form of church government practised by the Particular Baptists. The present work is an attempt to supplement an earlier work (Poh, 2000), by reference to primary sources.

1.7 METHODOLOGY

This study is made from within the Reformed Baptist theological tradition. The views of the Particular Baptists are determined from their Confessions of Faith in conjunction with John Owen's writings. These will be understood from the plain meaning of the texts, the Bible references and footnotes found in the original versions of the Confessions, and comparison in historiography. Du Plooy (undated, pp. 44-47) has defended the legitimacy of using confessions and the historical church orders as a definitive source of church polity.

The extant writings and church records of the Particular Baptists are analyzed to determine the extent to which their views and practices confirm or contradict the teaching of the Confessions of Faith. This is in line with the organic model of studying the origins of ideas and practices, which requires the establishment of ideas or structures based on official doctrine. This contrasts with the dynamic model advocated by Whittock (1985: 319) in which it is held that ideas may jump gaps, without any explicit trail by which to trace them.

The views and practices of the Particular Baptists and their theological heirs today are compared, and evaluated in the light of the Bible, with recommendations made for the Reformed Baptists. The contextual-grammatical-historical method of interpretation of the Bible will be used (Berkhof, 1990), with comparison in historiography.

✳ ✳ ✳ ✳ ✳

Two

AUTONOMY

2.1 INTRODUCTION

The distinguishing characteristic of the Separatists in 17th century
Britain was the belief in self-rule, or the autonomy of the local church.
This contrasted with the Church of England which was episcopal,
and the Church of Scotland which was presbyterial. The Baptists further distinguished themselves from the paedobaptist Independents
(or Congregationalists) by their tenet of believer's baptism. While
the General Baptists upheld believer's baptism from the perspective
of an Arminian soteriology, the Particular Baptists argued out their
case from the perspective of a Calvinistic soteriology. In common
with the mainline Protestant churches of the time, the Particular Baptists upheld a covenant (federal) theology that was developed in tandem with a Calvinistic soteriology. Theirs, however, was a covenant
theology that was worked out consistently with believer's baptism.
Believer's baptism is inseparable from the "matter" (or members)
and "form" of the local church. This is often treated as a distinct principle – called the gathered church principle – which, nevertheless, is
linked to the autonomy of the local church. To appreciate the principle of the autonomy of the church as understood by the Particular
Baptists, three things need to be examined: baptism, membership,
and the nature of the church.

This chapter will show how the Particular Baptists worked out the
principle of autonomy in the historical and ecclesiological climate
of the time. A number of men played key roles in the drama of

the development of their doctrine, which culminated in their settled views by the end of the 17th century.

2.2   THE KEY MEN

Among the men who played key roles in the early life of the Particular Baptist churches, six will be noted here. All of them were connected with the seven churches that published the 1644 Confession and its amended version in 1646. Two of them, Kiffin and Knollys, lived through the period from the publication of the 1644 Confession to the publication of the second London Baptist Confession in 1689, thus forming a link between the two generations of Particular Baptists. Kiffin was a signatory to the 1644 and the 1689 Confessions, while Knollys was a signatory to the 1646 and the 1689 Confessions. It is likely that Spilsbury also lived to the end of the seventeenth century, although the later years were spent in Bromsgrove. He signed the 1644 Confession but not the 1689 Confession. A description of this servant of God is given first.

2.2.1   John Spilsbury

John Spilsbury (or Spilsbery, 1593-1699) was pastor of a church that met in Wapping, London. The year of his death has not been clear. His recently discovered funeral sermon, preached by John Eccles in 1699, indicates that he died in that year (Eccles, 1699). The church at Wapping appears to have been the first to practise believer's baptism. The so-called Kiffin Manuscript records that in 1638 "Mr Tho: Wilson, Mr Pen & H. Pen, & 3 more being convinced that Baptism was not for infants, but professed Believers joined with Mr Io: Spilsbury the Church's favour being desired therein" (Burrage, 1912: 302). Spilsbury himself, probably a cobbler by trade, might have been a member of the J-L-J church at one point (Haykin, 1996: 28; Tolmie, 1977: 24-25). The church maintained good relationship with the J-L-J church. B. R. White (1977: 135) has observed that "there were no high walls of bitterness between them and even the withdrawals are recorded as brotherly". This is interesting in view of a number of similar break-away groups around that time, one of which was to have Kiffin as pastor. It would appear that Spilsbury's congregation practised baptism by either sprinkling or pouring at this point. In 1640, another member of the J-L-J church, Richard Blunt, began to question whether baptism should be by immersion. According to the Kiffin Manuscript, "Mr. Richard Blunt ... being convinced of Baptism yet also it ought to be by dipping ye Body into ye Water, resembling Burial & rising again ... Col 2:12, Rom 6:4, had sober conference about in ye Church" (Burrage, 1912: 302-303). Blunt, who spoke Dutch, went to the Netherlands to discuss the issue with a Mennonite body known as the Collegiants, and presumably saw a baptism performed. The Kiffin Manuscript tells us that on his return Blunt baptised a certain "Mr Blacklock who was a teacher amongst them, & Mr Blunt being Baptised, he & Mr Blacklock Baptised the rest of their friends that were so minded", forty-one in all (Burrage, 1912: 303-304). Two churches were formed, one pastored by Richard Blunt, the other by Thomas Kilcop. Soon after Blunt's return from the Netherlands, Spilsbury and his congregation also adopted immersion as the proper mode of baptism. Spilsbury seems to have removed from Wapping to Bromsgrove of the Midlands in or after 1656, rather than *to* Wapping, as claimed by Underwood (1947: 60 cf. 58). This was when Henry Cromwell, son of Oliver Cromwell, tried to get him over to Ireland to quell the more revolutionary Baptists there. Thurloe, Secretary of State of Oliver Cromwell, writing to Henry Cromwell in 1656, said that Spilsbury could not go as he had just accepted a call from "a very great people". The Wapping church continued to thrive under Spilsbury's successor, John Norcott. By 1670 around three hundred people assembled regularly in the church. The Bromsgrove church, which had Spilsbury as the pastor, was represented at least at the 1691 General Assembly of Particular Baptist churches (Narrative, 1691). Spilsbury was of too poor health to attend. John Eccles, who preached Spilsbury's funeral sermon in 1699, signed both the 1689 and 1691 Confessions of Faith (Eccles, 1699).

2.2.2 Samuel Richardson

The earlier church historians, Thomas Crosby (1738) and Joseph Ivimey (1811), do not record anything about Samuel Richardson. A latter historian, A. C. Underwood (1947: 78), devotes one paragraph to this man, consisting of two quotes from another source which is not identified, and ending with a short list of his writings. The first quote says that Richardson was "a substantial London tradesman and was certainly one of the shrewdest and most influential of the Baptist leaders in the capital. He appears to have been a member of the original Particular Baptist congregation. Richardson signed the three Baptist Confessions of 1643, 1644, and 1646, and was regarded both by his own Church and the Cromwellian Government as one of the most responsible leaders of his sect." The next quote says that "Richardson followed political and ecclesiastical developments with great acumen during an extremely critical decade, and devoted himself to the enlargement of religious liberty as the chief fruit of the revolution which England was then undergoing." Richardson appears to have been in the same church as Spilsbury, "the original Particular Baptist congregation". Furthermore, it seems that there was a Baptist Confession of 1643, apart from the celebrated ones of 1644 and 1646. Since the 1646 Confession was but an amendment of the one of 1644, it seems reasonable to assume that the 1643 Confession was an earlier version of the 1644 Confession. If this was the personal Confession produced by Spilsbury (Eccles, 1699), the quote above shows that it was signed by other Particular Baptists as well. This point is worthy of further pursuit. Richardson was to emerge as the principal Particular Baptist apologist (Bell, 2000: 88).

2.2.3   William Kiffin

Born in London, William Kiffin (1616-1701) was orphaned at the age of nine when his parents died of the plague. Apprenticed as a glover, Kiffin listened regularly to the Puritan preachers and was brought to faith by the preaching of the Arminian John Goodwin (Haykin, 1996: 43). In 1638, during the period when Archbishop Laud was imposing uniformity of ritual and doctrine in the Church of England, Kiffin left to join the independent congregation led by Samuel Eaton, who was at that time in prison. Eaton and his group had left the J-L-J church in 1633. It is not clear whether the group left because they rejected infant baptism or merely because they could not agree with the J-L-J church accepting the infant baptism of the Church of England. By 1638, Eaton had come to believe that baptism should only be for those able to profess their own faith (White, 1996: 60). Eaton seems to have been baptised by Spilsbury. A contemporary poem by John Taylor (1641: 6-7) reads:

> Also one Spilsbury rose up of late,
> (Who doth, or did dwell over Aldersgate)
> His office was to weigh Hay by the Truffe,

(Fit for the Pallat of Bucephalus)
He in short time left his Hay-weighing trade,
And afterwards he Irish stockings made:
He rebaptized in Anabaptist fashion
One Eaton (of new-found separation)
A zealous Button-maker, grave and wise,
And gave him orders, others to baptize;
Who was so apt to learne that in one day,
Hee'd do't as well as Spilsbury weigh'd Hay...

Upon Eaton's death in prison in 1639, Kiffin was invited to preach for the church, which met at Devonshire Square. Over the course of the next three or four years, he was appointed the pastor of the church. By the fall of 1642 he and the congregation had come to a decidedly Baptist position. Kiffin was to become a prominent figure in ecclesiastical and political circles in the seventeenth century. The second half of the century was a tumultuous period in which the English Civil Wars took place, during which time King Charles I was executed and a republican government was set up. Persecution of the dissenters followed not long after the restoration of the monarchy in 1660, until the Toleration Act was passed in 1688. The Calvinistic Baptist cause grew under such difficult circumstances, thanks to the able leaders of the period, the most notable of whom was Kiffin. He played a prominent role in the planting and establishment of new churches and associations of churches, spoke on behalf of them to the authorities, and intervened with personal advice in times of crises and difficulties faced by the church. Joseph Ivimey recorded that Kiffin was "one of the most extraordinary persons whom the [Calvinistic Baptist] denomination has produced, both as to consistency and correctness of his principles and the eminence of his worldly and religious character" (Haykin, 1996: 42). Thomas Edwards referred to Kiffin as "the Metropolitan of that Fraternity" of Baptists (Edwards, 1646: 87-88). Kiffin was a signatory to both the 1644 and the 1689 Confession.

2.2.4 Hanserd Knollys

Hanserd Knollys (c. 1599-1691) was a signatory to the second edition of the 1644 Confession, published in 1646. His name appears first in the list of signatories of the 1689 Confession, followed by that of Kiffin. Knollys may be regarded as a fruit of the publica-tion of the 1644 Confession. Unlike Kiffin and most of his fellow Baptists, Knollys had received a university education at Cambridge. Ordained as a minister of the Church of England, he made a com-plete break with the church in 1635 and left England for America. He ran into trouble with the New England Congregationalists and decided to return to England in 1641, joining himself to the J-L-J church. When the Confession was published, some members of the J-L-J congregation, which at that time had Henry Jessey as pastor, became convinced that the London Particular Baptists were not rad-ical Anabaptists, but true Christians. A group of "about 16 precious souls left", led by Knollys, to form a church that met at Broken Wharf (Anderson, 1979). Close to a thousand people regularly heard him preach in the late 1640s and 1650s (Tolmie, 1977: 60). Knollys was active not only in promoting the Baptist cause in London, but also in seeking to establish Baptist works in other parts of England and Wales. Throughout his life, Knollys was committed to the millenar-ianism of the Fifth Monarchists, but not to their militancy, believing that the power of Christ to usher in the Kingdom was "the power of the word, not the power of the sword" (Bell, 2000: 86).

2.2.5   Benjamin Keach

Benjamin Keach (1640-1704) was arguably the most notable lead-er among the second generation of Particular Baptists of the seven-teenth century. He has been described as "the single most important apologist for the Calvinistic Baptist views" (MacDonald, 1982: 77). Raised an Anglican, he joined the General Baptists at fifteen. He moved from Buckinghamshire to London in 1668, joining a General Baptist church in Southwark, London. He was soon ordained an el-der of the congregation. Before long, he made the acquaintance of Kiffin and Knollys. By the time of his second marriage in 1672 – his first wife having died in 1670 – he had become a Calvinist. Together with a few like-minded individuals, he began a Calvinistic Baptist church at Horsleydown. In addition to his labours as a pastor, Keach was active in planting churches in southern England and in defend-ing the Baptist cause with his pen. Although somewhat weak in his defence of the mode of baptism, he ably defended believer's bap-tism against a new generation of detractors to such an extent that it may be said that no new arguments are needed to establish the

Baptist position today (Riker, 2009). Keach was somewhat of a controversial figure among the Particular Baptists, probably because of the influence of his long association with the General Baptists. From early, he advocated the laying on of hands during baptism, a practice common among the General Baptists but resisted by many of the Particular Baptists (Parratt, 1966). He became embroiled in the hymn-singing controversy (MacDonald, 1982: 49-82), which soured relationship between the Particular Baptist leaders and contributed to the demise of the London annual General Assembly of Particular Baptists (see Chapter 6, later). His denial of the validity of ruling elders in the church was to have long lasting influence on the Particular Baptists (see Chapter 5, later). His son, Elias Keach (1667-1701) would play a key role in advancing the Baptist cause in and around Philadelphia in America, before returning to England (Jones, 1869).

2.2.6 Nehemiah Coxe

Apart from the Keaches, another father-and-son team is to be noted. Although the focus is on the son, Nehemiah Coxe (16??-1689), the father, Benjamin (1595 - c. 1664) is considered first. Benjamin Coxe (or Cox, also Cockes) hailed from Bedfordshire. His personal experiences paralleled those of Hanserd Knollys. Both men received a university education. Probably the son of a Church of England clergyman (Miller, Renihan & Orozo, 2005: 7), Benjamin received his BA degree from Oxford in 1613, and MA degree in 1617. Although appointed rector of a state church, Benjamin became a Baptist by 1643. Like Hansard Knollys, he joined one of the Calvinistic Baptist churches in the interval between the publication of the 1644 Confession and the second edition in 1646, becoming one of the signatories of the latter. In addition to these, he shared with Hanserd Knollys the similar experiences of having been Anglican clergymen, who became pastors of thriving Particular Baptist churches in London. The records of the Petty France church, of which Benjamin was pastor, shows that from 1675 to 1688/89 there were more than 530 people in membership (Petty France, 3). Benjamin Coxe published a number of treatises in defence of believer's baptism. His son, Nehemiah, was to inherit his mantle as a pastor and a defender of the Baptist cause. Indeed, it may be said that he outshone his father in the latter task.

Almost nothing is known of the birth and childhood of Nehemiah

Coxe. He joined the open-membership Bedford Church, made famous by John Bunyan, on 14 May 1669 (Bunyan Meeting 1928: 27). Though still relatively young, he rose to high esteem in the eyes of the church, frequently assisting in the pastoral oversight. He was not an elder, but was appointed one of the "ministers" or "gifted brethren" together with six other men on 21st December 1671. On that day John Bunyan was called formally to "pastorall [sic] office, or eldership" in the church. In May 1674, Nehemiah faced censure from the church for some "miscarriages". The church record book states (Bunyan Meeting, 1928: 54):

> Our Bro: Nehemiah Coxe did publickly make an acknowledgement of several miscarridges by him committed and declared his repentance for the same; and because he had bin faulty in such things heretofore therefore it was desired by som of the Bre that the form of his submission should be presented to us in writing, which also accordingly was, and was as followeth. Whereas several words and practices have been uttered and performed by me, that might justly be censured to have tendency to make rents and divisions in the congregation, I do declare myself unfeignedly sorry and repentant for the same. Ne. Coxe.

It has been suggested that Coxe's "words and practices" were related to the issue of open or closed membership, which was hotly debated at that time (Miller, Renihan & Orozo, 2005: 16). Not long after that incident, Nehemiah joined the Petty France church in London. On 21 September 1675, the Petty France Church Book (Petty France, 1) records that "bro Collins & Bro. Coxe were solemnly ordained pastors or elders of this church". Nehemiah Coxe was a qualified physician who was skilled in Latin, Hebrew and Greek. In 1676, when the influential Thomas Collier in the West Country began to deviate from the orthodoxy of the London churches, a team of men, including Coxe, was dispatched to attempt his recovery. Thomas Collier had been sent out as a minister by Kiffin's Devonshire church in the 1640s. He was now going astray doctrinally and needed to be reigned in. The Broadmead Records describe the incident as follows (Underhill, 1847: 359):

> ... five elders and brethren ... were coming down from

London, to visit a neighbouring church in the country about fifteen miles off, near Bradford or Trowbridge, to settle some disorder there, as the pastor thereof, T. C., holding forth some unsound doctrine, or new notions, contrary to the general reception of sound and orthodox men. The names of the London brethren were, brother Kiffin, brother Deane, brother Fitten, brother Cox, and brother Moreton.

The visit of this delegation failed to restore Collier, with the result that Coxe was enlisted to refute Collier's views in print. This he did in his work "Vindiciae Veritatis" (Coxe, 1677). Apart from other works, Coxe (1681) published a book on covenant theology, which is of interest to us here. Coxe and William Collins were most likely the compilers of the Second London Baptist Confession of 1677 (Miller, Renihan & Orozco, 2005: 20). Coxe died on 5 May 1689, four months before the General Assembly of 1689. Consequently, the man who had played such a significant role in the life of the Particular Baptists was not recorded among those who attended the meeting of 1689, or who subscribed to the Confession of Faith. He should rightly be numbered among the "mighty men" of the second generation of Particular Baptists.

2.3   THE CIRCUMSTANCES

Three periods of controversy over baptism may be discerned, in each of which the Particular Baptists propounded the subject in relation to a separate matter. These periods, of course, are not sharply defined by boundaries of time or subject matters. However, there are heuristic advantages to consider the subject under these periods:

(i) The years 1640-1660, in which baptism was debated in relation to church membership.

(ii) The years 1660-1680, in which baptism was debated in relation to participation at the Lord's Supper.

(iii) The years 1680-1700, in which baptism was debated in relation to the covenant of grace.

All three controversies dovetailed with the Particular Baptist principles of the gathered church and the autonomy of the local church.

2.3.1 Baptism and Church Membership (1640-1660)

In the mid-17th century, when the Particular Baptists were emerging as a self-conscious grouping, the stigma of being labelled "Anabaptists" had to be countered. Their increasing visibility caused alarm to the state church and the Presbyterians, calling forth a series of pamphlets denouncing them. Two anonymous pamphlets appeared in 1642, entitled "A Warning for England" and "A Short History of the Anabaptists of High and Low Germany". The latter clearly aimed to associate all English Baptists with the anarchisms of Münster. The authorship of the earlier pamphlet was later acknowledged by Daniel Featley. A brilliant liberal clergyman of the Church of England, Featley was to become a member of the Westminster Assembly, which convened in 1643 (Reid, 1983). In 1642 Kiffin and some others entered into a disputation with him. In 1643 Spilsbury published a confession of faith along with his "Treatise Concerning the Lawful Subject of Baptism". In 1644 Featley published "A Confutation of the Anabaptists and of All others who Affect Not Civill Government". Addressed to Parliament, Featley's work contained calumnies against the Baptists which were likely to unleash physical violence against them. The Baptists knew that the time had come for a concerted effort to defend themselves against the charges of Anabaptism.

The 1644 Confession, most likely compiled by John Spilsbury (Lumpkin, 1969: 145), was published by the seven Particular Baptist churches in London. Spilsbury, together with Samuel Richardson and William Kiffin, were to emerge as a circle of leaders active in promoting an organizational system of churches that encompassed England, Scotland, Wales, and Ireland. Kiffin was recognised as the key motivating force of this circle by virtue of his abilities and his standing in society. He was to become a trusted friend and counsellor of Oliver Cromwell and of King Charles II. The primary purpose of the confession was declared in its title, "The CONFESSION OF FAITH Of those CHURCHES which are commonly (though falsly [sic]) called ANABAPTISTS". The preface of the confession explained that it was meant to dispel the wild stories that were spread about the Particular Baptists and that they hoped that a statement of their orthodoxy would convince the public that they were not Anabaptists, "denying original sin, declaiming Magistracy, denying to assist them either in person or purse in any of their lawful Commands". Before concluding, the confession stated that "tributes, customs, and all such lawful duties, ought willingly to be by us paid and performed, our lands, goods, and bodies, to submit to the magistrate" who is "in every way to be acknowledged, reverenced, and obeyed". In this way, the Particular Baptists distanced themselves from the Anabaptists.

At the same time, the Particular Baptists were anxious to be distinguished from the General Baptists, who had come into prominence by the highly visible actions of their evangelists like Thomas Lambe and Samuel Oates. Many people were confusing the General Baptists with the Particular Baptists, blaming the shortcomings of either group equally on both. In the preface of the confession, the Particular Baptists stated that they wished to allay the accusations that they believed in "free-will" and the possibility of "falling away from grace". This last accusation they countered directly in Article XXIII by saying that "those that have this precious faith wrought in them by the Spirit, can never finally nor totally fall away". The Particular Baptists made their Calvinism clear by explaining that the blood of Christ was meant to "reconcile His elect only" and that the aim of God's church was the "preservation and salvation of the elect". This point was reiterated in Article XXI: "Christ by his death did bring forth salvation and reconciliation only for the elect". Additionally, faith was defined as the "gift of God wrought in the hearts of the elect". The Particular Baptists made it clear that they were neither Anabaptists nor General Baptists.

It is to be noted that the first wave of attacks against the Particular Baptists, while containing a political note insinuating Anabaptist anti-establishment sentiment, was theologically focussed on their re-baptism and separation from the Church of England. The Particular Baptists made their belief clear that "baptism is an ordinance of the New Testament, given by Christ, to be dispensed only upon persons professing faith". Their confession further stated that "the way and manner of the dispensing of this ordinance the Scripture holds out to be dipping or plunging the whole body under water". Thus, it was made clear that only believers are to be baptized, and baptism is to be performed by full immersion. These points are the teaching of "the New Testament" and "the Scripture". The sprinkling of infants was rejected by the Particular Baptists on biblical grounds.

The concept of the invisible church was acknowledged, while the membership of the visible church was specified as believers, and believers only (Lumpkin, 1969: 165):

> Christ hath here on earth a spirituall Kingdome, which
> is the church, which he hath purchased and redeemed
> to himself, as a peculiar inheritance: which Church, as it
> is visible to us, is a company of visible Saints, called &
> separated from the world, by the word and Spirit of God,
> to the visible profession of the faith of the Gospel, being
> baptized into that faith, and joyned to the Lord, and each
> other, by mutuall agreement, in the practical injoyment
> of the Ordinances, commanded by Christ their head and
> King.

The autonomy of each local church was made clear: "Every Church
has power given them from Christ for their better well-being, to
choose to themselves meet persons into office". The local congregations, while distinct from one another, are to walk by the same rule,
having fellowship for their mutual good (Lumpkin, 1969: 169):

> Although the particular Congregations be distinct and
> several Bodies, every one a compact and knit Citie in
> it self; yet are they all to walk by one and the same
> Rule, and by all meanes convenient to have counsell and
> help one another in all needfull affaires of the Church, as
> members of one body in the common faith under Christ
> their onely head.

The church was thus defined by the Particular Baptists as being
made up of baptized believers who voluntarily covenanted together
to be under the headship of Christ. The idea of a state church, with
a mixed membership of believers and unbelievers, and ruled by a
monolithic power structure that involved the civil authority, as exemplified in the Church of England, was rejected by the Particular
Baptists.

As noted above, the Confession was instrumental in winning Knollys and Keach to their cause. The "Kiffin Manuscript" (White, 1966)
recorded both the motivation and the results of the confession, stating that the Baptists "being much spoken against as unsound in doctrine as if they were Arminians, and also against Magistrates etc.
they joined together in a confession of their faith in fifty two articles
which gave satisfaction to many that had been prejudiced" against
them. While the Confession was successful in changing the miscon-
ception of some regarding the Baptists, others were not convinced.

They saw it as a trick, "a little ratsbane in a great quantity of sugar" (Featley, 1645: 220).

In the mid-1640s a new spate of pamphlets appeared which revived the charges of Anabaptism against the Baptists. One such was "The Anabaptist Catechisme: With all their Practices, Meetings and Exercises", produced by the Independents. It was claimed that the Anabaptists professed "that all goods, husband, wife, and all things whatsoever any Congregation have is in common to all", and that "no man is to lye with his brothers wife, whilst her husband is in presences, except he be fast asleep, or dead drunk". Further, the Anabaptists had for their leaders "Mr. Patient, and honest Glover; and Mr. Griffin [Griffith], a reverend Taylor; and Mr. Knowles [Knollys], a learned scholar; Mr. Spilsbery [Spilsbury], a renowned Cobbler; Mr. Barber, a Button-maker, and diverse others, most gallant teachers, well grounded in their opinions" (Bell, 2000: 87). The Particular Baptists were enraged enough to be mentioned by name, what more to be listed alongside well-known General Baptist leaders such as Griffith and Barber.

In the same year that "The Anabaptists Catechisme" appeared, Daniel Featley (1645) published his sensational "The Dippers Dipt, or, The Anabaptists duck'ed and plung'd over Head and Eares". This text proved immensely popular and quickly went through three editions. Samuel Richardson (1645), the principal Particular Baptist apologist at this time, quickly responded to Featley with his "Some Briefe Considerations on Doctor Featley". In addition to the numerous charges against the Baptists, Featley also articulated a series of criticisms aimed directly at the 1644 Confession, to which Richardson answered that "if God permit, we shall in the next impression of the Confession of our faith, more fully declare jointly what we believe".

The Particular Baptist leaders gathered again 1646 to revise and reissue the confession. To make clear they were not Anabaptists, the articles on the magistrate were condensed and two new articles included, in which it was stated that Baptists could hold public office and swear oaths, thus denying directly the two well-known characteristics of the Continental Anabaptists. To define themselves in contrast to the General Baptists, the Calvinism of the second edition was significantly strengthened. Reprobation and the nature of the elect were emphasized. Additionally, Benjamin Cox (1646) wrote "An Appendix to a Confession of Faith", which was meant to accompany and clarify the new edition of the confession. The "Appendix" further strengthened the Calvinism of the Particular Baptists by focusing on Christ's death for the elect only and the eternal punishment of the lost. Another point clarified by Cox was that only baptized believers should be allowed to the "use of the supper". Those who accepted this practice would have baptized believers only as members of their congregations and became known as "closed communion" Baptists. This was in contrast to the "open communion" churches, like those of Henry Jessey and John Bunyan.

Before a third and fourth edition of the confession appeared in 1651 and 1652, respectively, the position of the Baptists was greatly altered to their advantage. Baptists in the army of Crom-well had distinguished themselves and had risen to positions of leadership. The Army proved to be an excellent means of spreading their principles. When the brief wars were over, Baptists were everywhere in prominent positions, and no longer lived in fear of King or Parliament. By comparing the confession of the Particular Baptists with the newly published Westminster Confession, men could see that they belonged to the mainstream of Reformed life. However, a new challenge appeared, that of Quakerism, which was founded by George Fox. The Particular Baptists had to counter his "inward light" in the third and fourth editions of the confession. The Calvinism of Articles III and XXI was somewhat softened and the article on ministerial support was omitted, in response to Quaker criticism. A Baptist church had been founded at Leith in Scotland in 1650. To show their unity with the London Baptists and to advertise their beliefs, they issued in Leith, in 1653, a new edition of the 1644 Confession. Also in 1653, a "Fifth Impression Corrected" of the confession was issued by Henry Hills in London.

While the Quakers managed to win many converts away from the Baptists in the 1650s, the Seekers and Ranters posed less of a threat but were nevertheless troublesome. One John Marsh, a Seeker, wrote against the baptism practised by the Baptists. The Seekers, who began to appear in the 1620s, regarded all organized churches as corrupt and preferred to wait for God's revelation. John Saltmarsh produced his book, "The Smoke in the Temple" in 1646, in which he put forward thirteen "exceptions" against baptism as practised by the Baptists. This book was responded to in an irenic spirit by Hanserd Knollys, who providentially met Saltmarsh before the response was published. In the preface of his book, "The Shinning of a

Flaming Fire in Zion" (1646), Knollys said:

> I have resolved (before I see your face) to give you some
> answer unto those thirteen Objections touching Baptism.
> But meeting with you, by a good hand of Providence,
> I received much more encouragement to communicate
> to you that measure of understanding, which God hath
> given me His unworthy servant, to improve for His Glory.
> I entreat you, that love may cover mine infirmities therein,
> and if yourself, and others do receive any satisfaction
> thereby, God will have His Glory, and I have my end.

Saltmarsh's twelfth objection was:

> That these Churches who enjoy Christ's mind, as they
> think, most fully in the practice of Ordinances, yet have
> no greater gifts in their Churches then there are in those
> called Independent, or Brownists; Prayer, Teaching, Prophe-
> cying being as fully and powerfully performed in the one
> as the other. And being so, Whether must not the Churches
> of Christ be distinguished by some more visible glorious
> power and gifts as at first by which they may be discerned
> to excel all other Societies?

Knollys's answer, which seems to have given rise to the title of his
book, was as follows:

> There are Scriptural Rules to discern the Truth of Churches;
> to which Professors (who have their face towards Zion)
> shall do well to take heed, as a light that shines in a dark
> place, 2 Peter 1:19; &c. Rev. 11:1. And although we have
> no gifts in our Churches, but what we have received, and
> we have not received any Gifts of the Spirit, to boast of
> them: Yet I must bear this Testimony, we come behind
> in no Gift, what we have received, we are found to bless
> God for, and desire to honor Christ our Head with all the
> gifts, which we have received from Him.

Knollys's response to Saltmarsh was followed by a longer response from the pen of fellow Particular Baptist, Daniel King, entitled, "Stumbling Blocks Removed Out of the Way". When it was
published in 1650 (and republished in 1656), Saltmarsh had already

died in 1647, a point of which King was cognizant. Saltmarsh had argued that the Baptists were wrong to baptize in the name of the Holy Trinity, basing the practice on Matthew 28:18. Rather, the baptism practised by early church was in the name of Jesus Christ alone, as in Acts 2:38, 8:16, 10:48, 19:5, and Romans 6:3. King answered that neither Christ nor the apostles did anything in the name of Jesus Christ alone, excluding the Father and the Holy Spirit, that what was done in the name of Christ was done in the name of the Father, Son, and Holy Spirit, that the name of the Lord is one (Zech. 14:9), and that there is but one Lord, Father, Son, and Holy Spirit (Eph. 4:5):

> Seeing then, that the Father, Son, and Holy Ghost are one, to baptize in the name of the LORD, Acts 10:38 or in the name of the LORD JESUS, Acts 2:38, or into Jesus Christ, Rom. 6:3, or into the name of Father, Son, and Holy Ghost, Matt. 28:18, 19, is one and the same Baptism. And so to baptize is agreeable to, and no way contrary to the full practice of all that baptized by water.

Saltmarsh also claimed that the baptism mentioned in Matth-ew 28:18 is a baptism of gifts, as shown by comparison with Mark 16:15-17. King argued that, in Mark 16, the gifts were to follow them that believe, which has no connection with baptism. To equate baptism with the gifts "is to make this place dark and hard, and of a private interpretation". King concluded his arguments to this objection of Saltmarsh by saying:

> For Christ says Baptizing them, into the name of the Father, Son, and Holy Ghost, He gives order that the thing be done, not the words used. They having made profession of their faith in God, and Christ before, and upon that profession being dipped into water, they are dipped into the Name of the Lord, though no form of words be used at the doing of the action.

In passing, these words also show that immersion was the practice among the Baptists. It is seen, then, that by 1660 the doctrines of the closed communion Particular Baptists with regard to baptism and church membership were pretty much established. The same may be said of the open communion Particular Baptists, as will be seen in the next section.

2.3.2 Baptism and the Lord's Supper (1660-1680)

It has been noted how Benjamin Cox in his Appendix of 1646 made clear that only baptized believers should be allowed to the "use of the supper". Among the Calvinistic Baptists were those who practised open communion and open membership, meaning that believer's baptism was not regarded as a pre-requisite to partaking of the Lord's Supper and to church membership. One of the most prominent of these men was Henry Jessey, who had received his BA from Cambridge in 1623. In 1637 he was invited to be the pastor of the Jacob-Lathrop congregation, remaining in their service until his death in 1663. Bell (2000: 63) describes Jessey as follows:

> He was unquestionably one of the most fascinating and influential personalities at the center of religious radicalism in the mid-seventeenth century. Jessey began his public career as a Puritan, and then an Independent Puritan, but before the end of his life he could be called a Particular Baptist, a Fifth Monarchist, a Seventh-Day Baptist, and an Independent [open-communion] Baptist. In addition to his broad influence across a number of religious perspectives, Jessey was also a dynamic force in the politics of the period.

In 1645, Jessey was baptized by Hanserd Knollys, a former member of the J-L-J church. Many of the congregation did not agree with Jessey's new position on baptism. Not wanting to cause division, after having experienced a number of earlier divisions, Jessey allowed those who wished, to stay within the congregation, whether or not they had undergone believer's baptism. The church covenant, and not believer's baptism, united Jessey's mixed congregation of re-baptized and non-re-baptized Christians. Over time most members accepted believer's baptism and were re-baptized, but Jessey never made baptism a bar to church communion. This also was the practice of other open communion men, including John Tombes, John Bunyan and the Broadmead congregation at Bristol.

Henry Jessey could have been convinced finally of believer's baptism by John Tombes's writings, after seeing many men depart from the J-L-J church over this issue. On 22 June 1645, Jessey had written to the Puritans in New England concerning their harsh treatment "of some for being Anabaptists" (Bell, 2000: 64). Always an advocate of tolerance, Jessey explained that such actions only hurt the cause of the "Gathered Churches called Independents". Apart from the poor press such actions generated, Jessey maintained that such persecution was not godly and should be stopped. Along with the letter, Jessey enclosed some anti-paedobaptist literature that he found particularly persuasive. Among the literature that Jessey sent were the writings of John Tombes.

Tombes (1603-1676) had held strongly to believer's baptism, but never believed in separation from the state church. Michael Renihan (2001) has argued strongly that Tombes should be considered an Anglican Antipaedobaptist, instead of a Baptist, as has been done in the literature. Renihan argues that many writers have followed Thomas Crosby, "the father of Baptist history" (Renihan, 2001: 5), who presented Tombes as one who "gathered a separate church of those of his own persuasion, continuing at the same time minister of the parish" (Crosby, 1: 288). Renihan (2001: 4-5) argues that since Tombes was never a separatist, his "society" was not a gathered church, but a group within the church in Bewdley that met for mutual encouragement and edification. Yet Crosby reports that three men were trained up to be ministers by Tombes in his "society", one of whom was to become the eminent Particular Baptist pastor of the church in Bromsgrove, namely John Eccles (Bromsgrove Church Record). This would indicate that Tombes's "society" was more than just a fellowship within the Anglican congregation.

The present writer ventures the opinion that Renihan's classification of Tombes as not a Baptist but an Anglican Antipaedobaptist will be a matter of debate for some time to come. It seems that one needs to distinguish between Tombes's personal pilgrimage and the churches he founded. A. C. Underwood (1947: 69) records that Tombes became vicar of Leominster in 1630, but was driven out of his living by the Royalists in 1642, the year he adopted antipaedobaptist views as a result of a public disputation in Bristol. Throughout his life, Tombes saw no difficulty accepting public maintenance for various non-parochial appointments in which he could avoid baptizing infants. He was one of Cromwell's Triers. When the Presbyterian dominance ended, he was back in Leominster in 1649 and kept the living until he was ejected in 1662. The churches he founded were of the open communion type. The last years of his life were spent in Salisbury. There is no evidence that he had contact with the Baptist church in Salisbury. Under the Indulgence of 1672, he described himself as a Presbyterian. After his death, the Anglican rector wrote this about Tombes (Underwood, 1947: 70):

> When I attended him in his last sickness, he desired me to testify that though he was so unhappy as to differ from the Church of England on the point of Infant baptism, yet durst he not separate from her Communion on that account any farther than by going out of the Church whilst that office was performing and returning in again when it was ended.

Without questioning the integrity of the Anglican rector nor the accuracy of this record, it needs to be noted that these were words of one whose sympathy lay with the state church, concerning another who had returned to its fold, and that in the emotional setting of the deathbed. Its value is limited to showing that Tombes had returned to the fold of his former church. It was not uncommon to find men changing their views through their lives, as was the case with Henry Jessey. Careful historians like W. T. Whitley and B. R. White, while noting his peculiarities, classified Tombes as a Baptist for good reasons. For one thing, he was fully convinced of believer's baptism and was one of its strongest advocates. For another, he planted churches that were made up of believers, although not denying paedobaptist churches as true churches. Whitley made the observation (Renihan, 2001: 26):

> He saw the need of an educated ministry and trained three men who did good service. As he could not earn his living by manual work, he, therefore, showed some skill in finding positions where he could serve a Chapelry or a hospital or an inn of court, without being called upon to baptize infants, and yet could earn public maintenance. He linked together six or seven churches, due to his own efforts in the shires of Monmouth, Hereford, and Gloucester, and taught them how to co-operate. But he had a decided caste feeling, never co-operated with other Baptists and was content, once he had secured his financial position by marriage to describe himself as a Presbyterian; while the church at Salisbury, where he ended his days, has no tradition that he ever worshipped with them.

As can be seen, Tombes was not just baptistic in belief, but actually founded gathered churches, that is, churches made up of baptized believers. He must, therefore, be regarded as a Baptist, and being Calvinistic in soteriology, should be considered a Particular Baptist, for much of his life. His churches, however, were open communion and open membership ones. The closed communion Particular Baptists had many reasons to be wary of Tombes and the churches he founded. Apart from being closed communion, most of the Particular Baptists were against accepting public support for ministry, being lay-communicants at the Anglican eucharist, and serving as a Trier in Cromwell's government – all of which Tombes upheld. These were issues discussed in the various regional associations of churches of the closed communion Particular Baptists. For example, the Midlands Association, consisting of seven churches, dealt with these issues and even recommended that "baptized believers ought not to here the nationall ministers preach nor joyne with them in their publike worship" (White, 1971-7: Pt. 1: 25). White (1996: 104) describes the effects of the Act of Uniformity of 1662 in these words:

> Because, as has been seen, the vast majority of Baptists, whether Arminian, Calvinistic or Seventh Day, rejected on principle the whole concept of an established church and its methods of appointment and payment, even if they were qualified to receive them as, for example, was Hanserd Knollys, formerly a Chu-rch of England minister himself, only a tiny minority of their ministers was affected. In England these included John Tombes, perhaps the most learned of all the Baptists, vicar of Leominster; Henry Jessey, who held a lectureship at St George's Church, Southwark; Paul Hobson, who was chaplain at Eton College; John Skinner, who was rector of Weston-under-Penyard with Hope Mansell, Herefordshire; Richard Harrison, who led the gathered church at Netherton; and William Kaye, rector of Stokesley, Yorkshire. These six can reasonably, though not in every case with total certainty, be regarded as Baptists who had held paid appointments within the English church establishment of the 1650s, *who had led gathered congregations where believer's baptism was taught*, and who lost their posts dur-

ing the period 1660-62. [Emphasis added.]

Extant records show that Tombes was clearly the pastor of the church in Herefordshire in 1653. In 1657 the closed communion Particular Baptists debated whether to accept a church into association which had formed from members of Tombes's congregation in Leominster and Hereford. As late as 1689 a letter in the Leominster Church-book reported that there were still supporters of Tombes in the area (White, 1966).

The interest in Henry Jessey and John Tombes at this juncture is to show that the Particular Baptists had to work out their understanding of the gathered church in relation to the two sacraments of baptism and the Lord's Supper. Both the closed communion men and the open communion men were united in the beliefs of believer's baptism and the gathered church. They differed in the question of whether believer's baptism was necessary to the partaking of the Lord's Supper and to church membership. Over against Jessey and Tombes stood Benjamin Cox and Daniel King, who wrote in defence of closed communion. Cox's close association with Daniel King in the founding of the Midlands Association reflected their common stand on closed communion (White, 1966).

Benjamin Cox had asserted categorically in his Appendix to the 1646 Confession the closed communion position (Cox, 1646: Art. 20):

> Though a believer's right to the use of the Lord's Supper do immediately flow from Jesus Christ apprehended and received by faith; yet in as much as all things ought to be done not only decently, but also in order; I Cor. 14:40, and the word holds forth this order, that disciples should be baptized, Matt. 28:19, Acts 2:38, and then be taught to observe all things (that is to say, all other things) that Christ commanded the Apostles, Matt. 28:20, and accordingly the Apostles first baptized disciples, and then admitted them to the use of the Supper; Acts 2:41,42, we therefore do not admit any to the use of the Supper, nor communicate with any in the use of this ordinance, but disciples baptized, lest we should have fellowship with them in their doing contrary to order.

The debate over closed and open communion became intense in

the 1660s. John Bunyan, the open communionist, took up pen to espouse his view, while William Kiffin defended the closed communion position. Bunyan was born in Elstow, Bedfordshire, England in 1628. He worked as a tinker, that is, a tinsmith who repaired pots and kitchen utensils. He joined the Parliamentarian army in 1644, returning to his former trade after the Parliamentarians won the Civil War. After a traumatic conversion experience, he came under the ministry of the Nonconformist pastor, John Gifford. Upon the death of John Gifford in 1655, Bunyan began to preach. He was appointed a deacon in 1657. In 1660, during the Restoration of Charles II, Bunyan was arrested for preaching as a Nonconformist and imprisoned in Bedford Gaol. During his time in prison, he wrote his now famous allegory of the Christian life, "The Pilgrim's Progress". During Bunyan's incarceration, lax prison warders allowed him time out to preach and minister to his congregation. In January 1672 Bunyan was released under the Declaration of Religious Indulgence of Charles II.

In the Church Book of Bunyan Meeting (1928: 50), it is recorded that John Bunyan was appointed to be the pastor of the church on 21st of the 10th month, 1671 (based on the old calendar), which corresponded with the month of his release from prison. From his surviving parishioners, he organized an independent church which met at Bedford. The church grew strongly and many congregations were established for miles around Bedford. When the Declaration of Religious Indulgence was withdrawn in March 1675, Bunyan was again imprisoned for preaching. On being pardoned by the King subsequently, he continued actively to preach and to strengthen the congregations associated with the Bedford church. Bunyan died on 31 August 1688 and was buried in Bunhill Fields in London.

Some time before his release from prison, Bunyan published his "A Confession of My Faith and A Reason for My Practice in Worship". The first part showed Bunyan standing clearly as a Calvinist, while in the second part he put forward ten reasons for his practice of open communion. In the process, he castigated the closed communion Baptists for shutting out paedobaptist brethren from church membership, declaring that:

> To contest with gracious men, with men that walk with God, to shut such out of the churches because they will not sin against their souls, rendereth thee uncharitable.

Thou seekest to destroy the word of God; thou begettest contentions, janglings, murmurings, and evil-surmisings, thou ministerest occasion for wisperings, backbitings, slanders, and the like, rather than godly edifying; contrary to the whole current of Scriptures, and peace of all communities.

This was responded to by Thomas Paul (1673) in "Some Serious Reflections on the Part of Mr. Bunions", to which William Kiffin contributed a foreword. Kiffin commented that "The severe charges laid by Bunyan against those that are contrary minded, if true, would be sufficient to frighten them into his persuasion."

Bunyan immediately responded to Paul and Kiffin with his "Differences In Judgment About Water Baptism No Bar To Communion" (Bunyan, 1673), to which was appended the contribution of Henry Jessey in support of the open communion position. Bunyan defended his position that "the church of Christ hath not warrant to keep out of their communion the Christian that is discovered to be a visible saint by the word, the Christian that walketh according to his light with God." He was not denying believer's baptism, claiming, "I do not plead for a despising of baptism, but a bearing with our brother, that cannot do it for want of light", and, "I own water baptism to be God's ordinance, but I make no idol of it". Henry Danvers (or D'Anvers) was to published his "Treatise of Baptism" in the following year in support of closed communion, stating, "A seventh end of baptism is, that the baptized person may orderly thereby have entrance into the visible church. None were esteemed members, or did partake of its ordinances, before they were baptized, being so God's hedge or boundary." Danvers was a Baptist colonel in Cromwell's army who was appointed to the Barebone's (or Little) Parliament set up by Cromwell in 1653. A staunch Fifth Monarchist, he was involved in a rebellion against King Charles II. Called upon to surrender, he escaped abroad and died in Utrecht in 1687 (Underwood, 1947: 108).

By 1677, the Particular Baptists were aware that the controversy between themselves were not doing any good to their cause. They had good reasons to refrain from controversy among themselves. The Appendix to the 1677 Confession says:

We are not insensible that as to the order of God's house, and entire communion therein there are some things wherein

> we (as well as others) are not at full accord among our-
> selves, as for instance, the known principle, and state of
> the consciences of diverse of us, that have agreed in this
> Confession is such, that we cannot hold Church-communion,
> with any other then Baptized-believers, and Churches
> constituted of such; yet some others of us have a greater
> liberty and freedom in our spirits that way; and therefore
> we have purposely omitted the mention of things of that
> nature ...

When the General Assembly of churches convened in London in 1689, the open communion Broadmead church, Bristol, was represented. The closed communion churches, while maintaining a closed Lord's table and a closed membership, seemed more tolerant of fellowship with open communion churches (Poh, 2000: 292-296).

Before 1689, the paedobaptists had come into the fray of the controversy. Obed Wills published "Infant Baptism Asserted and Vindicated by Scripture and Antiquity: In Answer To a Treatise of Baptism lately published by Mr. Henry Danvers", which called forth a response from Danvers in a second edition of "A Treatise of Baptism" (Danvers, 1674). A new focus of argument was introduced, namely, that baptism is a sign and seal of the covenant of grace which, to the paedobaptists, included the baptism of infants by sprinkling. Kiffin (1681), in his "A Sober Discourse", had to come to the fore to re-assert the Particular Baptist position that the Commission given by Jesus Christ in Matthew 28:19, supported by the practice of the apostles in Acts 2:41-42, shows that baptism is for believers, and that it precedes communion. Although ostensibly countering the likes of Bunyan, who was not mentioned by name, Kiffin was engaging the paedobaptists indirectly concerning their infant sprinkling. A disproportionate amount of space was devoted to quoting from, and referring to, the paedobaptists, including John Owen, Jeremiah Burroughs, Theodore Beza, William Ames, Thomas Manton, Richard Baxter, and the early church fathers such as Athanasius, Nazianzen, Ambrose, Jerome, Augustine, and others. His overt arguments against the likes of Bunyan were that by accepting unbaptized believers to the communion table and to church membership, they were doing something that is without positive scriptural command, at the same time acting contrary to the order taught in such passages as Matthew 28:19 and Acts 2:41-42. How were they, while believing in believer's baptism, to demand scriptural warrant for the infant baptism of the paedobaptists? The paedobaptists had been consistent in their practice of insisting on baptism for initiation into church communion, and therefore, the Lord's table, while they admitted that their practice of infant sprinkling was without positive scriptural warrant. Furthermore, it was agreed by all that baptism is a sign and seal of the covenant of grace. A covenant, by its nature, requires consent from the parties concerned, which infants are incapable of giving. Said Kiffin:

> [T]he conclusion is, that infant Baptism is as much a nullity as the marrying or Ordination of infants, and being really so by the grant of the favorers of this opinion: It will unavoidably follow that there admitting persons, upon pretense of that baptism to the Lord's Supper, is neither more nor less, than an admission without Baptism, and a plain declaration that they esteem this ordinance to be unnecessary.

Rather than seeing Kiffin as prolonging the debate with the open communion Particular Baptists, as hinted at by Underwood (1947: 103), it could be said that he was engaging with the paedobaptists in his eirenic manner. The controversy over the terms of communion was to be revived among the Particular Baptists in the second half of the 18th century, which is beyond the ambit of the present work (Crosby, 1: 35).

2.3.3 Baptism and the Covenant of Grace (1680-1700)

It has been noted how the Act of Uniformity of 1662 caused the ejection of the Puritans from the state church. The Episcopalians who were in power passed a series of Acts which formed the Clarendon Code (1661-1665), bringing severe hardship to the dissenters. In 1672 King Charles was able to pass the Declaration of Indulgence, the aim of which was to favour the Roman Catholics under cover of toleration for the dissenters. The respite from persecution experienced by the dissenters was short-lived. Under pressure from Parliament, the Declaration of Indulgence was withdrawn in 1673. The renewal of persecution brought the Baptists, the Congregationalists, and the Presbyterians nearer together. To indicate their agreement with the Presbyterians and the Congregationalists, the Particular Baptists produced the Second London Baptist Confession of Faith of 1677, based on the Westminster Confession of the Presbyterians and the Savoy Platform of the Congregationalists.

The Particular Baptists, however, were not about to give up their belief in believer's baptism. Their conscience was bound to Scripture, and Scripture alone. In the Appendix of the Confession, they stated:

> Let it not therefore be judged of us (because much hath been written on this subject, and yet we continue this our practise different from others) that it is out of obstinacy, but rather as the truth is, that we do herein according to the best of our understandings worship God, out of a pure mind yielding obedience to his precept, in that method which we take to be most agreeable to the Scriptures of truth, and primitive practise.

The Appendix was long, taking up thirty-three printed pages, while the body of the Confession itself, covering thirty-two subjects, took up one hundred and seven pages. The Appendix unequivocally countered the paedobaptist contention that infant baptism is for the new covenant what circumcision was for the old. They rejected the paedobaptist claim that baptism is the seal of the covenant of grace and held, instead, the indwelling of the Spirit of Christ as the seal. Circumcision "was suited only for the Male children, baptism is an ordinance suited for every beleiver [sic], whether male or femal [sic]". The Confession, with the Appendix, most likely originated from the Petty France Church in London, of which Nehemiah Coxe and William Collins were the pastors (Ivimey, 3: 332).

In 1681, the year that Kiffin's "A Sober Discourse" appeared, Nehemiah Coxe published his book, "A Discourse of the Covenants that God made with men before the Law". The purpose was declared in the subtitle of the book, "Wherein, the Covenant of Circumcision is more largely handled, and the Invalidity of the Plea for Paedobaptism taken from there discovered". Carefully, Coxe delineated Abraham's dual role in the covenant God made with him (Coxe, 1681: 72):

> Abraham is to be considered in a double capacity: he is the father of all true believers and the father and root of the Israelite nation. God entered into covenant with him for both of these seeds and since they are formally

distinguished from one another, their covenant interest must necessarily be different and fall under a distinct consideration. The blessings appropriate to either must be conveyed in a way agreeable to their peculiar and respective covenant interest. And these things may not be confounded without a manifest hazard to the most important articles in the Christian religion.

Coxe concluded his discourse by saying (Coxe, 1681: 140):

The old covenant is not the new; nor that which is abolished, the same with that which remains. Until these become one, baptism and circumcision will never be found so far one that the law for applying the latter should be a sufficient warrant for the administration of the former to infants.

In the preface of the book, Coxe mentioned that he was intending to produce another work on "the covenant made with Israel in the wilderness and the state of the church under the law". He said:

But when I had finished this and provided some materials also for what was to follow, I found my labor for the clearing and asserting of that point happily prevented by the coming out of Dr. Owen's third volume on Hebrews. There it is discussed at length and the objections that seem to lie against it are fully answered, especially in the exposition of the eighth chapter. I now refer my reader there for satisfaction about it which he will find commensurate to what might be expected from so great and learned a person.

Just as Coxe was in agreement with John Owen's exposition on the old covenant *vis-à-vis* the new covenant, so also was his contemporary Particular Baptist colleague, Benjamin Keach. Keach wrote extensively on covenant theology and baptism. Riker (2009) has shown how Keach stood firmly with the likes of John Owen in Reformed orthodoxy as far as covenant theology was concerned, which he developed based on Isaiah 54:10, "For the mountains shall depart and the hills be removed, but My kindness shall not depart from you, nor shall My covenant of peace be removed, says the LORD, who has mercy on you." In the course of expounding his covenant theology,

Keach had to counter Antinomianism on the one hand and Baxter-ism on the other. The Antinomians denied the place of the law in the life of the Christian, while Richard Baxter argued for salvation as a synergistic act of God's grace coupled with human co-operation.

Much as Keach admired Owen, and shared with him the same basic understanding of covenant theology, they differed on baptism. Keach's paedobaptist opponents included the Episcopalian William Burkitt (1650-1703), the Presbyterians James Owen (1654-1706) and John Flavel (*circa* 1630-1691), and the Athenian Society. The Athenian Society existed to answer questions of all kinds, including secular and trivial ones, and stood on the side of paedobaptism in the debate on baptism. In his polemical interactions with his opponents, Keach showed how Christendom had defected from Scripture through the centuries, and the necessity of continuing with the work of reformation begun by the continental Reformers. To Keach, separation from any church which did not practise believer's baptism by immersion was urgent, otherwise the Reformation would not move forward. He saw the rite to be of cardinal importance to a properly constituted visible church, but not essential to salvation. He affirmed that paedobaptist congregations "are true churches, as well as we [i.e., the Baptists], they being godly Christians, tho I believe they are less compleat [sic] churches, than those who are baptised upon profession of faith, or not so orderly in their constitution" (Riker, 2009: 220).

In 1693, Keach published "The Ax laid to the Root", in which he reiterated that there were two covenants, also called a two-fold covenant, made with Abraham. One was with the fleshly seed of Abraham while the other was made with "the true spiritual Seed of Abraham under the Gospel". "These things being so, what reason there is for any to plead for Infants Church Membership, by vertue [sic] of the Covenant made with Abraham, let all men consider. See Heb. 8:13." He further said, "I never said no Infants were included in the Covenant of Grace God made with Abraham, but not as such: No doubt, all Elect Persons, both Infants and Adult, were included in the Covenant of Grace, and had or shall have the Blessings of Christ's Blood and Merits" (Keach, 1693: 14, 25). In this work, Keach directly countered Flavel's arguments for infant baptism, and engaged also with Burkitt, the Athenian Society, and even the Roman Catholic, Bellarmine. Keach and Coxe stood clearly in the orthodox Reformed position on covenant theology, exemplified in John Owen, but boldly extended the arguments to conclude that only believers, baptized by immersion, should make up the membership of the visible church.

When William and Mary came to the throne, the Toleration Act was passed in 1689. In the same year, the Particular Baptists published their 1677 Confession of Faith, but without the Appendix. One of the 37 men who signed to adopt the Confession on behalf of "upwards of one hundred baptized congregations in England and Wales (denying Arminianism)" was Thomas Vaux, the pastor of the open communion Broadmead church in Bristol. The 1689 Confession, as it is known today, was worked over and condensed by Benjamin Keach in 1697 and published with an appendix on church discipline which indicated a lack of agreement of the churches on closed communion, saying that "others of us have a greater liberty and freedom in our spirits that way" (Lumpkin, 1969: 239-240).

2.4   THE SETTLED VIEWS

From before the 1950s, the Particular Baptists had been recognized as among those who practised the system of church government called Independency, together with the "Independents" who were paedobaptists. In 1645, Hanserd Knollys had countered the Presbyterial form of church government propounded by John Bastwick (1593-1654), a physician and controversial writer, in his book, "A Moderate Answer unto Dr. Bastwicks Book; called Independencie not Gods Ordinance". Bastwick also questioned the perceived practice of the Independents of admitting individuals to church membership by requiring them to take a covenant, claiming that the biblical method is simply to admit those who are baptized. Knollys answered that the Independent churches that he was acquainted with would indeed admit to membership only those who had repented, believed and been baptized. With time, the distinction between "the matter" and "the form" of the church became clear – the right of membership belongs to those who believe and have been baptized, while the constituting instrument of the church is the church covenant. By the end of the 17th century, the Particular Baptists were pretty much settled in their views on the autonomy of the local church and the gathered church principle.

2.4.1 The Nature of the Church

The Particular Baptists saw clearly that the word "ekklesia" in the New Testament is used in only two ways in reference to the people of God: the universal church, and gathered congregations. In the chapter on the church, the 1689 Confession devotes only the first paragraph to the definition of the universal church, stating:

> 1. The Catholick or universal Church, which (with respect to the internal work of the Spirit and truth of grace) may be called invisible, consists of the whole (a) number of the elect, that have been, are, or shall be gathered into one, under Christ, the head thereof; and is the spouse, the body, the fulness of him that filleth all in all.
> (a) Heb. 12. 23. Col. 1. 18. Eph. 1. 10, 22, 23. & ch. 5. 23, 27, 32.

Two signatories of the 1689 Confession, William Collins and Benjamin Keach, had been assigned to draw up a Baptist Catechism, which was published in 1693. Keach's name soon became attached to the catechism, probably because he was active in promoting it through his bookshop. Keach's Catechism has a clear statement on the invisible church. That this "invisible church" is one and the same as the "universal church" spoken of in the 1689 Confession is clear from the similar words employed to describe it. It says:

> Q. 106. What is the invisible church?
> A. The invisible church is the whole number of the elect, that have been, are, or shall be gathered into one under Christ the head.

After defining the universal church, the 1689 Confession moves quickly to define the "visible church":

> 2. All persons throughout the world, professing the faith of the gospel, and obedience unto God by Christ, according unto it; not destroying their own profession by any errors everting the foundation, or unholyness of conversation, (b) are and may be called visible Saints; (c) and of such ought all particular Congregations to be constituted.
> (b)1 Cor. 1. 2. Act. 11. 26. (c) Rom. 1. 7. Eph. 1. 20, 21, 22.

In Keach's Catechism is found this question and its answer:

Q105. What is the visible church?
A. The visible church is the organised society of professing believers, in all ages and places, wherein the gospel is truly preached and the ordinances of baptism and the Lord's supper rightly administered.

In contrast to the episcopal and presbyterial forms of church government, which hold to the idea of the visible universal church, the Particular Baptists rejected connectional church government of any kind. Commenting on John Bastwick's Presbyterianism, Hanserd Knollys said (Knollys, 1645: 3):

[C]oncerning the Government of the Church, the Doctor acknowledgeth in the same 7th. page, that the Brethren on both sides [referring to the Presbyterians and Independents] agree, *that the Government of the church is a Presbyterian-Government, both acknowledging a Presbyterie.* But whether it be Dependent, or Independent is the maine thing in question, which the Doctor doth determine, and saith in the Title page of his book he hath evidently Proved. *'That the Presbyterian-Government-Dependent is Gods Ordinance, and not the Presbyterian-Government-Independ-ent.*

[I]f by Independent the Doctor indeede mean (as it doth appear so to my understanding by many passages in his booke, he doth intend) a Presbyterian-Government, which hath not Dependencie upon any in matters merely Ecclesiasticall (but upon the Lord Jesus Christ, Who is the Head of the Church) And if by Dependent hee also intendeth (as in many other passages in his booke seemeth to me to be his meaning) a Presbyterian-Government, which hath a Dependencie upon a supream Judicature of a Common-councell of Presbyters, and who must in matters Ecclesiasticall be subiect unto the Decrees, Sentences, Constitutions, and Commandments of Common-coun-cell, Colledge or Consistorie of Classicall, Provinciall, or Synodicall Presbyters; Then I do conceive the Doctor hath not proved, (nor will he ever be able to prove) That the Presbyterian-Government-Dependent is

God's Ordinance ...
[Emphasis original.]

Bastwick's arguments could be reduced to four propositions, namely, (i) that there were several assemblies of believers in Jerusalem; (ii) that these several assemblies made up one church; (iii) the apostles and elders ruled over this church jointly in a common council or presbytery; (iv) that the church of Jerusalem ought to be a pattern for all churches. Knollys showed that the many scriptures (enough to occupy "two sheets") used by Bastwick only prove that local congregations were ruled by presbyters. They do not prove that there were several congregations in each city, much less that the several presbyteries were united under "a Common-councell or Court of Presbyters".

The Particular Baptists declared their settled view in the 1689 Confession (Chapter 26: 7) as follows:

> 7. To each of these Churches thus gathered, according to his [Christ's] mind, declared in his word, he hath given all that (o) power and authority, which is any way needed, for their carrying on that order in worship, and discipline, which he hath instituted for them to observe; with commands, and rules for the due and right exerting, and executing of that power.
> (o) Mat. 18. 17, 18. 1 Cor. 5. 4, 5. with v. 13. 2 Cor. 2. 6, 7, 8.

Like the Particular Baptists, the paedobaptist Independents denied the existence of any form of government beyond the local congregation. However, since they upheld infant baptism, they had to uphold the idea of the visible universal church just like the Presbyterians. The Savoy Declaration contained this article (Chapter 26, Article 2):

> 2. The whole body of men throughout the world, professing the faith of the gospel, and obedience unto God by Christ according unto it, not destroying their own profession by any errors everting the foundation, or unholiness of conversation, are and may be called the visible Catholique Church of Christ, although as such it is not intrusted with the administration of any ordinances, or

have any officers to rule or govern in, or over the whole
Body.

2.4.2 The Matter of the Church

The principle of "the gathered church" arose from what was commonly called the "essence" of the church. All the Independents held
to the view that the essence of the church consisted of two elements,
namely, the matter and the form (Owen, 1976, Vol. 16: 11). As far
as the matter of the church is concerned, it is made up of saints, that
is, true believers in Christ. The kingdom of Christ is different from
all other kingdoms in the world. As is to be expected, its membership is unique. Not only are the obviously profane excluded from
Christ's kingdom, those admitted are limited to the regenerate. Although God alone knows who are truly regenerate, the church is
called upon to judge by the external life and profession of those who
seek membership in the church of Jesus Christ. John Owen (1976,
Vol. 16: 13) said:

> God alone is judge concerning this regeneration, as unto
> its internal, real principle and state in the souls of men
> (Acts 15:8; Rev. 2:23), whereon the participation of all
> the spiritual advantages of the covenant of grace doth
> depend. The church is judge of its evidences and fruits
> in their external demonstration, as unto a participation
> of the outward privileges of a regenerate state, and no
> farther (Acts 8:13).

Today, this is often called a "credible profession of faith". A
prospective church member must be examined as to whether his profession of faith is a believable one. How may a credible profession
of faith be determined so that the individual may be admitted into
membership of the church? John Owen (1976, Vol. 16: 15-17) gave
the following indications: a competent knowledge of the gospel; a
professed subjection to the authority of Christ in the church; a knowledge of, and consent to, the doctrine of self-denial and bearing of the
cross; a conviction and confession of sin, with the way of deliverance
by Jesus Christ; the constant performance of all known duties of religion; and a careful abstinence from all known sins. Owen (1976, Vol.
16: 17) added that this confession of one's faith is to be made in spite

of fear, shame, the course of the world, and the opposition of all enemies whatever. The church minute books and association records are
replete with accounts of the promotion of piety in the members, and
the maintenance of the purity of the church through corrective discipline. The promotion of piety included regular attendance at church
meetings to worship and to hear exhortations from Scripture. There
were also corporate fasting and prayer times, lasting a day to a few
days, especially when the association of churches met. The practice
of fasting seems to have been lost to the spiritual descendants of the
Particular Baptists from the 19th century onwards, corresponding to
the disuse of the 1689 Confession of Faith from the 1830s (Oliver,
2006: 336). The 1689 Confession also requires the setting apart of
an elder to office "by Fasting and Prayer, with imposition of hands
of the Eldership of the Church, if there be any before Constituted
therein", while the setting apart of a deacon does not require fasting
(1689 Confession: 26: 9). A typical example of prayer and fasting
is recorded in the church records of the Wapping church in London
(Kevan, 1933: 40):

> ...this 12th of ye 3 month or May 1680. At A Church
> meeting held at ould Gravell Laine it was Agreed that ye
> Ch. keep A Day of humiliation upon ye next fifth day com
> fortnight beginning at Six of ye Clock in ye morning and
> ending at six in ye afternoon.

The maintenance of the purity of the church included visitations,
often made by appointed men of the church, to admonish the way-
ward. The practices of the Broadmead church in Bristol, as well as
that of the Bunyan Meeting, as shown in their church records, were
typical of the churches of that time (Underhill, 1847; Bunyan Meeting, 1928). An entry in the church book of the Bunyan Meeting for
1656 says (Bunyan Meeting, 1928: 16):

> At a meeting of the Church the 1st day of the 8th mon-
> eth.
> It was agree that Two brethren should be made choyce
> of every monethly meeting, to go abroad to visit our
> brethren and sisters; and to certify us (how they doe in
> body, and soule; and to stirre them up to come (espe-
> cially at our monethly meeting [)] to us to Bedford: and

to let them know if they come not, the church will expect
an account of the reason of their absence.

The unrepentant would be suspended, and then excommunicated,
by the church, with the pronouncement of the church's decision being made by the pastor (Knollys, 1681: 54). The sins dealt with included swearing, theft, drunkenness, adultery, and the like (Kevan,
1933: 41). B. R. White, in his introduction to the Association Records
of the Western Association, said (White, 1971-7, Pt. 2), "there is a
continued emphasis upon the need for holy living, for evangelism,
for the member congregations to realize their fellowship in one body
and, sounding through them all, an undertone of expectancy, of millenarian excitement". The 1689 Confession states that (Chapter 26:
12):

> As all Believers are bound to joyn themselves to partic-
> ular *Churches*, when and where they have opportunity
> so to do; So all that are admitted unto the privileges of a
> *Church*, are also (b) under the Censures and Government
> thereof, according to the Rule of *Christ*.
> (b) 1 Thes. 5.14. 2 Thes 3. 6, 14, 15.

Isaac Watts (Milner, 1845: 197) confirmed the great care taken
by the early Independents to examine prospective members of the
church, saying:

> They think it not sufficient ground to be admitted a mem-
> ber, if the person be only examined as to his doctrinal
> knowledge and sobriety of conversation; but they require
> with all some hints, or means, or evidences of the work
> of grace on their souls, to be professed by them, and that
> not only to the minister but to the elders also, who are
> joint rulers in the church. Though this profession of some
> of their experience is generally made first to the minister,
> either by word or writing, but the elders always hear it,
> and are satisfied before the person is admitted a member.

> These relations, which the Independents require, are not
> (as some think) of the word or scripture, or time, or
> place, or sermon, by which they were converted ; for very
> few can tell this ; but only they discourse and examine
> them a little of the way of their conviction of sin, of their

55

being brought to know Christ; or at least ask them what evidences they can give why they hope they are true believers, and try to search whether there be sincerity in the heart, as much as may be found by outward profession, that they may, as much as in them lies, exclude hypocrites.

2.4.3   The Form of the Church

Apart from the matter, there is also the form of the church to consider. Chapter 26, paragraphs 2, 5 and 6 of the 1689 Baptist Confession are relevant. Paragraphs 2 and 5 tell us that only true believers should make up the membership of local churches. Paragraph 6 is virtually a full description of the "gathered church" principle. It reads, in full, as follows:

> 6. The Members of these Churches are (m) Saints by calling, visibly manifesting and evidencing (in and by their profession and walking) their obedience unto that call of Christ; and do willingly consent to walk together, according to the appointment of Christ; giving up themselves to the Lord & one to another by the will of God, (n) in professed subjection to the Ordinances of the Gospel.
> (m) Rom. 1.7. 1 Cor. 1.2. (n) Act. 2.41, 42. ch. 5.13, 14. 2 Cor. 9.13.

This statement clearly declares that both voluntary consent and covenant commitment are required for the formation of a church. Voluntary consent arises from the nature of discipleship, which is voluntary. It also arises from the headship of Christ. Christ is alone the head of the church, and the Lord of every member in that church. The believer submits himself to Christ, whose will it is that he should be joined to a local church. This is in accord with the liberty of conscience. Just as in other areas of the Christian life, no coercion from men should be permitted in the matter of church membership.

Covenant commitment is also involved. By this is meant that members of the church voluntarily bind themselves together to form a church based upon an accepted doctrinal statement, mutually agreeing to carry out all that is agreed upon as members of that church. Many Independent churches of the seventeenth and eighteenth centuries had covenants committed to writing and subscribed by their members (Deweese, 1990; George, 1996). For Scripture warrant they would point to the covenant theology of the Bible in general, and to 2 Corinthians 8:5 in particular: "They ... first gave themselves to the Lord, and then to us by the will of God." To these must be added the many instances when the nation of Israel committed itself afresh to God by covenant (Ex. 24:1-8; Dt. 29:10-15; Josh. 24:19-28; 2 Kings 11:4, 17; 23:3; 1 Chr. 11:3; 2 Chr. 15:12; 23:1, 3, 16; 34:31-32; Ezra 10:3-5; Neh. 9:38). Of the Independent churches in seventeenth century England, K. W. H. Howard (1976: 238) wrote:

> It is not putting matters too strongly to say that the covenant idea was the root principle of their church order; and from it, with due appeal to scripture, flowed the related principles of membership and discipline.

The theological basis for the church covenant had been provided by John Spilsbury in the second edition of his corrected and enlarged work of 1652, "A Treatise Concerning The Lawful Subject Of Baptism". Spilsbury argued that "matter and form constitute a Church":

> The matter is a company of Saints, or persons professing faith in the righteousness of Jesus Christ, and living accordingly, that is, in holiness of life ... The form is that by which these are united and knit up together in one fellowship, and orderly body, and that is the *Covenant of Grace* which lies between God and His people; by which God *visibly becomes the God of such persons, and they His people above all others.*" [Emphasis original.]

Spilsbury further argued that the constitution of the church is:

> [T]he orderly collection of conjoining of persons into the New Covenant or *visible union with Christ their head,* as their mutual faith and agreement in the truth to the practice of it, and so consequently into an orderly body among themselves; wherein the *Saints are the matter,* and the *covenant is the form*; from which these two concurring, the Church arises, and is by them constituted, as Ezek. 16:8; Jer. 31:33; Heb. 8:10; Gal. 3:18, 29; Heb. 6:17; Zech. 1:3, 9; with Deut. 26:16, to 19; Deut. 29:12, 13; & Romans 9:8; with Gal. 4:28. [Emphasis original.]

Similarly, John Owen wrote in "The True Nature Of A Gospel Church And Its Government" (Owen, 1976, Vol. 16: 11): "THE church may be considered...as unto its *essence*, constitution, and being... As unto its essence and being, its constituent parts are its *matter* and *form*." Owen further explained that (Owen 16: 29-30):

> [U]nder the old testament, when God take the posterity of Abraham into *a new, peculiar church-state*, he did it by a *solemn covenant*... This covenant was the sole formal cause of their church-state, which they are charged so often to have broken, and which they so often solemnly renewed unto God. This was that covenant which was to be abolished... as the apostle disputes at large, Heb. vii-ix. The covenant of grace in the promise will still continue unto the true seed of Abraham, Acts ii. 38, 39...
>
> The same way for the erection of a church-state for the participation of the more excellent privileges of the gospel, and performance of the duties of it, for the substance of it, must still be continued; for the constitution of such a society as a church is, intrusted with powers and privileges by a covenant or mutual consent, with an engagement unto the performance of the duties belonging unto it ...
> [Emphasis original.]

John Owen (1976, Vol. 16: 30) gave the further argument that "the constitution of such a society ... hath its foundation in the light of nature, so far as it hath anything in common with other voluntary relations and societies". In other words, the church, although a unique institution, shares certain things in common with other societies in the world in that a covenant, or mutual consent, is required of the constituting members for it to exist properly. For members, there are privileges to enjoy and duties to perform. Discipline needs to be maintained in that society. The discussion of church discipline among the Particular Baptists is beyond the scope of this work.

The practice of having the church covenant as the instrument that gives form to the church continued into the 18th century. The church covenant produced by Benjamin Keach, which was appended to his book, "The Glory of a True Church" (1697), was to be particularly influential among the Particular Baptists. Roger Hayden (2006) has given examples of churches that adopted church covenants, which were signed by all the original members as well as by those who joined subsequently, spanning the 17th and early 18th centuries. They included the churches at Bromsgrove in 1672, Hitchin in 1681, Horsleydown (Keach's church) in 1697, Great Ellington in Norfolk in 1699, Alcester in 1712, and Barnoldswick in 1744.

2.5 SUMMARY

The intra- and inter-denominational debates of the Particular Baptists over baptism were inextricably linked to their understanding of the church, covering its nature, matter and form. The Particular Baptists believed in "the gathered church principle", in which believers alone are to be baptized, by full submersion in water, and that they alone are qualified to be members of the local church. The closed communion churches believed that church membership and the Lord's Supper are restricted to such baptized believers, while the open communion churches would allow for sprinkled believers to partake of the Lord's Supper and become members. By 1689, many of the closed communion churches, while holding to a closed Lord's table and a closed membership, were becoming more tolerant of those who had fellowship with the open communion churches. Both the closed and open communion churches upheld the need of voluntary consent for membership, expressed in voluntary commitment to the church covenant.

The principle of "the gathered church" was inseparable from that of "the autonomy of the local church". The Particular Baptists did not countenance a visible universal church. The universal church is invisible, manifesting itself in the world as visible local churches. Christ has bestowed all the necessary power and authority to the local church to order itself and carry out all Christian services. Unlike the paedobaptist Independents (or Congregationalists), the Particular Baptists would not accept the children of believers into the membership of the church. The covenant theology of the Particular Baptists was worked out consistently with their belief in believer's baptism. Together with the paedobaptist Independents, the Particular Baptists rejected the synodical rule of the Presbyterians. It will be seen in the next chapter that the Dissenters – including the Particular Baptists, the (paedobaptist) Independents, the Presbyterians, the General Baptists, and the Quakers – rejected the interference of the civil authorities in the affairs of the church. To the Particular Baptists, the autonomy of the local church was linked closely to their understanding of the headship of Christ, which is the subject of the next chapter.

※ ※ ※ ※ ※

Three

THE HEADSHIP OF CHRIST

3.1   INTRODUCTION

The principle of "the headship of Christ" has been widely recognized as crucial in the discussion on church polity. Du Plooy (1982: 1-3) says:

> The idea of the kingdom of God occupies a pivotal place in Scripture. The New Testament explicitly describes the course from kingdom to church and the particular relationship between them. The concept *kingdom* deals specifically with the fact, domain and method of God's reign through Christ. The kingdom of God points to God's dynamic reign in and through Jesus Christ – a reign to which his children or subjects have to submit. We see the advent of the kingdom wherever the Word and the Spirit are obeyed, and this community of believers is known as the church.

Thus the church is the fruit of the kingdom and, in turn, the instrument through which the kingdom has to be proclaimed; in addition, the church itself has to grow until the manifestation of the kingdom at the end of the world. The church is charged with the mission to administer the keys of the kingdom, precisely to unlock the kingdom of heaven to believers and to lock it against unbelievers (Du Plooy, undated: 50).

Du Plooy further says that where people obey the Word and the Spirit, God creates a new order in an imperfect world, which is known as a new creation or church of Jesus Christ. Those who regard the kingdom of God as their point of departure acknowledge and confess that Christ is the only Head of the church, and that true church government should be nothing less than the reign of Christ.

In his view of the concept *justice*, Smit (1985:10-19) uses the kingdom of God as his point of departure, saying:

> Christ as the Head of the church, in other words, the reign of God through Christ, is crucial to the question of who determines justice in the church: not the pope, nor the statutes of a country, the churches in a synod, a local church or a majority of votes. Christ as the Head reveals in His word what is right. Christ is the Legislator, and the church is taught through his Spirit and Word how to behave with regard to doctrine and life, and what the order in the church should be. God's justice relates directly to love, grace and judgement, and to the will of God.
>
> We see then, that the kingdom of God is the only basis on which to build church polity. *The Headship of Christ is naturally the most important principle of church polity.* For this reason church polity should start its study and research on the church with the kingdom of God and not with the church.
> [Emphasis added.]

In this writer's book, "The Keys of the Kingdom" (Poh, 2000: 67), he wrote:

> The principle of "the headship of Christ" is central to the discussion on church government. On this rock stands the true church, and on this same rock the false church founders. The principle and its implications must be correctly understood, without which there will be no possibility of sifting the many claims of the various systems of church government. From this principle flows many, if not all, of the other principles that make up the system of church government taught in the Holy Scripture.

This chapter will consider the development and outworking of the headship of Christ among the Particular Baptists, together with the concomitant truths of the authority of Scripture, the liberty of conscience, the relationship between state and church, and the legitimacy of the civil magistrate. The key groups of people involved, however, must be identified first.

3.2 THE KEY MEN

Who exactly were the Particular Baptists? Most, if not all, of the literature to date assumes that they were the Calvinistic churches of the 17th century in England, Wales and Ireland that practised believer's baptism, affirmed the 1689 Confession, and were associated in a number of regional associations linked to the London churches, which played the leading role in their associational life. The impression portrayed is that these constituted all the Calvinistic Baptist churches there were, with a few sectarian groups scattered among them, and with the London churches acting as the standard bearers. While it is not the chief aim of the present work to challenge this conception, due cognizance must be taken of its possible falsity. The conception is true only if the period is limited up to the 1660s. Even in that limited period, there was no uniformity of belief among the number of Particular Baptist Associations. There were churches that would have to be considered Particular Baptist (both closed communion and open communion ones) which were not members of the regional associations. The churches connected with Henry Jessey, John Tombes, and John Bunyan have been referred to. There were certainly other churches that have escaped the purview of detailed studies. What Riker has said of Reformed theology and the Reformation of the 16th century may be said of the Particular Baptist movement in the 17th century. Said Riker (2009: 20, 21):

> Reformed theology ... was not monolithic from its inception; there was space for diversity within its boundaries. It is important to make a distinction between extra- and intra-confessional debates. The Reformed Orthodox disputed with those outside the family (Soci-nians, Papists, Anabaptists, Arminians, etc.) and also with those within.
>
> All of these many currents were accommodated within the broad confines of the orthodox Reformed stream. In

the light of this diversity, it is hardly possible to confer an *autorité papale* to Calvin as if he were the rule against which the whole Reformed tradition were to be measured.

Similarly, it is hardly possible to confer an *autorité papale* to the London Particular Baptist leaders nor to the 1689 Confession of Faith that they produced. Many of the early leaders changed their views on various issues and found themselves on opposite sides of controversies, as happened to William Kiffin and Hanserd Knollys in the hymn-singing controversy. While the 1689 Confession may be taken as an expression of the settled views of the Particular Baptists at large, it must not be wrongly assumed that all the articles of faith in the confession were accepted by everyone, or that the Confession was adopted by all the churches which shared its main doctrines. When discussing church autonomy, it has been noted how the Particular Baptists were divided into closed communion and open communion churches. In discussing the headship of Christ, it would be necessary to divide them along another plane, such that there were the conservatives and the radicals. Eschatology was a significant factor in the division between these groups (Bell, 2000).

3.2.1   The Conservative Particular Baptists

The conservatives among the first London churches were associated with William Kiffin, Samuel Richardson, and John Spilsbury who formed a threesome of respected leaders. The eschatology of this group can be seen to endorse society rather than to oppose it. It was concerned with apologetics and generally was more conservative in tone and action. These leaders dominated the London Particular Baptists during the interregnum and pushed radicalism to the perimeters, both geographically and theologically. Geographically, the radical Baptists had to go to the west of England or to Ireland to avoid the pressures of the Kiffin circle. Theologically, intensely apocalyptic Baptists were forced into the folds of the Fifth Monarchists or the Seventh-Day Baptists.

Among the London leaders, Hanserd Knollys embraced the radical theology of the Fifth Monarchists but not their violence. Knollys was the most thorough millenarian thinker among the Particular Baptists. He was the only Baptist of his time to undertake an exposition of the entire book of Revelation. His knowledge of Greek and Hebrew, combined with his familiarity with ecclesiastical histories, made his commentaries very forceful. Am-ong the members of his big congregation were many radical Fifth Monarchists. Knollys (1679), however, believed that the power of Christ to usher in the kingdom "is a ministerial, prophetical, stewardly power; that is, the power of the word, not of the sword". As such, he must be numbered among the conservatives.

The second generation of Particular Baptist leaders, such as Benjamin Keach, Nehemiah Coxe, and William Collins, would be regarded as conservatives as well. They were aligned with the older conservatives in supporting the king and adopted the policy of accommodation despite, and perhaps because of, the hardship experienced under the reigns of Charles II (r. 1660-1685) and James II (r. 1685-1688). It would be remembered that Coxe and Collins were probably the two men who drew up the 1677/1689 Confession of Faith (Ivimey, 3: 260), while Keach's name became attached to the Catechism drawn up for the Particular Baptists by himself and Collins. As will be seen, the third generation of Particular Baptists who served God into the first half of the 18th century were conservatives as well, praying constantly for king and nation whenever the throne was threatened by forces within or without the country.

3.2.2 The Violent Radicals

Before the 1650s, the Particular Baptists had to contend with the Levellers. Their opponents gave them their name, implying that they wanted "to level all men's estates, and subvert all government" (Wolfe, 1944: 238). The Levellers shared the Baptist desire for religious liberty and the removal of tithes. Common goals, mutual enemies, and shared experiences in the army of Cromwell allowed the Baptists and Levellers to cooperate in the mid-1640s, although their alliance was never stable. The Baptists, led by the threesome – Kiffin, Richardson and Spilsbury – eventually abandoned the Levellers, at the cost of being blamed for betraying them. In 1647, the Baptists published "A Declaration of Severall Congregationall Societies in, and about the city of London" in which they insisted that for the sake of the nation, the good of the churches, and the advancement of their cause, it was best that the members of the churches honour and submit to the present powers (Tolmie, 1977: 181-184).

By 1649, the relationship between the Baptists and the Levellers was totally severed (Wright, 2006). The Levellers faded away, while the Particular Baptists survived by changing their eschatological perspective to validate society instead of opposing it.

In the 1650s two new radical movements were to trouble the Particular Baptists, namely, the Fifth Monarchists and the Seventh-Day Baptists. The Quakers also caused them problems, claiming the necessity of the inner light while rejecting the ordinances as dead forms. However, the Fifth Monarchists and the Seventh-Day Baptists were the people who interacted with the conservatives in the development of their respective understanding of the headship of Christ, sharpening one another through the tumultuous events of the time. Historians in the first half of the 20th century, such as W. T. Whitley and L. F. Brown, saw a close connection between the Baptists and the Fifth Monarchists. In the latter half of the 20th century, historians such as B. S. Capp and B. R. White have downplayed the link between the movements. M. R. Bell in his book "Apocalypse How?" makes a convincing case for the link between them. He shows that a probable majority of Fifth Monarchists accepted believer's baptism. Out of a list of 242 Fifth Monarchists supplied by Capp (Bell, 2000: 167), the Particular Baptists outnumbered the General Baptists in the ratio of 4:1.

The Fifth Monarchist movement was so named by their belief that the fifth monarchy – the rule of Christ and His saints – was at hand. The seventh chapter of Daniel served as their primary proof text. It was believed that the Assyrian, Persian, Greek and Roman empires would be replaced by the reign of Christ in the fifth monarchy. The time was at hand, now that Rome was undone by the Revolution. The Fifth Monarchists found some supporters among the Presbyterians, but their membership was drawn mainly from the Baptists and Independents. Numbered among them were Paul Hobson and Thomas Gower. The two had led the Particular Baptist church at Newcastle and had signed the 1644 and 1646 Particular Baptist Confessions together. They soon left the company of other Baptist signatories such as Kiffin and Richardson, being heavily involved with the Levellers and the Fifth Monarchist movement. In 1663 Hobson's name appeared on an arrest warrant for "seditious and treasonable practices". Gower and Hobson managed to elude the authorities in London. Hobson continued to organize various radicals and lived in hiding among friends. After a series of aliases and near captures,

Hobson's hiding ended in the summer of 1663, when he was arrested for his involvement in the Yorkshire Plot. According to one of the conspirators, the Yorkshire Plot was intended to force Charles II to honour the promises made at Breda, to grant liberty of conscience to all but Roman Catholics, to abolish certain taxes, and to reform the ministry of the state church (Katz, 1988: 42).

It is to be noted that the distinction between Fifth Monarchists and other members of gathered churches was amorphous. Many of those who held to Fifth Monarchy views were actually members of the churches led by the conservatives. Conservative leaders who held to their radical eschatology, although not sharing their belief in the use of force, included Hanserd Knollys in London and Thomas Collier in the West Country. Collier was later disowned, and condemned for heresy, by other Particular Baptists. Paul Hobson and Thomas Gower also dissociated from the conservative Baptists because of their Fifth Monarchy radicalism. Other notable Fifth Monarchists included Vavasor Powell, John Pendarves, Nathaniel Strange, and Thomas Tillam.

3.2.3   The Passive Radicals

As the Fifth Monarchy movement died out towards the close of the 1650s, the Seventh-Day Baptists increasingly became a problem. Though they remained small in number they were a source of worry for the conservative Particular Baptists. Losses to the Seventh-Day Baptists as well as to the Quakers were so significant that the issue had to be seriously addressed. Women seemed to be particularly vulnerable. It was not until 1654 that the West Country Association officially ruled on the role of women in the church. They decided that "a woman is not permitted at all to speak in the church, neither by way of praying, prophesying, nor inquiring". It is little wonder that women left the Particular Baptists for the "errors of the times viz. the people called Quakers and those that hold the Seventh-Day Sabbath" (White, 1971-7: Pt. 2: 55; Pt. 3: 190-191, 209, 211-214). On the wider front, the Seventh-Day Baptists' call for further reformation placed them in opposition to a society recently shaken by revolution. As people sought peace and avoided conflict, the Seventh-Day Baptists refused to be silent. Even if some attended both Sunday and Saturday services, the observance of the seventh day connected them to a select group of saints.

There was considerable overlap in the membership of the Fifth Monarchy movement and the Sabbatarian movement. Bern-ard S. Capp's book, "The Fifth Monarchy Men", is regarded by Mark R. Bell as the best source available for the study of the Fifth Monarchists. Of the list of 242 Fifth Monarchists supplied by Capp, Bell (2000:167) noted that there were between 43 and 49 Seventh-Day Baptists compared to the Particular Baptists, who were between 35 and 43 in number. A number of Particular Baptists were to remain or become Seventh-Day Baptists even after the demise of the Fifth Monarchy movement. Henry Jessey, the open communion Particular Baptist, was eventually to turn Seventh-Day Baptist, although he practised Saturday observance privately with a small group of people. Thomas Tillam, who was initially associated with the closed communion Particular Baptists, became a Fifth Monarchist, and finally a leading Seventh-Day Baptist.

The Seventh-Day Baptists believed that the Sunday Sabbath was a popish innovation that replaced the apostolic practice of observing the Saturday Sabbath. They interpreted the prophecy of Daniel 7:25, that Antichrist shall "change times and law", as proof for their argument. Rome had usurped God's authority by corrupting the fourth commandment. To complete the Reformation and expose the Antichristian Rome, they insisted that the Sabbath must be returned to Saturday. The observance of the Saturday Sabbath not only complied with Christian obedience, but was also a battle against Rome, in defence of true religion. It can be seen that eschatology was at the foundation of the movement, in line with the Baptist apocalypticism, in seeking to return to original purity in order to move forward to the eschatological end.

The conservative Particular Baptists rejected the Saturday Sabbath, as may be seen in their Association Records. The Midlands Association Records (White, 1971-7: Pt. 1: 32) gave three grounds for the rejection of the Saturday Sabbath. First, the Sabbath was given to the children of Israel as a sign between them and the Lord in their generation. Second, Colossians 2:16ff clearly shows that the Sabbaths were shadows not meant for gospel times, as is confirmed in Hebrews 4, rightly understood. Third, in Galatians 4:10ff the apostle speaks (disapprovingly) of the observance of days that had been appointed by the law of Moses, which are a reference to the weekly or Sabbath days, as is clear by comparison with verse 21. Although somewhat frowned upon, the Sabbatarians seemed to be accepted by the main Particular Baptist body, prior to the General Assembly of the Particular Baptists in London in 1689. The Records of the Abingdon Association answered the query, "Whether it be expedient for us to hold communion with them [the Sabbatarians] and, if yea, then how and how farr [sic]" as follows: "...in case nothing else should be found amisse [sic] but the bare observing of the 7th day Sabbath, then the saying of the apostle in Ro. 14:1,5f. might be well minded" (White, 1971-7: Pt. 3: 195).

A change of attitude to Sabbatarianism took place in the years following, probably due to the tumultuous events that unfolded, as described below. In a discussion of London Baptist life M. D. MacDonald (1982: 34) says this of the General Assembly of the Particular Baptists in London in 1689:

> No invitation... was extended to the seventh day Calvinistic Baptist churches of which there were two in London in 1690... representatives had evidently been invited to meetings of the London Elders in 1688... but were now told that they could not be admitted without verification that all the churches of the association were willing to receive them.

It will be seen that the Particular Baptists dissociated themselves from the more radical Seventh-Day Baptists, like Thomas Tillam, for their actions. By the end of the 17th century, they declared their rejection of the theology that gave rise to those actions.

3.3   THE KEY ISSUES

The root of the agitations among the Particular Baptists lay in their biblicism, arising from their submission to the headship of Christ. Disagreement lay in the following areas:

(i) How does eschatology impinge upon the the headship of Christ, as it is worked out in the life of the church now?

(ii) Is the restoration of the Saturday Sabbath related to the calling in of the Jewish elect and, therefore, in the hastening of Christ's return to establish the eschatological kingdom?

(iii) How do the liberty of conscience and the priesthood of all believers relate to the divine rights of the magistrate and civil
authority?

The crossroads of their struggle came with the publication of the
Confession of Faith of 1644 and the subsequent editions. The Confession marked the beginning of their movement from a more opposi-
tional to a relatively more accommodationist movement. Before the
Particular Baptists came to the settled views of the 1689 Confession,
the conservatives had had to win over or subdue the radicals. Three
periods may be discerned, corresponding to those in which baptism
was debated. Again, it is to be noted that these periods were not
sharply defined by boundaries of time or issues. The three periods
were:

(i) The years 1640-1660, in which understanding on the headship
of Christ was worked out in relation to the violent radicalism
of the Levellers and the Fifth Monarchists.

(ii) The years 1660-1680, in which the understanding on the headship of Christ was worked out in relation to the passive radicalism of the Seventh-Day Baptists.

(iii) The years 1680-1700, in which the understanding of the headship of Christ, as refined under severe persecution, arrived at
the settled view expressed in the 1689 Confession.

3.3.1   Christ's Headship and Violent Radicalism (1640-1660)

John Smyth taught that the English Reformation had struck a fa-
tal blow upon the temple of the Antichrist, but there remained the
work of undermining its very foundation. He declared "the error
of baptizing infants, [is] a chief point of antichristianism, and the
very essence and constitution of the false church" (Whitley, 1915:
576, 659). Baptists like Thomas Collier identified the Antichrist, the
Beast, and the Devil as the sources of infant baptism (Collier, 1645:
18-22). The practice of believer's baptism brought the Baptists into
extremely high tension with society. Before the Baptist challenge,
infants were being baptized to symbolize entry into the Christian
community, which was seen as comprehensive. This was the essence
of sacralism. By rebaptizing themselves, Baptists were declaring that

faith and piety were matters that concerned the individual and God. They were declaring their belief in the priesthood of all believers. Many otherwise law-abiding citizens were so threatened by the Baptists that they resorted to both symbolic and physical violence against them. Baptists, on their part, saw such treatment as the Beast's defences as its final garrison was attacked. The Beast was taking on the dual nature of baptism of infants and persecution for religion. The idea developed that Christ had given temporal authority to the magistrate, but still retained all authority in matters of conscience. While it was true in the Old Testament that the magistrate was responsible for the morality of the people, under the gospel, Christ alone was the King of the church. All who opposed His authority in this matter were usurpers, the Beast, Antichrist. This perspective helped Baptists to see their persecution and alienation as a confirmation of their favour with God. As William Kiffin explained, "the afflictions and persecutions that are imposed by the wicked men upon the Saints, causes them to see a spirit of glory reflecting upon them" (Kiffin, 1641).

Most Baptists were millenarians who believed that a future millennium was described in Revelation. They debated whether it was literal or spiritual, but they agreed that it was close at hand. Another facet of Baptist eschatology was the idea of bearing witness against the Beast. While most Baptists did not believe in the revolutionary politics of Müntzer, they believed that the Beast had to be combated. Soon Christ would return to judge all in their struggle against the Beast. Knollys wrote, "Consider I beseech you, there is a world to come, and Christ will come, and everyone shall give account of himself to God" (Knollys, 1681b: 32). Witnessing against the beast requires some form of action beyond mere faith, putting faith into motion against the Beast. In the meeting of messengers of the churches of the Abingdon Association in the tenth month of 1656, the following was published (White, Pt. 3: 169):

> It is not lawfull for saints to joyne with the national church assemblyes or the nationall church ministers (viz., those that preach and pray as men authorised to act as ministers of the nationall church commonly called the Church of England, as namely, parsons, vicars, curates and parish lecturers) in any part of their nationall worship, or so to heare the said national church ministers in their preach-

ings or ministeriall exhortations whether in their churches, so-called, or at burialls or in any other like way, as in any appearance to countenance the same or to seeke edification thereby, the nationall church worship and the nationall church ministrie being antichristian and Babylonish. Consider 2 Cor. 6.17 with Rev. 18.4.

The association records of the Midlands churches similarly published, after their meeting in June 1656, the following: "baptised believers ought not to here the nationall ministers preach nor joyne with them in their publike worship, their pretended ministery being Babylonish, Rev. 18.4" (White, Pt. 1: 25).

Some Baptists thought that witnessing against the Beast required radical, even military action. They saw their war against King Charles in an apocalyptic light, where bloodshed was not only permitted but required. Still others came to see Oliver Cromwell as the Beast and advocated his violent overthrow. These conclusions were easily drawn in an age when politics and religion were inseparable. Numerous Baptists joined the Parliamentary forces during the civil wars of the 1640s, both as soldiers and as chaplains. They proved to be good preachers as well as good fighters in both the civil wars. Unlike the pacifist Anabaptists, the Particular Baptists had few reservations about war. The army provided a vehicle for the spread of Baptist beliefs. Richard Baxter observed in despair that there were "swarms of Anabaptists in our armies" (Woodhouse, 1938: 388). Soldiers were not the only converts. The inhabitants near the stations of the armies were reached by the gospel so that churches were established. It was only after their activities had abated that planned missionary efforts were required, through further organization on the part of Baptist leaders after the wars.

While the Presbyterians shared the Baptists' belief that the army was a divine tool for bringing about the Kingdom, they did not share the Baptists' hope that it would establish religious liberty. This hope, however, was shared by the Levellers. Originating around 1645, the movement came to advocate various radical reforms, including a widening of the franchise, the opening of enclosed lands, the abolition of monarchy, and the equality of men under the law, as well as a social contract as the foundation for government. Bell (2000: 99) suggests the possibility that the Levellers' egalitarian policies derived in part from General Baptist theology, particularly the idea of universal equality and accountability before God. While the Levellers shared much in common with the Baptists, including religious liberty and the removal of tithes, the differences between them were stark. It became clear to the Particular Baptists that the Levellers were more a liability than an asset. An example of the initially shared vision of the Baptists with the Levellers was the sermon preached by Thomas Collier at Putney. Collier was a great Baptist leader and a fervent evangelist who spent most of his life in the western sections of England establishing Baptist churches. He published the sermon that he preached to the soldiers at Putney on 29 September 1647 under the title "A Discovery of the New Creation". For Collier, a new day had truly burst forth in England. The soldiers' success, the religious freedom, the new light in many saints, and the Levellers' proposed reforms all pointed to the dawn of the New Jerusalem (Hill, 1972: 59). What was missed in the Levellers' agenda Collier supplied, namely, that reforms were to come about not through new laws based on rationality and natural rights, but by "the abundance of light" that accompanies Christ's coming. Collier explained that it was

> only the glorious light of this new creation that will put an end to these divisions amongst Christians. It is not magisterial power ... but that one Spirit of light and truth that must bring the Saints into this unity ... And the truth is that nothing else will be able to put an end to these divisions but this spiritual dispensation, this new creation of God ... and this is and shall be the glory of this heaven, unity and peace amongst Saints (Collier, 1647: 3-40).

Eschatology lay at the heart of the Baptist-Leveller alliance. The Levellers, however, went one step beyond the Baptists' acceptance of the division of church and state as a temporary expediency until the coming of King Jesus. The Levellers rejected any form of godly rule. Instead, they advanced the "secular" state as legitimate in its own right, based on rationality as opposed to divine grace. When the second Civil War began in 1648, Parliament passed a strict blasphemy ordinance calling for the imprisonment of all those who denied infant baptism. Presbyterians were barred from the "Rump" Parliament. The Independents who were decidedly in control set about the trial and execution of the king. By this time, the conservative Baptist leaders were confident of pursuing their goals without the Levellers. A number of Leveller leaders were arrested and imprisoned in the

Tower, including Richard Overton, John Lilburne and William Walwyn. They had criticised the government in a petition published under the title, "The Second Part of England's New Chaines Discovered". The Particular Baptist leader, Samuel Richardson, went to see them and asked that they abandon their critiques of the government, but failed in his mission. The Particular Baptists issued their own petition, entitled, "The Humble Petition and Representation of Several Churches of God in London, Commonly (though Falsly) called Anabaptists" (1649), in which they condemned the Levellers' petition and agenda. The Particular Baptists were now defining their movement in contrast to the Levellers as well as the Anabaptists. This petition was presented to Parliament on 2 April and William Kiffin was allowed to address the House. What a relief it was to Kiffin and his companions, when the Speaker returned the House's answer (Humble Petition, 1649: 4-8): "That for yourselves and the other Christians walking answerable to such professions as in this petition you make, they do assure you of liberty and protection." The tie between the Particular Baptists and the Levellers had been cut. The Levellers faded out of the scene, while some individuals from among them were drawn into the Fifth Monarchist movement.

After the collapse of the Levellers the next serious challenge to the Particular Baptist cause came from the Fifth Monarchists in the 1650s. When the Barebone's Parliament collapsed and gave powers to Cromwell, the "hotter" saints were outraged. The Particular Baptists in Ireland shouted the loudest. In response, Kiffin, Spilsbury and Joseph Fansom (Samson) sent a letter to the Baptists in Ireland, chastising them and demanding their immediate acquiescence to the new government. The Fifth Monarchists in London, including those in Knollys's and Jessey's churches signed a "Declaration of Several of the Churches of Christ and Godly People ... Concerning the Kingly Interest of Christ" (Bell, 2000: 154). Knollys and Jessey themselves did not sign. Kiffin and his circle went all out to denounce the Fifth Monarchists by visiting numerous congregations and by sending letters to congregations they could not visit (Bell, 2000: 180). It quickly became apparent that the majority of conservative Particular Baptists were not willing to go into direct opposition against the post-regnum regime, regardless of its character. They thought it best to wait for the manifestation of God's will. As a result, the Fifth Monarchists now defined themselves in contrast to the main Baptist movements, just as the Baptists tried to define themselves against the Fifth Monarchists. The Baptists still believed in the apocalypse, but it was now an event placed in the distant future. For the Fifth Monarchists, on the other hand, it was still an urgent and imminent reality (White, 1996: 57-58). The eschatology of the Fifth Monarchists also affected their ecclesiology. They rejected any semblance of "ecclesiastical tyranny" and, therefore, deliberately avoided creating any organizational structure. The Baptists were able to distance themselves from the Fifth Monarchists because of a combination of their nascent denominational identity, a distinct core of leaders, and an organizational system.

An example of the agitation caused by the Fifth Monarchists was the petition put forward by the open communion Particular Baptist, Vavasor Powell in 1655 (Bell, 2000: 185-191). Powell was a radical itinerant evangelist who was influential in the establishment of a number of congregations in Wales. He was closely associated with Henry Jessey. In his petition, entitled "A Word For God", Powell strongly criticized Cromwell, warning him to repent of his apostasy and return to "doing your first works ... lest God's fury break forth like fire upon you, and there be no quenching of it". By 1656 Samuel Richardson put forth his "Plain Dealing" to defend the Protectorate. This work at the same time showed the difference in perspectives on Revelation between the radical Baptists, like Powell, and more conservative Particular Baptists like Richardson. They both still sought the millennium, only Richardson argued that the Beast, for the time being, had been sufficiently defeated. The *status quo* was an acceptable substitute, if not an avenue for, the Kingdom of Heaven. Powell and his supporters, however, believed there was little good in coming half way out of Babylon.

Apart from Powell and his followers, the Particular Baptists in areas outside the direct influence of the Kiffin-Knollys-Richardson circle took a stand similar to that of their London brethren (White, 1966: 224-225). An example was the Midlands Association which published, after their meeting in October 1656, the following in answer to the question, "What is the duty of beleivers [sic.] at this day towards the present powers, whether in civill things to submitt unto them and to live what in them lyeth peacable under them":

[W]ee must desire and indeavour to leade peaceable life
under the civill power and these things among others
in like manner commanded are still to [be] taught and

learned and obeyed as may soundly be inferred from 2 Tim. 2.2. And if the magistrate shall now give forth unto us unlawfull commands wee ought rather to suffer patiently for our just refusing to yeald any acttive obedience to them then to rise up in rebellion against the magistrate. If, doing well, wee suffer for it and take it patiently this is acceptable with God, I. Pet. 2.20.

... Shall not kings then be the churches' nursing fathers and their queens their nursing mothers, Is. 49.23? Wee offer it to the searious consideration whether it be not implied in Ro. 11.12,15 that the Gentile churches shall be in a low condition till the calling of the Jewes and whether it may not be gathered from Mic. 4.8, that the Jewish Church shall have the kingdom and the first dominion, Japhet being to dwell in the tents of Shem, Gen. 9.27. If so, then whether it doth not behove us with patience and quietness to waite for the time (White, 1977: Pt. 1: 30).

By spring of 1657, even the conservative Particular Baptists in London were growing anxious, for "The Humble Petition and Advice" had been put forward in Parliament as the foundation for a new government. In addition to providing for an "other house" to the House of Commons, the Humble Petition also proposed that Cromwell be named king. The Particular Baptists and the Independents drafted a letter urging Cromwell to reject the crown. They maintained that since God's chosen instrument had as recently as 1649 declared that monarchy was "unnecessary, burdensome, and destructive to the safety of the people", then it should not be reinstated. All the leading men of London signed, except for Kiffin. Cromwell ended up refusing the crown (Bell, 2000: 190-191).

As the Fifth Monarchist movement began to wane due to sporadic arrests of some men by the government and the counteractive influence of the conservative Baptists, some members were driven to even more radical extremes. Thomas Venner was one of the leaders of the Fifth Monarchist congregation in Swan Alley, Coleman Street, in London. Like many others, he had left for the New World but returned after the calling of the Long Parliament. Venner was briefly employed as the cooper (that is, one who made barrels) at the Tower of London, but was dismissed for a number of reasons, including his suspected intention to blow it up. By the beginning of 1657, his congregation was preparing for a final revolution. The plan was for a new kingdom to be set up, ruled by a Sanhedrin selected by the saints and governed by laws taken from the Bible. The conspirators decided on midnight 9 April 1657 as the date and time of attack. The plot, however, was discovered in the nick of time and scuttled. Venner was imprisoned in the Tower of London, which he had apparently planned to blow up before. His stay was not long, for he was released before the Restoration.

Upon the death of Cromwell, his son replaced him as Lord Protector. Recognizing that the Revolution was unravelling, a meeting of Particular Baptist and General Baptist leaders took place. These representatives united to issue a joint, blanket, promise of civil obedience to "whatever Government is, and shall be established in this Nation" (Declaration, 1659: 1). Charles Stuart did indeed come back and was proclaimed king on 8 May 1660. Shattered by the Restoration of the king and the failure of all of their prophecies, a group of Fifth Monarchists gathered around the recently freed Thomas Venner. They decided to make one last bid to bring about the Kingdom of God on earth by force. In January 1661, they attacked London twice with great ferocity, plunging the city into chaos. After the majority of the Fifth Monarchists had been shot or captured, some semblance of order was restored. Venner himself had been shot three times before he was captured. Venner and twelve of his leading disciples were swiftly executed and their heads displayed on London Bridge. In an attempt to mop up the remaining Fifth Monarchists, many innocent Baptists, Independents and Quakers were arrested. Within days, conventicles were banned. A time of great persecution and harassment began for dissenters. The intensity of this persecution would wax and wane over the next two decades and further transform the Baptist movements. The Fifth Monarchists had extinguished themselves in anything but a blaze of glory.

3.3.2 Christ's Headship and Passive Radicalism (1660-1680)

With the collapse of Venner's Fifth Monarchist uprising in 1661, one last significant manifestation of Baptist eschatology appeared. The authorities made an example of John James, a Seventh-Day Baptist who was arrested for allegedly advocating a change of government. He was brutally executed, with his heart removed and his head skewered on a pole and placed opposite his meeting house. While the Baptists had frequently seen infant baptism and religious persecution as the "last bastions of Antichrist", the Seventh-Day Baptists saw another obstruction in the doctrine of the Sabbath. They were convinced that removing this last design of the Man of Sin would finally allow them to complete the Reformation. It was also widely believed that the conversion of the Jews was a necessary precondition for the return of Christ. Sunday worship was seen as a great obstacle for the Jews, since it was unscriptural. If the Sabbath were returned to its proper day of the week, the Jews would be more speedily converted. Notable leaders among the Seventh-Day Baptists included Thomas Tillam, Richard Denton, John Spittlehouse, Christopher Pooley, Peter Chamberlen, John James, Francis Bampfield, and Edward Stennett.

Tillam was a restless apocalyptic radical who was initially connected with the church in Hexham. Like John Smyth and Henry Jessey, his commitment to finding his own truth forced frequent changes in his religious perspective. Tillam was at the beginning a Particular Baptist, then a Fifth Monarchist, and ended as a Seventh-Day Baptist. In his earlier years, the London churches disapproved of his close association with the open communion churches of John Tombes. Because of his complicated involvement with a certain Joseph Ben Israel, who turned out to be not a Jew, but a Scotsman by the name of Thomas Ramsey, the Particular Baptists disowned him in 1655. Together with Christopher Pooley, Tillam had founded churches in the North Country that were Fifth Monarchist and distinctively Baptist, and usually Seventh-Day Baptist. The Restoration was the final blow to the attempts of the radicals to prepare England for the return of Christ. England was no longer the New Jerusalem, but the new Babylon. Tillam now wanted to remove the godly remnant from England to start a community in the Palatinate, in southwestern Germany, in order to salvage the revolution of the saints. He and Pooley became embroiled with Paul Hobson in recruiting saints for the colony in the Palatinate. As noted already, Hobson was arrested, imprisoned, and released shortly before his death. He evidently believed that the Baptists' long-term goal of religious liberty could still be achieved through radical action. Tillam and Pooley were back in England by 1664 to gather more Sabbatarians for their Palatinate colony. A spy obtained a copy of "Solemn Covenant" that was being distributed by Pooley. Those who desired to go to the colony had to sign the covenant. The covenant declared that all power was given to "Christ our king [and] we do utterly renounce all powers and rulers". Those who agreed swore to obey all the laws of God "which he hath commanded for all Israel, and particularly those first foundation truths, the seventh day Sabbath and marriage". By June 1667 Pooley was apprehended and imprisoned. He refused to swear an oath of obedience to the king or acknowledge himself a subject to the present government. He seems to have escaped from prison, for he was spotted again in his efforts to recruit the saints for the Palatinate. Tillam and Pooley finally settled in the colony in Germany, when the last known boatload of passengers sailed there on March 1668.

Another Seventh-Day Baptist was Edward Stennett. He was a Baptist in Abingdon and had been an active Fifth Monarchist in the 1650s before becoming a Seventh-Day Baptist. Along with Francis Bampfield, Stennett was the most influential Seventh-Day Baptist in the later years of the reign of Charles II. Stennett actively published in defence of the seventh-day cause, and kept in contact with the nine or ten seventh-day churches he knew of in England, as well as in Rhode Island. In 1667 he met with some of the best-known advocates of the seventh-day cause to denounce the actions of Thomas Tillam.

The Particular Baptists were troubled by the Sabbath question. In 1657, the church of Tewkesbury raised the question of the Saturday Sabbath at the Midlands Association (White, Pt. 1: 32-33). The messengers gave a thorough response to the question, "Whether the last day of the week comonly called Satterday be to bee observed as a sabbath now under the gospell of Christ".

> Answer: the messengers answere in the negative, only one brother declaring himselfe to bee enquiring and not yet fully satisfied. The grounds for the negative are these among others:
> ground 1, the sabbath given to the children of Israell was to be a signe betweene the Lord and them in theyre generation. Ex. 31.13; Ezek. 20.12; 40.4.
> ground 2, from that cleare place, Col. 2.16f., provs that the sabbath[s] that the law had required to be observed to bee shadowes and for the nonobserving when in gospel times the saints are not to regard the censure of any man, the same apeares alsoe in Heb. the 4th, if rightly under-

stood.

ground 3, from Gal.4.10f. The apostle certainly speaks of the observing of dayes that had beene apoynted by Moses' law: compare it with v. 21 to be weekly or sabbath dayes.

A meeting of the Abingdon Association in 1656 reveals how the Particular Baptists were being affected by the Seventh-Day radicals in their view of the headship of Christ, submission to civil authorities, and the apocalypse (White, Pt. 3: 158). The church at Oxford proposed that the churches consider "what the beast is which is spoken of in the Revelation of John, what is his image, and what it is to worship him and to receive his marke upon their forehead or in their right hand". This was followed by the suggestion that the churches similarly consider the questions:

i. Whether the seventh-day sabbath, as it was given in Ex. 20.10, be in force to be observed by the saints under the Gospell.

ii. Whether, if the churches shall be satisfyed of the unlawfullnes of paying tithes to the maintenance of the nationall ministerie and the payment of church rates they are free joyntly to publish their apprehensions in print.

iii. Whether, if any member suffer for non-payment of tithes or church rates it be not the duty of the respective churches concerned in this testimonie against the Antichrist to bear a proportionable share with the member or members so suffering making it as a publike charge.

While these issues were not resolved, they show the impact of the sabbatarian movement upon the beliefs of the Particular Baptists.

Many Baptist leaders wrote to affirm the Sunday Sabbath and to refute the Saturday Sabbath. Thomas Collier wrote against the Saturday Sabbath as early as 1658, hoping that Baptists would not fall into this error. At the Whitehall debates in 1649, Collier had denounced Jewish laws as a foundation for magisterial power in religion. In 1658, he denounced Jewish laws as the foundation for the observance of the Seventh-Day Sabbath when he published "The Seventh Day Sabbath Opened and Discovered" (Collier, 1658). John Bunyan joined in the denunciation of Saturday observance, setting out his objections in "Questions About the Nature and Perpetuity of the Seventh-Day-Sabbath" (Bunyan, 1685). In his typically thorough style, arguments were given one after another to show that the first day of the week, which is the day of Christ's resurrection, has replaced the seventh day as the Christian Sabbath. Objections were answered one after another. Bunyan showed that the Saturday Sabbath was a part of the old covenant, the resurrection of which for Christians would tend toward the resurrection of the other rites of the Old Testament, as some were known to have done. It seems that the Seventh-Day teaching was being taken to the extreme by some, prompting this late work of Bunyan. Said Bunyan (1685: 281):

> The truth is, one thing that has moved me to this work is, the shame that has covered the face of my soul when I have thought of the fictions and fancies that are growing among professors; and when I see each fiction turn itself to a faction, to the loss of that good spirit of love, and that oneness that formerly was with good men.

The Seventh-Day Baptist movement barely survived the 17th century for various reasons. These included their persistent alienation from society, economic hardship, constant government harassment, the writings of the conservative Baptists against their beliefs, and their own lack of interest in organizational structure. By the middle of the 18th century the movement in England had become virtually extinct. But they had left their influence upon the conservative Baptists in their settled views on the headship of Christ, the relationship between church and state, and the liberty of conscience.

3.3.3   Christ's Headship through Persecution (1680-1700)

The principle of the headship of Christ was forged in the fires of intense persecution that came to the Puritans from 1660 to 1688, of which the last two decades were most crucial to the Particular Baptists. The state rulers were determined that the Puritans would never again exercise the sort of political power they had during the 1640s and the 1650s. From 1688, the Puritans in England – who included Presbyterians, Independents, Baptists, and Quakers – would be known to history as Nonconformists or Dissenters.

With the return of King Charles II, who disembarked at Dover on 25 May 1660, the balance of power within the Church of England shifted almost immediately. The Anglicans linked most closely with the court regarded both the Presbyterians and all those to their left as not only hostile to the true interests of the Church of England but also as potentially revolutionary. On 1 and 2 May 1660 riots against Dissenters broke out across the city of London. William Kiffin's meeting house in Thames Street on St Dunstan's Hill was destroyed. Despite the petitions submitted to the House of Lords, appealing for religious freedom and toleration, tension remained high (Cross & Wood, 2010: 81-99). The uprising in London led by Thomas Venner in January 1661 galvanized the public perception that the "Anabaptists" were violent disturbers of the peace. The John James trial made it clear that the authorities regarded any kind of Fifth Monarchy view as politically dangerous, with no distinction made between the violent and the passive radicals. If to these are added Paul Hobson's deep involvement with the abortive Yorkshire Plot in 1663, government unease with the Baptists in particular is understandable. Nor did the 1663 plot mark the end of Baptist involvement in revolutionary plotting.

The day after Thomas Venner's arrest, the government moved against the "anabaptists, quakers and other sectaries", warning them not to meet at "unusual hours, nor in great number", nor leave their homes for "any spiritual exercise, or serving of God after their own way, but that they do the same in their own parish" (Underhill, 1846: 313). Both the Calvinistic and General Baptists, led by William Kiffin and Henry Denne, publicly repudiated Venner and his people. In 1661, a twenty-page pamphlet entitled "The Humble Apology of some commonly called Anabaptists" was issued by a broad coalition of thirty Baptists (Bell, 2000: 198; Cross & Wood, 2010: 89). They pointed out that, as far as they knew, all but one of his followers had believed in infant baptism. Furthermore, Venner's supporters had bitterly attacked the Baptists for their faith in, and practice of, submission to the civil power. They also argued that it was unjust to impute the failing of the continental Anabaptists at another time and in another place to the English Baptists (White, 1996: 99).

Between 1661 and 1665, Parliament passed a series of Acts, known as the Clarendon Code, which were designed to enforce conformity to the worship of the state Church. The Corporation Act was passed in December 1661, requiring all government officers to take the Oath of Allegiance and Supremacy and that they "do declare and believe that it is not lawful upon any pretence whatsoever to take up arms against the king," and make a formal disavowal of the Solemn

League and Covenant (1643) which had committed England to a Presbyterian church settlement. Anyone who refused to make these oaths and declarations was regarded as removed from office from that moment. The Act also required the appointee to take the sacrament of the Lord's Supper of the Church of England. The provisions of this act would be very difficult for the great majority of Baptists to meet (White, 1996: 100).

The Act of Uniformity of 1662 required all ministers to receive episcopal ordination and that, upon pain of deprivation of every ecclesiastical office held, each minister must, upon some Lord's Day before the feast of St. Bartholomew (24 August), publicly assert his "unfeigned assent and consent to all and everything contained and prescribed in and by ... the Book of Common Prayer". As has been noted, some 2,000 ministers were ejected, swelling and strengthening the cause of Dissent. The government, however, envisaged one church with no toleration of alternative forms of worship. The courts were soon kept busy with cases of unlawful assembly under the first Conventicle Act of 1664. This Act made it illegal for more than five persons over the age of sixteen (apart from members of the same household) to assemble together for worship except according to the rites of the Book of Common Prayer. Disobedience would result in heavy fines. Spies were employed to report on the preachers who convened secret assemblies.

After the first spurt of persecution encouraged by the Conventicle Act of 1664, a slow but marked easing of the situation occurred in the late 1660s. This has been attributed to various factors, including the devotion shown by the ministers during the Plague of London in 1665 and its aftermath, and the government's unwillingness to provoke the Calvinists at home during the 1665-7 war with their close friends in Holland (White, 1996: 109). After the fall of Clarendon in 1667 some members of the government with the more moderate Anglicans sought a new measure of comprehension, for the Presbyterians at least, within the established Church. The more rigid Anglicans, however, managed to manoeuvre things to their advantage, so that a much more severe Conventicle Act came into force in 1670. Despite the persecution, the life of the congregations continued, as exemplified by the Broadmead church in Bristol. The impact of the fines for minister and congregation can be judged both from the salary proposed for the Broadmead pastor, Thomas Hardcastle, in 1671 and from the sum promised by members towards it. It was decided that he should be paid £80 per year to provide for him and his family comfortably. Individual pledges ranged from 6 shillings to £6 per year (Underhill, 1847: 134, 136).

While the Dissenters suffered under the cruel provisions of the second Conventicle Act, the king and his ministers were planning a Declaration of Indulgence. It is not clear why the king and his ministers made the Declaration of Indulgence on 15 March 1672, which suspended the penal laws against both Protestant Dissenters and Roman Catholics. It was received with very mixed feelings by the Dissenters. There was the belief that the king had no extra-parliamentary powers to make such a declaration. There was also the suspicion that the Declaration was a covert attempt to allow the Roman Catholics to come to power. There were those who suspected that the registration of teachers and meeting places under the Indulgence was a pretext to identify the Dissenters for the next round of persecution. The king, however, needed money and so, in February 1673, Parliament had to be recalled. The members of Parliament made it clear that unless the king withdrew the Declaration there would be no supplies. On 8 March, the king capitulated. Persecution against the Dissenters was resumed. John Bunyan, who had been imprisoned before 1660, was cast into prison again when the Declaration of Indulgence was withdrawn (Underwood, 1947: 104).

The Popish Plot and the parliamentary exclusionist crisis of 1678-1681 did not help the Dissenters. The essence of the Popish Plot was that a group of Roman Catholics had been planning to murder the king in order to put his brother, the Duke of York, who had become a convert to Roman Catholicism, on his throne. It was an age of plots and counterplots, and the government gave in to popular hysteria by executing some of the alleged plotters. In March 1679 the House of Commons passed a bill to exclude James, Duke of York, from the succession. To prevent it becoming law, the king dissolved Parliament. Further attempts were made by the House of Commons to introduce the bill of exclusion, which the king blocked each time by dissolving the parliament. Once the king successfully secured the financial assistance he needed from Louis XIV of France, Parliament was not to meet again. He did not now need the money which only parliamentary taxes had previously provided. The easing of persecution after the excitement of the Popish Plot, for four and a half years in the late 1670s, enabled the Calvinistic Baptists "in London and the country" to publish their new Confession in 1677, which was based on the Savoy Confession of the Congregationalists and the Westminster Confession of the Presbyterians.

The second period of persecution lasted from the summer of 1680 until the death of Charles II. G. R. Cragg wrote of the Dissenters after 1681, "never had their sufferings been so bitter or so prolonged" (Cragg, 1957: 26). During this period, nearly 4,000 London Dissenters were arrested or convicted for being present at what the state regarded as illegal religious meetings (Harris, 1987: 485). Other parts of England also felt the brunt of attacks. Hercules Collins was imprisoned in Newgate Prison in 1684 (Piggot, 1702: 33-36). Colonel Danvers fled abroad and died in Utrecht in 1687 (Underwood, 1947: 108). Hanserd Knollys was one of those incarcerated in Newgate Prison in consequence of the Venner uprising but was pardoned during the coronation. For a while afterwards, he brought his family into self-exile in Holland and Germany. He returned to London in 1666 to share with Edward Harrison in setting Thomas Patient apart as co-pastor with William Kiffin but was sent to prison again as a result of the Second Conventicle Act. He was apparently freed in time to marry Benjamin Keach to his second wife in April 1672. In the new bout of persecution, he was cast into prison again for six months during 1684 (White, 1996: 129-130). William Kiffin was jailed a number of times in the two or three years following Charles's restoration, but for short periods of time. His influence in the court stood him in good stead. He used his wealth and position to intervene on behalf of the Dissenters. However, he was unsuccessful in seeking the freedom of his two grandsons, William and Benjamin Hewling, who were charged with conspiracy against James, who came to power upon the death of Charles II in 1685 (Haykin, 1996: 48).

The Glorious Revolution of 1688 placed King William III and Queen Mary II on the throne as co-regents. After Mary died in 1694, William ruled alone until his death in 1702. The beginning of the reign of William III and Mary inaugurated a decade of considerable vitality before spiritual decline came upon the Dissenters. The Act of Toleration of 1689 exempted dissenting Christians from the penalties of certain laws, but they must be Trinitarian and Protestant, sign loyalty oaths, and have their practice approved by the state. Catholics and non-Trinitarians were excluded from this exemption. For Benjamin Keach, toleration "opened a great door for the gospel and sent us blessed harvest weather" (Keach, 1689: 102). The Toleration Act meant that, once again, they could meet freely without fear of the well-rewarded informers or the irate magistrates. The new reign "put a new life in those who before were sunk in despair" (Burnet, 1833, Vol. IV: Bk. VI: 550). William himself believed that "conscience was God's province and that it ought not to be imposed on". His experience in Holland "made him look on toleration as one of the wisest measures of government" (Burnet, 1883, Vol. IV: Bk. V: 21).

The heady exhilaration and relief under the rule of William and Mary was abruptly followed by some renewed tension and threatened persecution under Anne, the last of the Stuart sove-reigns. Mob violence against the Dissenters occurred throughout the country, resulting in considerable damage to Nonconformist meeting-houses. At the time of the Jacobite rebellion in 1745 the Independent minister Philip Doddridge acknowledged the highly tentative nature of their freedom. He knew how easily the Dissenters might lose the liberties they had enjoyed since the accession of William III:

> We have long enjoyed halcyon days ... how soon clouds may gather. [Y]ounger brethren may live to see ... our religious liberties trampled under foot, and with them undoubtedly our civil, for they are twins that will live and die together (Doddridge, 1745: 53-54).

In France, Louis XIV revoked the Edict of Nantes in 1685. The liberties earlier guaranteed to French Protestants were cruelly withdrawn. This confirmed in the mind of the average Englishman that Catholicism and freedom of religion were incompatible partners. William's military campaigns meant that he was constantly on the continent fighting alongside his troops. To the Englishman, it was not simply a war for England, but an essential struggle against popery and oppression.

In 1727 the London ministers revived a practice commenced in 1702 of presenting a Loyal Address to the sovereign and joined together for meetings of the General Body of the Three Denominations. Five years later, London ministers were joined by lay members of Presbyterian, Independent and Baptist churches for the first Protestant Dissenting Deputies. Both these organizations kept a vigilant eye on parliamentary legislation, anxious lest their work should again be restricted by oppressive laws. There was need for this, for the Anglicans were to maintain the monopoly of the political power throughout the 18th century and were unwilling to restore the full rights of citizenship to the Dissenters (Brown, 1986: 34-54).

To the Dissenters, submission to the monarchy was always conditional. Loyalty to God was paramount. John Piggot (d. 1713) told his fellow Baptists that "no pretence of allegiance or duty will justify our trust in a prince whose arts of government are levelled against the law of God". Should a king "once break his coronation oath and invade the liberties of his people, he is no longer a prince but tyrant" (Piggot, 1714: 132).

The last two decades of the 17th century were crucial years in which the Particular Baptists forged the principle of "the headship of Christ" through persecution, expressing it in the 1689 Confession and applying it in the associational life of the churches. These two decades included the second period of persecution under Charles II, which began in 1680 till his death, and extended into the period of toleration under the reign of William III (r. 1688 - d. 1702).

3.4   THE SETTLED VIEWS

It is no exaggeration to claim that the principle of the headship of Christ is the foundation upon which church polity is built. Differences in understanding this principle lie at the base of the various forms of church government, which manifest in different understandings of church-state relationship, different ways of worship, and different approaches to corrective discipline (Poh, 2000: 67-83). The headship of Christ as understood by the Particular Baptists may be considered under the headings of His mediatorship, His word, and His lordship over the conscience.

3.4.1   Christ the Mediator

In the 1689 Confession, a whole chapter, consisting of ten articles, is devoted to the subject of Christ as Mediator. The substance corresponds, almost word for word, with the equivalent chapter in the Westminster Confession. It is declared that by the eternal covenant made between the Father and the Son, Jesus Christ has been appointed to be the Mediator between God and man, and the Head of His church. As Mediator, and therefore also as Head of the church, He occupies the offices of prophet, priest and king. This is expressed in the 1689 Confession as follows (Chapter 8: 1, 9, 10):

1. It pleased *God* in his eternal purpose, to chuse and ordain the *Lord Jesus* his only begotten Son, according to the Covenant made between them both, (a) to be the *Mediator* between *God* and *Man*; the (b) Prophet, (c) Priest and (d) King; Head and Saviour of his Church, the heir of all things, and judge of the world: Unto whom he did from all Eternity (e) give a people to be his seed, and to be by him in time redeemed, called, justified, sanctified, and glorified.

(a) Is. 42.1. 1 Pet. 1. 19, 20. (b) Act. 3. 22. (c) Heb. 5. 5, 6. (d) Ps. 2. 6. Luk. 1. 33. Eph. 1. 23. Heb. 1. 2. Act. 17. 31. (e) Is. 53. 10. Joh. 17. 6. Rom. 8. 30.

9. This office of Mediator between God and Man, is proper (q) onely [sic.] to Christ, who is the Prophet, Priest, and King of the Church of God; and may not be either in whole, or any part thereof transfer'd from him to any other.

(q) 1 Tim. 2.5.

10. This number and order of Offices is necessary; for in respect of our (r) ignorance, we stand in need of his prophetical Office; and in respect of our alienation from God, (s) and imperfection of the best of our services, we need his Priestly office, to reconcile us, and present us acceptable unto God; and in respect to our averseness, and utter inability to return to God, and for our rescue, and security from our spiritual adversaries, we need his Kingly office, (t) to convince, subdue, draw, uphold, deliver, and preserve us to his Heavenly Kingdome.

(r) Joh. 1. 18. (s) Col. 1. 21. Gal. 5.17. (t) Joh. 16. 8. Ps. 110. 3. Luk. 1. 74-75.

Christ's mediatorial work is for the church – His redeemed people. All the redeemed people constitute the universal church, over which Christ is the Head. The universal church manifests itself in the world as local congregations, or visible churches. Chapter 26 of the 1689 Confession states these truths as follows:

1. The Catholick or universal Church, which (with respect to the internal work of the Spirit and truth of grace) may be called invisible, consists of the whole (a) number

of the elect, that have been, are, or shall be gathered into one, under Christ, the head thereof; and is the spouse, the body, the fulness of him that filleth all in all.
(a) Heb. 12. 23. Col. 1. 18. Eph. 1. 10, 22, 23. & ch. 5. 23, 27, 32.

4. The Lord Jesus Christ is the Head of the Church, in whom by the appointment of the Father, (g) all power for the calling, institution, order, or Government of the Church, is invested in a supream & soveraigne [sic.] manner, neither can the Pope of *Rome* in any sense be head thereof, but is (h) that Antichrist, that Man of sin, and Son of perdition, that exalteth himself in the Church against Christ, and all that is called God; whom the Lord shall destroy with the brightness of his coming.
(g) Col. 1. 18. Mat. 28. 18, 19, 20. Eph. 4. 11, 12. (h) 2 Thes. 2. 3-9.

5. In the execution of this power wherewith he is so intrusted, the Lord Jesus calleth out of the World unto himself, through the Ministry of his word, by his Spirit, (i) those that are given unto him by his Father; that they may walk before him in all the (k) ways of obedience, which he prescibeth to them in his Word. Those thus called he commandeth to walk together in particular societies, or (l) Churches, for their mutual edification; and the due performance of that publick worship, which he requireth of them in the World.
Joh. 10.16. chap. 12. 32. (k) Mat. 28. 20. (l) Mat. 18. 15-20.

This view of Christ as Head and Mediator of the church is standard Reformed truth, and was upheld across the board by the Independents, of which Owen was representative. In discussing the "hypostatical union", that is, the union of the divine and human nature in the person of the Son of God, John Owen has this to say: "So is he [Christ] said to be the Head, the King, Priest, and Prophet of the church; all which offices he bears, and performs the acts of them, not on the singular account of this or that nature, but of the *hypostatical union* of them both" (Owen, 1976, Vol. 1: 235). Christ continues to exercise the mediatory office in heaven: "He lives as the Mediator of the church; as the King, Priest, and Prophet thereof" (Owen, 1976, Vol. 1: 252).

The headship of Christ is inextricably linked to the ecclesiology of the Particular Baptists. Their attempt to restore believer's baptism was due to their understanding of a regenerate membership of the church, which was seen as the purpose and product of Christ's mediatorial work. The work of reformation involves bringing every facet of church life under the headship of Christ, which encompasses the three offices of prophet, priest, and king. It is significant that Chapter 8, Article 10 of the 1689 Confession states that, "This number and order of offices is necessary". This clause is not found in the Westminster Confession. It came, instead, from Article XIV of the 1644/46 Confession. This does not mean that the three offices have to be handled or referred to in that number and order all the time. However, the three offices are to be seen as inseparable from the headship of Christ. In a general meeting of messengers of the Northern Association in 1699, the question was posed, "What are the most dangerous errors of the Church of Christ falling into at this day?" The answer given, apparently to counter the Arianising tendency of certain General Baptists of the time, was, "That we think those errors are most dangerous that strikes most at ye Person of Christ in his two Natures and Offices." Scripture references were then given to prove Christ's two natures in one Person, His priestly office, kingly office, and prophetic office, respectively (Copson, 1991: 84 cf. 70).

The churches of the Abingdon Association were similarly conscious of the practical importance of the three offices of Christ, which is inextricably bound to the headship of Christ. In the general letter sent out to the churches after the messengers met from the 13th day to the 16th day of the 8th month in 1657, the following admonition was given (White, 1971-7: Pt. 3: 179):

> It is likewise our earnest request unto the Lord that you may rightly understand not only the propheticall and priestly office of Christ but his kingly office also: that he is over all and Lord of all, Ro. 9.5, Acts 10.36. That the Father hath put all things under his feet and given him to be the head over all things to the church, and hath committed all judgement unto him having given him all power both in heaven and in earth, Eph. 1.22, Jn. 5:22, Mt. 28.18. And that you, knowing this, may be allwayes

carefull to obey all the commands of this your Lord and King Christ Jesus, not forgetting his saying in Jn. 14.15, If ye love me, keep my commandments. And upon this account we desire you to take heed that you doe not sin against Christ and to remember that they doe sin against Christ which sin against the brethren and wound their weak conscience, I Cor. 8.12, which put a stumbling block or an occasion to fall in their brother's way, Ro. 14.13.

The headship of Christ was thus applied within the church and with respect to those they disagreed with. Together with the other Dissenters, the Particular Baptists stood against Rome and the Church of England over their idea of the state church. Benjamin Keach, for example, blamed Rome for creating state or national churches, saying, she has "made void the laws and constitutions of the Gospel, forming whole nations into churches, though the greatest part shew themselves the worst of men" (Keach, 1682: 113). The Particular Baptists went beyond the other Dissenters in the effort at reforming the church by insisting on the immersion of believers as the biblical mode of baptism and admission into the visible church. William Kiffin, for example, wrote (Kiffin, 1681: 27):

Now that this was the order of administration with respect to these ordinances, viz. 1. To Teach, then Baptize, and then admit to Church-Communion, is else where full evidenced from precept and example, Matt. 28:19; Acts 2:41; &c. And if that be the stated method of God, and the universal practice of the Primitive Christians, we may rationally infer that the contrary practice is a deviation from the Divine Rule, and a thing which God commanded not.

Similarly, Benjamin Keach saw the restoration of believer's baptism as a continuing work of the Reformation (Riker, 2009: 127). He lamented that "many very holy and pious men, yea, pastors of churches that are for the baptising of little infants" (Keach, 1689: 154). However, the Scriptures, not human beings, are to be one's guide. History has shown that "some godly men who have had great light and were glorious Reformers too in their day, yet lay short of some great things and duties; as Jehosapht, & c. who 'did not removed nor pulled down the high places' (1 Kin.22.43)". Moreover, "light and knowledg of divine truths have broken forth *gradually*. When Reformation first began, those godly men laboured to restore the doctrinal part of the Gospel and yet great corruptions remained in point of discipline (which errors God hath since by degrees discovered)" (Keach, 1689: 155).

In view of the constant emphasis placed by the Particular Baptists on the necessity of returning to biblical purity while furthering the Reformation (Riker, 2009: 122), the practical implications of "the number and order of offices" of Christ seem to have been overlooked in the literature, and in the outlook of their present-day counterparts (Poh, 2000: 67-83). The number and order of Christ's offices should be a guiding principle in the work of reformation today.

3.4.2   The Authority of Scripture

The church, over which Christ is her Head, is made up of His redeemed people. The Particular Baptists countenanced only a pure membership in the church, that is, a membership that is made up of baptised believers alone, and not including the children of believers who are as yet incapable of professing faith. Membership with the church is distinguished from attendance in the congregation. A congregation may be made up of believers and non-believers, a portion of the former being covenanted together as the members of the church. The purity of the church begins with ensuring a regenerate membership to the best of human ability, by looking for a credible profession of faith. That purity continues to be maintained by the positive work of teaching the word and the negative work of corrective discipline. In Chapter 2, it has been noted that corrective discipline featured prominently in the Particular Baptist churches, as witnessed in the Association records and the church records of the Broadmead Church in Bristol and the Bunyan Meeting. The church that submits to the headship of Christ would be ruled by His law. Individuals who are converted have an obligation to be joined to the local church, and accept the Reformation principle of *sola scriptura*. Chapter 26 of the 1689 Confession expresses these truths in the following way:

> 2. All persons throughout the world, professing the faith
> of the Gospel, and obedience unto God by Christ, accord-

ing unto it; not destroying their own profession by any Errors everting the foundation, or unholiness of conversation, (b) are and may be called visible Saints; (c) and of such ought all particular Congregations to be constituted.

(b) 1 Cor. 1. 2. Act. 11. 26. (c) Rom. 1. 7. Eph. 1. 20, 21, 22.

6. The Members of these Churches are (m) Saints by calling, visibly manifesting and evidencing (in and by their profession and walking) their obedience unto the call of Christ; and do willingly consent to walk together according to the appointment of Christ, giving up themselves, to the Lord & one another by the will of God, (n) in professed subjection to the Ordinances of the Gospel.

(m) Rom. 1. 7. 1 Cor. 1. 2. (n) Act. 2. 41, 42. ch. 5. 13, 14. 2 Cor. 9. 13.

12. As all Believers are bound to joyn [sic.] themselves to particular *Churches*, when and where they have opportunity so to do; So all that are admitted unto the privileges of a *Church*, are also (b) under the Censures and Government thereof, according to the Rule of *Christ*.

(b) 1 Thes. 5.14. 2 Thes. 3. 6, 14, 15.

These articles must be seen in conjunction with Chapter 1 of the Confession:

6. The whole Councel [sic.] of God concerning all things (i) necessary for his own Glory, Mans Salvation, Faith and Life, is either expressely [sic.] set down or necessarily contained in the *Holy Scripture*; unto which nothing at any time is to be added, whether by new Revelation of the *spirit*, or traditions of men.

Nevertheless we acknowledge the (k) inward illumination of the Spirit of God, to be necessary for the saving understanding of such things as are revealed in the Word, and that there are some circumstances concerning the worship of God, and the government of the Church common to humane actions and societies; which are to be (l) ordered by the light of nature, and Christian prudence according to the general rules of the Word, which

are always to be observed.
(i) 2 Tim. 3. 15, 16, 17. Gal. 1. 8, 9. (k) John 6. 45. 1
Cor. 2. 9, 10, 11, 12. (l) 1 Cor. 11. 13, 14. & ch. 14. 16
& 40.

The emphasis on submission to the law of Christ was shared
by John Owen, who described Christ as "the only 'lawgiver' of the
church, James iv. 12; Isa. xxxiii. 22". "He builds his own house,"
and he is "over his own house," Heb. iii. 3-6. "He both constitutes
its state, and gives laws for its rule" (Owen, 1976, Vol. 15: 237).
Since Christ alone is the Head of the church, Owen rejected the interference of any civil and ecclesiastical authority in the affairs of the
church, saying (Owen, 1976, Vol. 15: 237-239):

> [T]he bishops of the fourth and fifth centuries took upon
> themselves power to make laws, canons, and constitu-
> tions for the ordering of the government and rule of the
> church, bringing in many new institutions on a pretence
> of the same authority.
>
> This authority was first usurped by *synods*, or *councils
> of bishops*. ... This was the fatal event of men's invad-
> ing the right of Christ, and claiming an interest in au-
> thority to give laws to the church. This, therefore, is
> absolutely denied by us, – namely, that any men, under
> what pretence or name soever, have any right or author-
> ity to constitute any new frame or order of the church,
> to make any laws of their own for its rule or govern-
> ment that should oblige the disciples of Christ in point
> of conscience unto their observation. ... there is noth-
> ing in this assertion that should in the least impeach the
> power of magistrates, with reference unto the outward,
> civil, and political concerns of the church, or the public
> profession of religion within their territories, – nothing
> that should take off from the just authority of the lawful
> guides of the church, in ordering, appointing, and com-
> manding the observation of all things in them, according
> to the mind of Christ ... In these things "the LORD is our
> judge, the LORD is our statute-maker, the LORD is our
> king; he will save us."

Owen (1976, Vol. 15: 244) similarly acknowledge that '[t]here are in the Scripture general rules directing us, in the application of natural light, unto such a determination of all circumstances, in the acts of church rule and worship, as are sufficient for their performance "decently and in order."' The Particular Baptists did not treat such matters as baptism and the Lord's Supper, the day in which to worship, church discipline, and the autonomy of the local congregation, as belonging to the "some circumstances concerning the worship of God, and the government of the church common to humane actions and societies".

3.4.3 The Liberty of Conscience

The headship of Christ is also tied to the liberty of conscience. The believer is bound only to obey what he believes to be the teaching of the Bible. He may not be forced to believe anything that is against, or not taught in, the Scripture. He may not be forced to obey such commands, by either ecclesiastical or civil authorities. This is stated as follows in Chapter 21 of the 1689 Confession:

> 2. God alone is (m) Lord of the Conscience, and hath left it free from the Doctrines and Commandments of men, (n) which are in any thing contrary to his Word, or not contained in it. So that to Believe such Doctrines, or obey such Commands out of Conscience, (o) is to betray true liberty of Conscience;and [sic] the requiring of an (p) implicit Faith, and absolute and blind Obedience, is to destroy Liberty of Conscience, and Reason also.
> (m) Jam. 4. 12. Rom. 14. 4. (n) Act. 4. 19 & 5. 29. 1 Cor. 7. 23. Mat. 15. 9. (o) Col. 2. 20, 22, 23. (p) 1 Cor. 3. 5. 2 Cor. 1. 24.

The 1689 Confession declares God as "the supream Lord, and King of all the World" (Confession, 1689: Ch. 24: 1). Civil magistrates have been ordained to be "under Him, over the people, for His own glory and the public good". The belief in the separation of church and state does not mean isolation from society. Unlike the Continental Anabaptists, the Particular Baptists declared the legitimacy of Christians becoming magistrates (Confession, 1689: Ch. 24):

> 2. It is lawful for Christians to Accept, and Execute the Office of *Magistrate*, when called thereunto; in the management whereof, as they ought especially to maintain (b) Justice, and Peace according to the wholesome Laws of each Kingdome, and Commonwealth: so for that end they may lawfully now under the New-Testament (c) wage war upon just and necessary occasions.
> (b) 2 Sam. 23.3. Ps. 82. 3, 4. (c) Luk. 3. 14.

Further, to show that they were not anti-establishment or anarchists, it was declared:

> 3. *Civil magistrates* being set up by God, for the ends aforesaid; subjection in all lawful things commanded by them, ought to be yielded by us, in the Lord; not only for wrath (d) but for Conscience sake; and we ought to make supplications and prayers for Kings, and all that are in Authority, (e) that under them we may live a quiet and peaceable life, in all godliness and honesty.
> (d) Rom. 13. 5, 6, 7. 1 Pet. 2. 17. (e) 1 Tim. 2. 1, 2.

Peter Toon has shown that Owen was an indefatigable defender of religious toleration and the liberty of conscience. One example of this is seen in his reply to Samuel Parker, archdeacon of Canterbury who, in 1669, wrote violently against the Nonconformists. Owen's reply, in his book published in 1976, "Truth and Innocence Vindicated" (Owen, 1976, Vol. 13: 344ff.), was based on the premise that Holy Scripture is God's only final, authoritative word to man. Scripture clearly taught that the church should be pure and subject, in matters of doctrine and worship, only to Christ the King. Liberty to worship God according to the New Testament pattern was absolutely essential to those whose minds and hearts rejected, for Christ's sake, the government and liturgy of the Church of England. The worship of God was the highest duty of man and could not be placed in the realm of secondary matters (Toon, 1971: 137). Said Owen (1976, Vol. 13: 462, 463, 464):

> [A] principle which is termed the "foundation of all Puritanism,"... is, "That nothing ought to be established in the worship of God but what is authorized by some precept or example in the word of God, which is the complete and adequate rule of worship."

There are yet other general maxims which Nonconformists adhere unto ... And they are these that follow:– 1. That whatever the Scripture hath indeed prescribed and appointed to be done and observed in the worship of God and the government of the church, that is indeed to be done and observed ...

2. That nothing in conjunction with, nothing as an addition or supplement unto, what is appointed ought to be admitted, if it be contrary either to the general rules or particular preceptive instructions of the Scripture ...

3. That nothing ought to be joined with or added unto what in the Scripture is prescribed and appointed in these things without some cogent reason, making such conjunction or addition necessary ...

4. That if any thing or things in this kind shall be found necessary to be added and prescribed, then that and those alone be so which are most consonant unto the general rules of the Scripture given us for our guidance in the worship of God, and the nature of those institutions themselves wherewith they are conjoined or whereunto they are added ...

These sentiments are expressed in the 1689 Confession. Owen published many tracts, most of which were anonymous and even without the printer's name, in the years of persecution to protest the impolicy and injustice of persecution for conscience's sake (Owen, 1976: Vol. 13).

The Great Ejection of 1662, the persecution of the Dissenters, and the fierce extra- and intra-confessional debates were all due to the belief in the liberty of conscience and the sole authority of Scripture, arising from subjection to Christ the Mediator and Head of the church – doctrines held in common by the Dissenters.

3.5 SUMMARY

In the years 1640-1660, the Particular Baptists' view of the headship of Christ was worked out in relation to the violent radicalism of the Levellers and the Fifth Monarchists. While they shared in common certain ideas such as religious liberty and the abolition of tithes, the

Levellers were opposed to any idea of a godly government. In consequence, the conservative Particular Baptists had to abandon them in favour of working through the army and government of Oliver Cromwell. The Fifth Monarchists insisted on using violence to establish the rule of Christ on earth, and rejected any organizational structure in the church which they thought smacked of "ecclesiastical tyranny". The conservative Particular Baptists, however, saw the rule of Christ on earth as imminent but in the future, such that the church has to exist side-by-side with the state. Meanwhile, Christ asserts His headship over the church through a church government that is sufficiently defined by His word.

In the years 1660-1680, the Particular Baptists worked out their understanding of the headship of Christ in the face of the passive radicalism of the Seventh-Day Baptists. The Seventh-Day Baptists, or Sabbatarians, set themselves up as thorough reformers who were intent on following the Bible by their insistence on restoring the sixth-day Sabbath, the drawing in of Jewish believers, and the renunciation of all earthly powers. The Particular Baptists countered their understanding of the Christian Sabbath and distanced themselves from these radicals in the tense religious atmosphere of the time, when the powers-that-be did not distinguish between violent and passive radicals.

In the years 1680-1700, the Particular Baptists worked out their view of the headship of Christ through persecution and toleration. Severe persecution came upon the Dissenters as Charles II imposed a series of Conventicle Acts to curb their liberties from 1680. Rather than submit to the restrictions imposed upon them, the Dissenters risked imprisonment by continuing to meet, while the preachers travelled to preach. From the Glorious Revolution in 1688, following the reign of William III and Queen Mary II, to the death of King William in 1702, the Particular Baptists formulated their beliefs in the 1689 Confession of Faith, met in annual General Assemblies, and revived the flagging regional Associations of churches.

The 1689 Confession of Faith showed the Particular Baptists as belonging to the same theological milieu as the Presbyterians and the Independents, in upholding the headship of Christ. Any differences between the Particular Baptists and other communions, such as in the form of church government and baptism, were a result of their persistent (and consistent, they would claim) outworking of the headship of Christ – in His role as Mediator, in the submission of the church to His word, and in His lordship over the individual conscience. In particular, Chapter 26 of the 1689 Confession was based on the Savoy Platform of Church Polity of the Congregationalists, of which John Owen was the chief architect. The substantial agreement between the Particular Baptists and John Owen on the headship of Christ is therefore obvious.

Bell (2000: 257) ably summarized what the Baptists shared in common:

> The Baptists were not born fully formed, but developed within a historical context. Taking the Reformation heritage of a priesthood of all believers and *sola scriptura*, the Baptists had added their own unique beliefs. Most distinguishing was believer's baptism – a symbol of a life in Christ and the faith of the individual. To the ideas of the gathered congregation under the kingship of Christ as the only authority of the church, the centrality of the Bible and believer's baptism was added the idea of religious liberty. In the midst of Reformation, Revolution and Civil War, they had found these timeless truths which would be the rock from which Baptists would spread throughout the world.

The headship of Christ must be seen to be at the base of the church polity of the Particular Baptists. The autonomy of the visible church is possible only because Christ is her Head. It will be examined next the Particular Baptist insistence that Christ exercises His headship through the rule of elders in the church.

※ ※ ※ ※ ※

Four

RULE BY ELDERS

4.1   INTRODUCTION

The substantial agreement between the Particular Baptists and John Owen on the headship of Christ has been established. Did this agreement extend to the way Christ exercises His headship in the churches? In other words, was the nature, form, and manner of church government of the Particular Baptists substantially the same as those of the paedobaptist Independents, baptism excepted? In answer to this question, it will be necessary to determine how the Particular Baptists understood the nature of church authority, who the church officers should be who wield that authority, and how that authority is to be executed. Three particular areas will be explored, namely, (i) the nature of church authority; (ii) the rulers of the church; and (iii) the manner of rule. The extant writings, the church books, and the association records will need to be examined in the light of the historical and theological situations of the time, and compared with the 1689 Confession of Faith, to determine the settled and dominant views of the Particular Baptists touching their ecclesiology.

4.2   THE NATURE OF CHURCH AUTHORITY

As head of the church, Jesus Christ exercises His power over the local, visible, congregations. The 1689 Confession says, in Chapter 26, Articles 4 and 5:

> 4. The Lord Jesus Christ is the Head of the Church, in

whom by the appointment of the Father, (g) all power for the calling, institution, order, or Government of the Church, is invested in a supreme & soveraigne manner... (g) Col. 1.18 Mat. 28.18, 19, 20.

5. In the execution of this power wherewith he is so intrusted, the Lord Jesus calleth out of the World unto himself, through the Ministry of his word, by his Spirit, (i) those that are given unto him by his Father; that they may walk before him in all the (k) ways of obedience, which he prescribeth to them in his Word. Those thus called he commandeth to walk together in particular societies, or (l) Churches, for their mutual edification; and the due performance of that publick worship, which he requireth of them in the World.
(i) Joh. 10.16. chap. 12, 32. (k) Mat. 28.20. (l) Mat. 18. 15-20.

The 1689 Confession declares that power is vested in Christ supremely, which He executes in the calling to existence local churches. The called out saints are constituted as covenanted communities of baptized believers, "giving up themselves, to the Lord and one another by the will of God". This is expressed in Chapter 26, Article 6 as follows:

6. The Members of these Churches are (m) Saints by calling, visibly manifesting and evidencing (in and by their profession and walking) their obedience unto that call of Christ; and do willingly consent to walk together according to the appointment of Christ, giving up themselves, to the Lord & one another by the will of God, (n) in professed subjection to the Ordinances of the Gospel.
(m) Rom. 1.7. 1 Cor. 1.2. (n) Act. 2. 41, 42. ch. 5. 13, 14. 2 Cor. 9.13.

The Particular Baptists had, from the beginning, held to the view that all needful "power and authority" to carry out its duties had been given to the church by Christ, together with "commands and rules" to execute that power – a reference to the teaching of the Scripture. This is the essence of their belief in the autonomy, or self-rule, of the church, which they held in common with the paedobaptist Independents. There is no individual, no body of individuals, and no institution on earth outside the congregation of God's people who has the right and power to exert rule over that congregation. Civil and ecclesiastical authorities of any sort are precluded from interfering with the government of the church. This is expressed as follows in Chapter 26 of the 1689 Confession:

> 7. To each of these Churches thus gathered, according to his mind, declared in his word, he hath given all that (o) power and authority, which is any way needfull, for their carrying on that order in worship, and discipline, which he hath instituted for them to observe; with commands, and rules, for the due and right exerting, and executing of that power.
> (o) Mat. 18.17, 18. 1 Cor. 5. 4, 5. with v. 13. 2 Cor. 2. 6, 7, 8.

Although Benjamin Keach held to a slightly different view on the rulers of the church compared to the majority of the Particular Baptists, his understanding of the nature, government and discipline of the church was, in the main, representative of the other Particular Baptists. Keach, in his discussion on church discipline, said (Dever, 2001: 71):

> The Power of the Keys, or to receive in and shut out of the Congregation, is committed unto the Church: ... it is exercised in the Name of Christ, having all lawful Rule and Government within itself ... This Power of Christ is exerted as committed to them by the Hands of the Elders appointed by Christ, the due management whereof is in and with the Church ... And that the Power of the Keys is in the Church, appears to me from Mat. 18. *If he will not hear the Church*; it is not said, if he will not hear the Elder, or Elders. As also that the Apostle, in directing the Church to cast out the Incestuous Person, he doth not give this Counsel to the Elder or Elders of the Church, but to the Church; so he commands the Church to withdraw from every Brother that walks disorderly. *Purge out the old Leaven, that you may be a new Lump.* [Emphasis original.]

Many Particular Baptist churches were organized into regional associations, of which more will be said in a later chapter of this study. The messengers of the eighteen churches of the West Country Association met in Chard from the 24th to the 27th days of the 8th month, 1655, at which the following query was raised (White, Pt. 2: 60): "Whether the power of the keys spoken of in Mat. 16.19, John 20.23, Mat. 18.18, be given to the church or to the eldership in the church?" The answer given was: "the exercise of the power of Christ in a church having officers, in opening and shutting, in receiving in and casting out, belongs to the church with its eldership, Mat. 18.17f., I Cor. 5.4f., III John 9ff., Acts 15.4,22." The answer shows that the church is the seat of church power, fundamentally speaking, while the eldership wields that power, practically speaking. This is confirmed by the next query: "Whether a church of Christ in her election of elders are vested the power of teaching and ruling in them all alike or to appoint some for teaching and some for ruling sutable [sic] to their gift?" The answer given being: "it is the office of an elder both to teach and rule. The church, therefore, ordaining a person to that office do thereby invest him with the power both to teach and rule. Tit. 1.9ff., I Tim. 3.2, Acts 20.17,28, Heb. 13.7,17, I. Peter 5.1f. Yet sutable to the gift are they to be most exercised, I.Tim. 5.17."

Comparing with John Owen, he is found declaring that (Owen, 1976, Vol. 16: 31, 33):

> The rule of the church is, in general, *the exercise of the power or authority of Jesus Christ, given unto it, according unto the laws and directions prescribed by himself, unto its edification.* This power in *actu primo*, or fundamentally, is in the church itself; in *actu secundo*, or its exercise, in them that are especially called thereunto ... This is the especial nature and especial end of all power granted by Jesus Christ unto the church, namely, *a ministry unto edification* ... Wherefore there is no rule of the church but what is ministerial, consisting in an *authoritative declaration* and application of the commands and will of Christ unto the souls of men; wherein those who exercise it are servants unto the church for its edification, for Jesus' sake, 2 Cor. iv. 5.

It can be seen, then, the agreement between the Particular Baptists and John Owen that the source of church power is Christ, and the seat of power is the church, while the authority of executing that power lies with the elders. In Owen's words, in the church is "power in *actu primo*" and in the eldership is "power in *actu secundo*". Owen actually distinguished between the *right* or *power* of the church, and the *authority* to execute the duties of office (Owen, 16: 37):

> The things before mentioned are all of them acts of right and power, but not of authority ... Wherefore the Lord Christ hath ordained *offices*, and appointed officers to be established in the church, Eph. iv. 11-15. Unto these is all church authority granted; for all authority is an act of office-power, which is that which gives unto what is performed by the officers of the church the formal nature of authority.

4.3 THE RULERS OF THE CHURCH

The Particular Baptists held to the view that the offices of apostles, prophets and evangelists were extraordinary offices given by Christ for the foundation of the church, after which they have been withdrawn. Daniel King's view may be regarded as representative of that of the Particular Baptists.

In Chapter 2 of the present work, it is seen how Daniel King wrote "Stumbling Blocks Removed Out of the Way" to counter John Saltmarsh's book, "The Smoke in the Temple", which was published in 1646. The Seekers, of whom John Saltmarsh was one, regarded all organized churches as corrupt and spoke against church offices, church organization, and the ordinances. Saltmarsh had put forward thirteen "Exceptions" against baptism as practised by the Baptists. Hanserd Knollys quickly countered Saltmarsh by publishing, "The Shinning of a Flaming Fire in Zion", in 1646. This was followed by King's book, published in 1650, and the second edition in 1656, in which he acknowledged that his work was in addition to that of Knollys, having gathered most of the material for publication before he saw Knollys's book. King was actually planning to publish a trilogy, beginning with "A Way To Sion", followed by "Stumbling Blocks Removed Out Of The Way", and ending with "Some Beams Of Light For The Further Clearing Of The Way".

A large section of Daniel King's first book, "A Way to Sion", was on the nature and government of the church. King distinguished between the extraordinary offices and the ordinary ones (King, 1656):

> The gifts of the Apostles, Prophets, and Evangelists, as such, are ceased, Therefore there must needs be a cessation of the Office also ... what they said by way of Doctrine, was infallible Scripture: they laid the foundation: Eph. 2:20.

Daniel King regarded the pastors and teachers of Ephesians 4:11 as ordinary officers who continue in the church. Among the many arguments raised in support of this are the following:

> ... the Apostle Paul writes to Timothy diverse charges, to see to the Doctrine others teach, and that Himself teaches; ... 1 Tim. 1:3. ... 2 Tim. 2:2. Here He speaks of ordinary gifts, and He shows, chapter 3:14,15, that the man of God is thoroughly furnished for every good work, not only from an infallible Spirit, but from the Scripture, and as certainly; for He says, ALL SCRIPTURE WAS GIVEN BY INSPIRATION OF GOD.
>
> The qualifications that Paul required Timothy and Titus to look to be in Bishops or Elders, and Deacons (1 Tim. :2-8; Titus 1:5-10) shows it; which may all be in a man that is not infallibly inspired by that pure anointing.
>
> The Bishops and Deacons admittance and trial is the same, they must be both proved, verse 8. Therefore the one administers no more by an infallible Spirit than the other.

Benjamin Keach also held to the view that the extraordinary offices have ceased and only elders and deacons remain in the church. In his book "The Glory Of A True Church, And Its Discipline Display'd" (1697), he said:

> A Church ... constituted ought ... to choose them a Pastor, Elder or Elders, and Deacons, (we reading of no other Officers, or Offices abiding in the Church) and what kind of Men they ought to be, and how qualified, is laid down by *Paul* to *Timothy*, and to *Titus*. Moreover, they are to take special care, that both Bishops, Overseers, or Elders, as well as the Deacons, have in some competent manner all those Qualifications; and after in a Day of solemn Prayer and Fasting, that they have elected them, (whether Pastor, &c., or Deacons) and they accepting the Office, must

be ordained with Prayer, and laying on of Hands of the Eldership; being first prov'd, and found meet and fit Persons for so Sacred an Office ...

The works of John Owen will now be considered. In 1667 his book "A Brief Instruction in the Worship of God and Discipline of the Churches of the New Testament" was published without the names of the author or printer, for the Court was at that time striving for universal ecclesiastical practice throughout England. The book became particularly helpful to the many dissenting congregations that were springing up in different parts of the country. It was so much appreciated that a second edition, with slight amendments, was published that year, and became known as the "Independents' Catechism". Question 24 of this work asks, "What are the principal differences between these two sorts of officers or rulers in the church, extraordinary and ordinary?" The answer given is as follows (Owen, 15: 492-293):

> The former were called to their office immediately by Jesus Christ in his own person, or revelation made by the Holy Ghost in his name to that purpose; the latter by the suffrage, choice, and appointment of the church itself. The former, both in their office and work, were independent on, and antecedent unto, all or any churches, whose calling and gathering depended on their office as its consequent effect; the latter, in both, consequent unto the calling, gathering, and constituting of the churches themselves, as an effect thereof, in their tendency unto completeness and perfection. The authority of the former being communicated unto them immediately by Jesus Christ, without any intervenient actings of any church, extended itself equally unto all churches whatever; that of the latter being derived unto them from Christ by the election and designation of the church, is in the exercise of it confined unto that church wherein and whereby it is so derived unto them. They differ also in the gifts, which were suited unto their several distinct works and employments.

Question 25 asks, "What is required unto the due constitution of an elder, pastor, or teacher of the church?" The answer given is:

That he be furnished with the gifts of the Holy Spirit for the edification of the church, and the evangelical discharge of the work of the ministry; that he be unblamable, holy, and exemplary in his conversation; that he have a willing mind to give up himself unto the Lord in the work of the ministry; that he be called and chosen by the suffrage and consent of the church; that he be solemnly set apart by fasting and prayer, and imposition of hands, unto his work and ministry.

In "Two Discourses Concerning The Holy Spirit And His Work", published posthumously in 1693, John Owen showed that four things constitute an extraordinary officer: (i) an extraordinary call; (ii) an extraordinary power communicated unto persons so called; (iii) extraordinary gifts; and, (iv) extraordinary employment as to its extent and measure (Owen, 1976, Vol. 4: 439).

From the above discussion, it can be seen that the Particular Baptists shared in common with John Owen the views that: (i) the extraordinary offices of apostles, prophets and evangelists have been withdrawn after the laying of the foundation of the New Testament church through their teaching and writings; (ii) the ordinary officers remaining in the church are elders (also called bishops) and deacons; (iii) elders and deacons must be those who are suitably qualified for office, have been chosen by the congregation, and ordained with prayer and the laying on of hands of the existing elders. The 1689 Confession states these points in Chapter 26, Articles 8 and 9:

8. A particular Church gathered, and compleatly [sic] Organized, according to the mind of *Christ*, consists of Officers, and Members; And the Officers appointed by Christ to be chosen and set apart by the Church (so called and gathered) for the peculiar Administration of Ordinances, and Execution of Power, or Duty, which he intrusts them with, or calls them to, to be continued to the end of the World are (p) Bishops or Elders and Deacons.
(r) [sic.] Act. 20:17, with v. 28. Phil.1.1.

9. The way appointed by *Christ* for the Calling of any person, fitted, and gifted by the Holy *Spirit*, unto Office of Bishop, or Elder, in a Church, is, that he be chosen thereunto by the common (q) suffrage of the Church it-

self; and Solemnly set apart by Fasting and Prayer, with imposition of hands of the (r) Eldership of the Church, if there be any before Constituted therein; And of a Deacon (s) that he be chosen by the like suffrage, and set apart by Prayer, and the like Imposition of hands.

(q) Act. 14.23. See the original. (r) 1 Tim. 4.14. (s) Act. 6.3. 5.5.

4.3.1 Teaching and Ruling Elders

It has been noted that Chapter 26 of the 1689 Confession was based largely on the Savoy Platform of Church Polity (Murray, 1965: 275-280). At first sight, the Savoy document seems to say that there are four continuing offices in the church. Article IX of the Savoy Platform says: "The officers ... to be continued to the end of the world, are pastors, teachers, elders, and deacons." However, on comparison with Article XI, it is seen that the office of pastor, teacher or elder is one: "The way appointed by Christ for the calling of any person, fitted and gifted by the Holy Ghost, unto the office of pastor, teacher or elder in a church ..." The word "office" is in the singular, and the word "or" shows that the terms are used interchangeably. Rightly understood, the Savoy Platform is teaching a two-office view similar to that in the 1689 Confession. Confirmation of this is to be found in John Owen, the chief architect of the Savoy Platform.

In his posthumously published work of 1689, "The True Nature Of A Gospel Church And Its Government", John Owen said (Owen, 1976, Vol. 16: 42):

> The organizing of a church is the placing or implanting in it those officers which the Lord Jesus Christ hath appointed to act and exercise his authority therein. For the rule and government of the church are the exertion of the authority of Christ in the hands of them unto whom it is committed, that is, the officers of it; not that all officers are called to rule, but that none are called to rule that are not so.

> The officers of the church in general are of two sorts, "bishops and deacons," Phil. i. 1; and their work is distributed into "prophecy and ministry," Rom. xii. 6, 7.

> The bishops or elders are of two sorts: – 1. Such as have authority to *teach* and administer the sacraments, which is commonly called the *power of order*; and also of *ruling*, which is called a power of jurisdiction. corruptly: and, 2. Some have only *power for rule*; of which sort are some in all the churches in the world.
>
> Those of the first sort are distinguished into *pastors* and *teachers*.
>
> The distinction between the elders themselves is not like that between elders and deacons, which is as unto the whole kind or nature of the office, but only with respect unto work and order, whereof we shall treat distinctly.

On the pastors of the church, Owen said (Owen, 1976, Vol. 16: 79):

> No church is complete in order *without teaching officers*, Eph. iv. 11, 12; 1 Cor. xii. 27, 28. ... A church not complete in order cannot be complete in administrations ... Hence the first duty of a church without officers is to obtain them, according to rule.

On the teachers of the church, Owen said (Owen, 1976, Vol. 16: 105):

> I will no deny but that in each particular church there may be many pastors with an equality of power, if the edification of the church do require it. ... the absolute equality of many pastors in one and the same church is liable unto many inconveniences if not diligently watched against. Wherefore let the state of the church be preserved and kept unto its original constitution, which is congregational, and no other, and I do judge that the order of the officers which was so early in the primitive church, – namely, of one pastor or bishop in one church, assisted in rule and all holy administration with many elders teaching or ruling only, – doth not so overthrow church-order as to render its rule or discipline useless.
>
> But whereas there is no difference in the Scripture, as unto office or power, intimated between bishops and presbyters, as we have proved, when there are many teaching

elders in any church, an equality in office and power is to be preserved. But yet this takes not off from the due preference of the pastoral office, nor from the necessity of precedence for the observation of order in all church assemblies, nor from the consideration of the peculiar advantages which gifts, age, abilities, prudence, and experience, which may belong unto some, according to rule, may give.

On the ruling elders, Owen said (Owen, 1976, Vol. 16: 112, 113):

> To the complete constitution of any particular church, or the perfection of its original state, it is required that there be *many elders* in it, at least more than one. ... Where the churches are small, the number of elders may be so also; for no office is appointed in the church for pomp or show, but for labour only ... But the church, be it small or great, is not complete in its state, is defective, which hath not more elders than one, which hath not so many as are sufficient for their work. ... The pattern of the first churches constituted by the apostles, which it is our duty to imitate and follow as our rule, constantly expresseth and declares that many elders were appointed by them in every church, Acts xi. 30, xiv. 23, xv. 2, 4, 6, 22, xvi. 4, xx. 17, etc... Where there is but one elder in a church, there cannot be an *eldership* or *presbytery*, ... which is contrary unto 1 Tim. iv. 14.

Of deacons, Owen said (Owen, 1976, Vol. 16: 147):

> This office of deacons is an office of service, which gives not any authority or power in the rule of the church ... Extraordinary collections from or for other churches are to be made and disposed by the elders, Acts xi. 30. ... Hereon are they obliged to attend the elders on all occasions, to perform the duty of the church towards them, and receive directions from them.

In Owen's book, "A Brief Instruction in the Worship of God and Discipline of the Churches of the New Testament", the question is asked (Owen, 1976, Vol. 15: 504): "Are there appointed any elders in the church whose office and duty consist in rule and government only?" The answer given is: "Elders not called to teach ordinarily or administer the sacraments, but to assist and help in the rule and government of the church, are mentioned in the Scripture.– Rom. xii. 8; 1 Cor. xii. 28; 1 Tim. v. 17." In the explication, Owen had this to say (Owen, 1976, Vol. 15: 504-505):

> ... there is in the gospel express mention of persons that were assigned peculiarly for rule and government in the church, as 1 Cor. xii. 28. And it is in vain pretended that those words, "helps, governments," do denote gifts only, seeing the apostle expressly enumerates the persons in office, or officers, which the Lord then used in the foundation and rule of the churches as then planted. He that ruleth, also, is distinguished from him that teacheth and him that exhorteth, Rom. xii. 8; and is prescribed diligence as the principal qualification in the discharge of his duty. And the words of the apostle to this purpose are express: 1 Tim. v. 17, "Let the elders that rule well be counted worthy of double honour, especially those who labour in the word and doctrine." For the words expressly assign two sorts of elders, whereof some only attend unto rule; others, moreover, labour in the word and doctrine. ... bishops that attend to the rule of the church ... the apostle expressly preferreth before and above them those that attend constantly to the word and doctrine ... The qualification of these elders, with the way of their call and setting apart unto their office, being the same with those of the teaching elders ...

It has been noted that "the office of bishop, or elder" of the 1689 Confession is equivalent to "the office of pastor, teacher or elder" in the Savoy Platform. The explication of John Owen reveals that there are two types of elders in the one office of rule – the pastor who teaches and rules, and the ruling elder who only rules. While one would have no difficulty accepting Owen's explanation of the elder's office as applied to the Savoy Platform, it is another matter to claim that the same applies to the 1689 Confession. Could it be that the 1689 Confession was advocating one type of elders only, namely, elders who both teach and rule? Put another way, could it be that the Particular Baptists did not accept the validity of the ruling elder?

Note that the discussion here is not the intricacies of whether the ruling elder's office is distinct and different from that of the teaching elder's, nor whether the ruling elder is, in fact, a biblical presbyter or merely a lay representative. These queries had been debated hotly by the Presbyterians when the Westminster Assembly met, but no definitive conclusions were arrived at (Murray, 1983). The concern here is only to determine whether the Particular Baptists believed in the validity of the ruling elder, and if so, how extensively this view was held to. The answers will have to be sought from the extant writings, Church Records, and Association Records of the Particular Baptists.

4.3.2 Daniel King's Eldership

Consider, next, Daniel King who wrote on the nature and government of the church in "A Way To Sion". In the section, "What Officers are to be in the Church" he has this to say (King, 1656):

> ... the Officers in a Church, seem to me, to be ranked into two sorts, or heads in general, which Paul calls Bishops and Deacons, Phil. 1:1. And Paul names the same, 1 Tim. 3. And Rom. 12:6,7. He sets them down under the general head of Prophesying and Ministering, and He distributes them into particulars.

> Now the Bishop is He which the Scripture in other places calls the Elder, Tit. 1:5-7. And it is a general name to Teachers, Pastors, or Overseers, as these Scriptures make clear, Acts 20:17, with 28. And this word Elder, or Bishop, is a general name to all that feed the Church, and takes in as well Apostles as others into the work of overseeing, or feeding, 1 Pet. 5:1,2; 2 John 1:3; 3 John 1; yea, sometimes Christ Himself, 1 Pet. 2:25.

> Again, these two are distributed into particulars, as the Bishop or Elder, is distributed into Pastor and Teacher, and Ruling Elder, or He that Rules, 1 Tim. 5:17; Rom 12:7,8. There we have a distribution of two generals into particulars: He that prophesies, verse 6, into Teacher, Exhorter, and Ruler. And He that ministers, into giver, and shower of mercy.

> 1. For Pastor and Teacher, we read of them, Eph. 4:11.

And I hinted to you, it is the same with Bishop or Elder, which I proved ordinary Officers.

2. For ruling Elder, see Rom. 12:8; 1 Cor. 5:17. And this office is called helpers in Governments, 1 Cor. 12:8.

In the subsequent section, King considered "What Their Officers Are", saying:

The Pastor's office is to feed the Flock, Jer. 3:15 ... And this is He that is to wait upon exhortation or application, and bringing home the Word to the heart and conscience, Rom. 12:7. Therefore His Word is called, the Word of Wisdom, 1 Cor. 12:8. And this man is to administer other Ordinances, as Baptism and the Supper, in the Church; because it is the Church's right, and so a part of feeding, Matt. 24:45. The ruler over the house must give His fellow-servants their meat, Luke 12:42.

The Teacher's office is to wait on Teaching, Rom. 12. That is, I conceive, principally to expound the Scripture, and lay down sound Doctrine, and confute Errors, that so the Church may be established in the Truth, Tit. 2:8. ... But I conceive Pastor and Teacher may be understood for one and the same, and may perform the same Offices in the Church; but only where the church is large and mul-tifarious, they may choose more Officers for the better ordering of things, and so have several titles given them according to their several gifts, and they fall both under the general name of Bishop or Elder ...

The ruling Elder is to feed, guide, or go before, and no otherwise to rule, Matt. 2:6; 1 Tim. 3:5 and 5:17; Heb. 13:17. to oversee the manners and lives of men, that none walk disorderly, and to warn them that do; and to see where any are disconsolate, and to comfort them; and to assist in Censures, if any be to be cast out, 1 Thes. 5:14. But I conceive the ruling Elders are to be, only in the necessity of the Church, being many, and spread abroad; for otherwise, all these things the preaching El-der may do... And that such are to be in case of neces-sity (I conceive) appears from that order, Rom. 12:7, 8, where is, first Pastor, then Teacher, then Deacon; Afterward those that rule, and show mercy; showing that they were to be in case of necessity to help the others.

The Deacon's office is to receive and distribute the contribution of the Church, as they see need and occasion, Acts 6:1-6. And this is He that gives, Rom. 12:8 and also to see the Church's members walk not idly.

Under the section, "How Many Officers are to be in the Church", King said:

Some say, every Congregation is to have a Pastor and a Teacher, and two ruling Elders, and two Deacons, and Widows: But I conceive the number is left to the Church, and her necessity: For, in the Church at Jerusalem were many Elders, Acts 21:18, the Church being great; And had seven Deacons, Acts 6, THE POOR BEING MANY; and so many were neglected until they were chosen: and need requiring that there should be a daily Ministration, as you may see, verse 1, which could not be done by one or two; neither do I read how many were in Ephesus, Acts 20, nor how many they ordained in every Church, Acts 14.

It can be seen that Daniel King believed in the validity of ruling elders. The view expressed by him is exactly that of John Owen, the points held in common being: (i) the office of elder or bishop is one, to be filled by officers who share the same basic office of rule; (ii) the pastor or teacher, who is "the ruler over the house" (said King), rules primarily by teaching the word of God; (iii) the pastor is assisted in ruling the church by the ruling elder; (iv) the needs of the church determine whether more than one pastor and/or ruling elder are to be appointed; and, (v) the pastor has the priority over the ruling elder, the former being the officer generally appointed first in a church, and is the leading elder if there are more than one elder. Owen made the additional point that the pastor should be assisted by at least one ruling elder because: (a) the biblical pattern is a plurality of elders, (b) at least two elders are needed to form a presbytery; (c) the many needs of any church would normally require an elder to help the pastor. Owen's plurality of elders – constituting the presbytery or eldership – consists of at least a pastor who was also known as the teaching elder, and a ruling elder.

115

The question that arises at this point is whether Daniel King's view of the eldership was peculiar to himself or representative of other Particular Baptists? A contrary view was to be propounded by Benjamin Keach (1640-1704), who published "The Glory of a True Church and its Discipline display'd" in 1697. In the book, Keach wrote (Dever, 2001: 65, 68-69):

> A Church thus constituted ought forthwith to choose them a Pastor, Elder or Elders, and Deacons, (we reading of no other Officers, or Offices abiding in the Church)... Therefore such are very disorderly Churches who have no Pastor or Pastors ordained, they acting not according to the Rule of the Gospel, having something wanting.
>
> Query, *Are there no ruling Elders besides the Pastor? Answ.* There might be such in the Primitive Apostolical Church, but we see no ground to believe it an abiding Office to continue in the Church, but was only temporary.
> 1. Because we have none of the Qualifications of such Elders mention'd, or how to be chosen.
> 2. Because we read not particularly what their Work and Business is, or how distinct from preaching Elders; tho we see not but the Church may (if sees meet) choose some able and discreet Brethren to be *Helps in Government*. We have the Qualifications of Bishops and Deacons directly laid down, and how to be chosen, and their Work declared, but no other Office or Officers in the Church, but these only.

To Keach, the pastor is to be equated with elder, bishop and overseer. He countenanced no ruling elders. Keach would not call the pastor the teaching elder, for that would imply a belief in the validity of the ruling elder. While allowing for the possibility of having more than one pastors, as has been noted above, Keach anticipated a single pastor most of the time, as he intimated by the constant use of the singular, "pastor". When the first edition of King's book, "A Way to Sion" was published in 1650, Keach was only ten years old. Keach was a second generation leader among the Particular Baptists in London, who gathered the Horsleydown church at Southwark only in 1672. While it may be argued that there could have been other Particular Baptists of the first generation who had held to his view of the eldership, no convincing proofs have been put forward from their writings (see, for example, Renihan, 1998: 177-239; Waldron, *et al.*, 1997). Calling the variant to King's view of the eldership by Keach's name is, therefore, an anachronism. The present writer's contention is that Keach's view of the eldership (as well as of a number of other matters, which will be discussed in the next chapter) was not the view of the majority of the Particular Baptists, while that of Daniel King was the predominant view. To determine the correctness of this, the extant documents of the Particular Baptists will have to be carefully weighed up.

While examining the documents of the Particular Baptists, care must be taken to understand correctly the view of the churches or individuals concerned. Since the appointment of pastors and ruling elders was to be based on the needs of the church, according to Daniel King and John Owen, there would be churches that had a pastor or teaching elder but no ruling elders, or had ruling elders but not a pastor. There would also be churches that had more than one pastor, but usually not more than two, with or without ruling elders. Furthermore, the constant persecution accompanying the political turmoil of the time, and the general poverty of the members, resulted in the inability of many churches to support a full-time ministry (Knollys, 1812: 2-7). This was recognized by the General Assembly of 1689 which met in London, at which it was proposed that a public fund be started to strengthen the ministry among the churches (Narrative, 1689: 48-49). Small churches in close geographical proximity were urged "to join together for the better and more comfortable support of their Ministry, and better edification of one another". Combined with the mission-mindedness of the churches, which resulted in many churches having satellite congregations, the need for preachers was pressing. The situation was overcome to some degree by the appointment of suitable helpers known as "gifted brethren", or just "ministers", who did not hold office as elders.

The 1689 Confession expresses the beliefs and practice of the churches in these matters in Chapter 26, Articles 10 and 11:

> 10. The work of Pastors being constantly to attend the Service of *Christ*, in his Churches, in the Ministry of the Word, and Prayer, (t) with watching for their Souls, as they that must give an account to him; it is incumbent on the Churches to whom they Minister, not only to give

them all due respect, (u) but also to communicate to them of all their good things according to their ability, so as they may have a comfortable supply, without being themselves (x) entangled in Secular Affairs; and may also be capable of exercising (y) Hospitality toward others; and this is required by the (z) Law of Nature, and by the Express order of our Lord Jesus, who hath ordained they they that preach the Gospel, should live of the Gospel.
(t) Act. 6.4. Heb. 13.17. (u) 1 Tim. 5.17, 18. Gal. 6. 6, 7. (x) 2 Tim. 2.4. (y) 1 Tim. 3.2. (z) 1 Cor. 9. 6-14.

11. Although it be incumbent on the Bishops or Pastors of the Churches to be instant in Preaching the Word, by way of Office; yet the work of Preaching the Word, is not so peculiarly confined to them; but that others also (a) gifted, and fitted by the Holy *Spirit* for it, and approved, and called by the *Church*, may and ought to perform it.
(a) Act. 11.19,20,21. 1 Pet. 4.10, 11.

From the foregoing, it can be seen that the following situations might be encountered, especially before Keach came upon the scene, that is, before 1672, when he gathered together a Calvinist church, or even up to 1697, when he published "The Glory of a True Church":

1 A church that indicated the existence of, or belief in, either a teaching elder or a ruling elder would be holding to the view of eldership propounded by Daniel King and John Owen, regardless of whether the other sort of elder had been appointed yet.

2 A church that indicated the existence of, or belief in, a pastor with one or more elders would be holding to the view of King and Owen.

3 A church that indicated the existence of either elders only, or pastors only, might be holding to King's view or Keach's view. In such a situation, it is more likely that King's view was held to in the period before the publication of Keach's view of the eldership in 1697, because of the prevalence and influence of King's book, "A Way to Sion", and the writings of John Owen on the subject. It was only from the beginning of the 18th century that uncertainty may be entertained as to whether such a church held to King's or Keach's view.

4 In a situation where there is an assistant pastor, it would have to be concluded definitely that it is King's view that is in mind, and not that of Keach. Only King explicitly allowed for an order of priority among the equal elders: "... where the church is large and multifarious, they may choose more Officers for the better ordering of things, and so have several titles given them according to their several gifts, and they fall both under the general name of Bishop or Elder." This, as seen already, was in line with Owen's view.

To summarize, it may be said that in Keach's view, all pastors are elders and all elders are pastors, while in King's view, all pastors are elders but not all elders are pastors.

4.3.3   Hanserd Knollys's Eldership

Hanserd Knollys has been referred to as he interacted with Dr. Bastwick, in Chapter 2 of the present work. In his book, "A Moderate Answer Unto Dr. Bastwicks Book", Knollys wrote as an Independent over against Dr. Bastwick's Presbyterianism (Knollys, 1645). His view on the eldership would have been that advocated by Daniel King and John Owen. Commenting on Revelation 2:1, Knollys said (Knollys, 1698):

> ... by Angel in this and all the other epistles written to the seven churches in Asia, we are to understand the episcopacy, presbytery, and ministry in each particular church, unto whom the charge, oversight, care and government thereof was committed by the Holy Spirit ... *elders and bishops, among whom none were lords over God's heritage,* (1Pe 5: 1, 2, 3) ... So the word "Angel" in all these seven epistles, is a noun collective, comprehending all the bishops and presbyters, called elders, (Ac 20:17) in this Church of Ephesus, so in all other churches of Christ in Asia, and elsewhere. [Emphasis original.]

The duties of the presbytery – specified here as having "the charge, oversight, care and government" of the church – was also stated in another book, "The World that Now Is, and The World That is to Come" (Knollys, 1681: 56-57):

> The Office of a *Pastor, Bishop,* and *Presbyter,* or *Elder* in
> the Church of God, is to take the Charge, Oversight, and
> Care of those Souls which the Lord Jesus Christ hath com-
> mitted to them, to feed the Flock of God; to watch for
> their Souls, ... to Rule, Guide and Govern them (*by virtue
> of their Commission, and Authority received from Christ,
> Mat.* 28.28, 19, 20. & *Titus* 2.15.) according to the Laws,
> Constitutions and Ordinances of the Gospel. [Emphasis
> original.]

Believing that the church at Jerusalem set the pattern for other
churches, Knollys (1681: 44-45, 50-51) argued that ideally – "Gospel-
Oneness which maketh very much for the Well-Being of a particular
church" – there should be one church in one city, which consists of a
number of congregations bearing but one name. Further, the church
in each city should choose one of the elders of the congregations to
have "Priority, Presidence, and Pre-eminence" over the other elders
(Knollys, 1681: 68-69):

> I mean and intend any one of the Bishops, Pastors, Teach-
> ers, Presbyters, or Elders, who are, or shall by the Con-
> sent, Approbation and Choice of the rest be appointed,
> ordained, and set over them as Chief Bishop or Presbyter
> of the Church in any City and Villages adjacent, who
> for Order sake in Gospel-Government, hath Priority, Pre-
> eminence, and Authority above the rest of the Presbyters
> or Bishops of the same Church, not alone, *nor without
> them,* but when *Convened* with them, to Act, Rule, Guide,
> Order and Govern with their Consent, Suffrage and As-
> sistance, according to the Laws of the Lord Jesus Christ,
> the Constitutions and Commandments, the Practice and
> Example of his Holy Apostles, *Act.* 15.2, 6, 19, 22. [Em-
> phasis original.]

It will be discussed in Chapter 5 of the present work the widespread practice of the Particular Baptists in having a number of satellite congregations under one church, in which Knollys's system of
church government was applied. For now, it must be noted that
Knollys's view of the eldership is basically that of King's, namely: (i)
a presbytery consisting of at least two elders rule in a church; (ii)
they rule according to the word of God; and (iii) one of the elders

is to be recognized as the leading elder. Knollys did not specifically differentiate between the teaching and the ruling elders, but placed the responsibilities of teaching and caring for souls, that is, "to rule, guide and govern" the church, in the eldership or presbytery, which was consistent with King's view. This view allowed for the appointment of ruling elders. Confirmation of this is found in the records of the church in later days.

Upon the death of Knollys in 19 September, 1691, Robert Steed succeeded him. The church which had met at Broken Wharf, Thames Street, moved to Bagnio Court, Newgate Street, and then to Currier's Hall, Cripplegate, where it remained for a century. In 1705, Steed was succeeded by David Crossley who had been baptized by John Eccles of Bromsgrove, remaining in the London church until about 1710 (Ivimey, Vol. 3: 360-361; Bromsgrove CRB, Vol. 1: 50). An entry in the Church Minute Book concerning procedures to be adopted for bringing matters to the church meeting included the following points (Bagnio/Cripplegate CMB: 12):

> 5 That no stranger be present when any declare ye dealing of God with their Soules: or any other matter in ye church but members only (unless allowed by ye *pastor*)
> 6 That all those members yt frequently are absent from their comunion wth the church, be carefully and constantly observed, and our **Elders** acquainted therewith; that they may be visited, & admonished according to rule.
> 11 That every member that doth not contribute towards the maintenance of *ye Ministrie* &c. according to their ability be visited & admonished according to rule.
> 13 That ye power of determining & concluding all matters & things be in & by the Church: The actuall exercise of all power (ministerially) &c. be by ye **Elders** or those the Church shall appoint, According to ye rule of our Lord and Law-giver Christ Jesus in ye Holy Scriptures.
> [Italics original. Emphasis in bold added.]

The "pastor" is mentioned as a distinct individual, while the "Elders" could have included, or not included, him. The maintenance of "the ministry" would indicate that the pastor was supported full-time. Knollys emphasized the "Priority, Presidence, and Pre-eminence of any one Bishop above other Bishops, Pastors, Teachers, Presbyters, or Elders, and Ministers of Christ", at the same time also emphasizing that it "is not any *Lordly* Prelacy, with *coercive* Power over the Conscience, or *Dominion* over the Faith of God's Clergy". In fact, it can be said that the whole of Chapter 2 of his book, entitled "Of Gospel-Ministry", consisting of fifteen pages out of the book of forty-eight pages, was devoted to emphasizing these two points. A little before his death, Knollys wrote a letter of admonition to his church, in which he began by saying, "To the Church whereof I am Pastor ..." (Knollys, 1812: 58). He referred to his assistant as "my reverend and beloved brother Steed", and urged "our honoured and beloved Elder [Steed]", and "our ministering brethren who are helps in government, to join together to set in order these things" (Knollys, 1812: 59, 66). His last piece of counsel was for the church to "look out a Minister of Jesus Christ, whom he hath in some competent measure qualified with such ministerial gifts and graces, as make him worthy of so great honour as is due to a Pastor, and Elder of the church of God; yea, of double honour, 1 Tim. v. 17; both of maintenance and obedience, Heb. xiii. 17" (Knollys, 1812: 67). Since the pastor was clearly distinguished from the assistant pastor and the other elders, Knollys's eldership had to be that of King's and Owen's.

Apart from Daniel King's book, "A Way to Sion", Knollys's book, "The World that Now Is; and the World that is to Come", may be said to portray the definitive views of the Particular Baptists of the 17th century. These books were not specifically on church government, unlike Owen's books of 1667 and 1689, but they may not be casually disregarded. The emphasis on the priority of the gospel ministry, that is, of the full-time pastor, was in line with Owen's view (Owen, 1976, Vol. 16: 105):

> ... the absolute equality of many pastors in one and the same church is liable unto many inconveniences if not diligently watched against. Wherefore let the state of the church be preserved and kept unto its original constitution, which is congregational, and no other ... namely, of one pastor or bishop in one church, assisted in rule and all holy administration with many elders teaching or ruling only ...

4.3.4 Eldership in the South Wales Association

Many Particular Baptist churches were organized into regional associations, of which more will be said in Chapter 6. Messengers from the five churches of the Association of South Wales met on 30 to 31 August 1654. The record for the meeting not only differentiated between the extraordinary and the ordinary officers, but also delineated the duties of the continuing officers. After specifying the duties of the "joint office" of those called Elders, Bishops, Watchmen, etc., it stated the following (White, 1971-7, Pt. 1: 11):

> These were the duties of all the elders, though the greatest charge lay on the pastors, as appears in that, though there were many elders in the church at Ephesus, yet the epistle in the Revelation the second chapter, is directed but to one, viz., the angel of the church, and the charge given to, and the account required of him wholly. Now more particularly:
>
> First, the pastor's office is to do all that tends to the feeding of the flock, Jer. 3.15; Mt. 24.45 as to 1. Exhort ...; 2. Reprove ...; 3. Cast out ...; 4. Lead the sheep ...; 5. Watch ...; 6. Administer all ordinances ...; 7. Give himself wholly to the word and doctrine ...; 8. Rule well ...
>
> Secondly, the teacher's particular office is, to wait on teaching, to expound scriptures, and confute errors. Tit. 2.7f. 2 Tim.4.2. And this is no less the pastor's office.
>
> Thirdly, the ruling elder's, or helping office is, to oversee the lives and manners of men: to who also double honour is due, I Tim. 5.17; Ro.12.8. He also must take care of God's house, Heb.13.17. I Tim. 3.5.

The agreement of the churches of South Wales with the view of Daniel King and John Owen is obvious, the points held in common being: (i) the office of elder or bishop is one; (ii) the pastor is the teaching elder; (iii) the pastor is assisted in ruling the church by the ruling elder; and, (iv) the pastor has the priority ("the greatest charge") over the ruling elder (who has the "helping office").

In the 18th century, the Welsh churches were in close touch with the Bristol Academy, starting with Bernard Foskett's close interaction with the indefatigable church-planter, Miles Harry. Hugh and Caleb Evans were to contribute to the teaching in the Academy, which further strengthen ties between the two regions. Over the century, at least eighty-seven Welsh students from twenty-five different Welsh churches studied at Bristol. The-se, and a larger number of other students of Bristol, were to exert an influence over the whole nation, including London, the effects of which have not been fully appreciated (Hayden, 2006: 93). It is to be expected that the view of eldership held by the Welsh churches and the Broadmead church, in which the Bristol Academy was based, was spread far and wide in the 18th century.

4.3.5   Eldership in the Midlands Association

In his book "A Way to Sion", Daniel King described himself as "Preacher of the Word Near Coventry". The Association Records of the Midlands (White, Pt. 1: 20) show that during the second General Meeting of messengers, held on 26 June 1655, seven churches were represented. Daniel King who represented Warwick together with one Henry Vencent, was obviously the pastor of the church there. Furthermore, King published a tract in 1651, entitled "A Discovery of some Troublesome Thoughts", in which was mentioned that he was "neer related" to the following churches (White, Pt. 1: 39; 1966a): "the Churches of Christ in London meeting usually at the glasse-house in Broad Street, the Church in Coventry, the Church in Warwick, the Church at Hook Norton in Oxfordshire and the Church meeting neer Morton-Hinmarsh in Gloucestershire". The last three mentioned churches were among the seven that formed the Association of Churches of the Midlands. It is safe to say that King's view on church government extended to all seven churches of the Midlands Association as well as to the other churches he was "near related" to in London.

Of the seven churches that formed the Midlands Association in 1655, one was located at Alcester (or Alchester) in Warwickshire. In the early 18th century, it had Bernard Foskett as the pastor. Foskett later removed to the open communion Calvinistic Baptist church at Broadmead, Bristol. The church held clearly to King's view of the eldership, as shall be seen below. Foskett's easy transition into Broadmead church shows that he had held to the same view of eldership in Alcester. Foskett was later involved in the ordination of Benjamin Beddome in the church at Bourton-on-the-Water in the Midlands.

The church at Bourton-on-the-Water was another of the seven

original churches of the Midlands Association (White, Pt. 1: 20). During the ordination of Benjamin Beddome on 23 September, 1743, Bernard Foskett of Bristol gave the charge to the pastor. To the church the new pastor was a "teaching elder", thus showing that it held to King's view of the eldership. This may be seen in the document drawn up by the church a week before the ordination, stating: (Brooks, 1861: 27):

> We, the church of Christ meeting at Bourton-on-the-Water, Having solemnly called, and set apart, our be-loved brother, Benjamin Beddome, to the office of *teaching elder* to us, do hereby declare, that we don't intend to bring him under any such special obligation to us; but that if the providence of God calls him elsewhere, or he upon valuable considerations, doth desire his release from us, we will give up our right in him, as if he had never stood in any such relation to us. In witness whereof we have put our hands, &c. [Emphasis added.]

In later years, Beddome had "an assistant, or co-pastor, in the Rev. William Wilkins" and after Wilkins, "an assistant was found in Mr. Reed" (Brooks, 1861: 55-56). As noted earlier, this would indicate that the church held to King's view of the eldership.

4.3.6 Eldership in London

Daniel King's book, "A Way to Sion", was accompanied by "The Epistle Dedicatory" which bore the signature of Thomas Patient, William Kiffin, John Spilsbury, and John Pearson. In it, these men said,

> This book has been above a year since in our hands to put in the press. But, we may say as Paul says, Satan hindered, that we could not timelier put it forth. But to our knowledge, such a Treatise as this has been much longed for by many of the people of God in most of the counties in England. And now it's God's time, which we judge is a seasonable time, that this Treatise will come into many of their hands.

This is of interest in that these men approved of and, indeed, recommended the views put forward by King which, in this first volume, included the nature and organization of the church. There was no disclaimer of any kind, and no reservation indicated, but commendation instead. They expressed the hope, regarding those influenced by the Seekers, "if God have not given over persons to much hardness of heart, that the reading of this may be of singular use to convince them of the truth". They added that "for those that are in the practice of the way and true order of Christ, it will be of singular use to settle and establish them more fully". Would it be amiss in claiming that Thomas Patient, William Kiffin, John Spilsbury, and John Pearson held to the same views as Daniel King on the matters explained in his book?

It has been noted that King's tract of 1651, entitled "A Discovery of some Troublesome Thoughts", mentioned that he was "neer related" to "the Churches of Christ in London meeting usually at the glasse-house in Broad Street". The churches in London must have included those of the four men who contributed the "Epistle Dedicatory" of King's book, "A Way to Sion". Of the four men who contributed the "Epistle Dedicatory", Kiffin was the pastor of the church at Devonshire Square, while Spilsbury was the pastor of the church meeting at Wapping. Nothing is known of John Pearson. Thomas Patient was the co-pastor with Kiffin at Devonshire Square.

William Kiffin led the Devonshire Square church for the whole of his life, from the time he became its pastor from round about 1644. In 1690, Richard Adams was ordained into "sayd works & office of an elder amongst them, in conjunction wth Bro. Wm Kiffin" (Devonshire Square CMB: 21). Similarly, in 1706 when Mark Key was ordained into office with him, Adams was instructed to say, "... my Br: Mark Key is by this church appointed or ordained a joynt elder Pastor or overseer wth my self over her" (Devonshire Square CMB: 159). As noted already, the appointment of two pastors need not necessarily mean that the church held to Keach's view of eldership (cf. Renihan, 201). Rather, based on what is known of Kiffin's connection with Daniel King and his book "A Way to Sion", it is more likely that the church held to King's view. Furthermore, Kiffin was known to sustain a close relationship with Hanserd Knollys, editing and publishing the biography of the latter on his demise (Knollys & Kiffin, 1692). Kiffin most likely shared Knollys's and King's view of the eldership. It must be noted that Knollys was also based in London.

The same can be said of the Petty France church. When the church ordained William Collins and Nehemiah Coxe as co-pastors, it was stated that, "On ye 21th of ye 7th M: bro Collins & Bro: Coxe were solemnly ordained pastors or elders in this church" (Petty France CMB: 1). As with the Devonshire Square church, this need not necessarily mean that the church believed in Keach's view of the eldership (cf. Renihan, 1998: 200-201). By assuming that the church held to Keach's view, a case can be made out that Nehemiah Coxe was expressing this view of the eldership when he said, "Elders, ... Bishops or Overseers, ... Pastors and Teachers ... it is evident the Holy Ghost intends no distinction, or preeminence of Office among those that bear these Characters, by any of these different Terms" (Coxe, 1681: 18). In reality, Coxe was explaining the one office of elder – a point held in common by Keach's view and King's view – without denying the validity of the ruling elder. It is likely that Coxe was expressing the view of the Petty France church, which probably corresponded to King's view. The point here is that it cannot be claimed with certainty which view the Petty France church had held to, based upon Coxe's ordination sermon alone. Coxe's "Ordination Sermon" was published in 1681. The Petty France church had interacted with the churches of the Abingdon Association on a similar issue in 1656, as will be seen below. Keach's "The Glory of a True Church" was yet to be published, in 1697. Keach was a relatively late comer, whose personality and views seemed to have been weighed with caution by the other Particular Baptists (see next chapter).

4.3.7 Eldership in the Abingdon Association

The Abingdon Association began in 1652, with three churches, and soon expanded to five. From 1654, when the Midlands churches were beginning to associate, Abingdon began to sort out the issue of church order. The original five churches in the association met on 26 December 1654, proposing that the following points be discussed in their subsequent meeting (White, Pt. 3: 134):

> 1. That the offi[ces of E]lders and deacons are ordained of the Lord for the [good] of his church and, therefore, it is the duty of everie church verie diligently to endeavour, and very earnestly to seeke unto the Lord, that they may enjoy the benefit of these his gracious appointments, remembering God's promise to give his people pastors according to his owne heart, Jer. 3.15.

2. That the office of pastors, elders and overseers or bishops is but one and the same and that it is the duty of everie elder as well to teach as to rule in the church whereof he is elder.

Representatives of the Abingdon Association met again on the 19th and 20th day of the 4th month, 1655, at which the proposals of the previous meeting was not adopted because of the dissenting voice of one of the messengers (White, Pt. 3: 138). At this meeting, four other churches joined the membership of the Association. In the meeting of 18 October, 1655, the churches expressed their desire to appoint elders and deacons according to the biblical pattern. On the 11th of the first month of 1656, the associated churches, now twelve in number, concluded, "That the office of pastors, elders and overseers or bishops is one and the same and that it is the duty of everie elder as well to teach as to rule in the church whereof he is an elder" (White, Pt. 3: 145). Since there is no explicit denial of the ruling elder, unlike the case of Keach, it is not possible to state with certainty which view this is. Both King's view and Keach's view share in common the belief that the office of the elder is one, and the pastor both rules and teaches. Following the meeting on the 30th of the tenth month of that year, the letter requesting advice from the Petty France church which was referred to earlier was sent, the specific questions over which they wanted help being: "i. Who have authoritie to ordaine elders and deacons? ii. How they are to be ordained?" As noted above, when considering the Petty France church in London, the reply included the statement on the office of elder or pastor which did not specifically repudiate the validity of the ruling elder. It seems that, throughout this period stretching from the end of 1654 to the end of 1656, the desire of the churches was to be convinced of, and to implement, the biblical teaching on elders and deacons.

Throughout this period, the Midlands churches were seeking the help of the Abingdon Association to form an association of their own (White, Pt. 3: 134-135, 166-167). Benjamin Cox, a leader of the Abingdon Association, was assigned to communicate with the churches in the Midlands with the view of helping them to associate. In view of the key role played by Daniel King in the Midlands Association, and the fact that the second edition of his book, "A Way to Sion" was published both in London and Edinburgh, there is the strong likelihood that his view had had an influence on the Abingdon Association. King had explicitly upheld the validity of the ruling elder.

The church at Reading was one of the three founding churches of the Abingdon Association in 1652, the other two being those of Henly and Abingdon (White, Pt. 3: 126). After Charles II returned in triumph in 1660, the Abingdon Association ceased to be active. The new government was extremely sensitive to the threat posed by left-wing political plottings. Too many Baptists had been linked with the Fifth Monarchists for them to run Association meetings without being suspected of planning subversion. When better days came following the Act of Toleration, the churches in London initiated the first General Assembly of the Particular Baptists, held from 3rd to 12th September, 1689. The letter sent out to the churches after the Assembly was signed by a number of leaders, including representatives of the church at Reading, namely, William Facey and Reyamire Griffin, as pastor and messenger respectively. In 1707, the Abingdon Association began functioning actively again, with the participation of the church at Reading. The spirituality of the church, however, declined, especially after the death of its pastor. There was an attempt made at uniting the General Baptist church with the Particular Baptist church in Reading, which probably took place in 1712, or some years earlier. The merger of the two congregations led "to the complete adoption and prevalence of the calvinistic theology" (Hinton, 1826), and the resulting church was still a member of the Abingdon Association (White, 1968: 262). The Association ceased meeting after the gathering held on 19 May, 1714. The church at Reading continued to function, however, declaring in its church book the following (Reading CB: 124):

> The Church having undergon many alterations, being destitute for some time of one to under take the Pastoriall Charge there of: at length through Divine goodness providing for it, did unanemosly agree, to give a Call to Mr. Johnathan Davis to undertake the saide Charge: who having readelly accepted of the saide Call of the Church tooke upon him the Care there of, as it's Minister & Pastor about ye beginning of July –1715–
> About Septembr. In serving the Church proceeded to the Chose of Ellders and Deacons, to asist the saide Pastor in

Disiplin and other affares of the Church, as is incombant
on them in their proper stashons: and the under named
was then unanimosly Chose to the offices hear after Men-
shon
Mr Johnathon Davis – Pastor
George Elliott Ambrose Freeman – Ruling Ellders
Thomas Goodwin John Collier John Glover Jur John
Legg – Deacons

The church at Reading obviously held to King's view of the eldership, with a pastor, two ruling elders, and four deacons. With
its longstanding association with the other churches, would it not be
reasonable to conclude that all the other churches in the Abingdon
Association had held to the same view on the eldership?

4.3.8   Eldership in Ireland

Thomas Patient (or Patience), the other man among the four who
contributed the "Epistle Dedicatory" to King's book, was one of those
who had gone to New England. While there, he had come to reject infant baptism and had consequently found it best to leave Mas-
sachusetts in 1642. His experience seemed to parallel that of Hanserd
Knollys. Hanserd Knollys and Edward Harrison set apart Thomas Patient as co-pastor with William Kiffin in 1644. Patient and Kiffin had
signed the London Confession of 1644 and 1646, and "Heartbleed-
ings for Professors Abominations", sent out by the London leaders in
1650 (White, 1966). Probably after 1644, but before he signed the
1646 edition of the Confession, he was involved with Kiffin in an unsuccessful mission to Kent where the converts were taken over by the
General Baptists. He apparently stayed in London until early 1650
when he joined the English invasion of Ireland. There he played a
prominent role in building Baptist congregations. He was one of the
signatories representing ten congregations which sent a letter to the
London churches in 1653, asking for joint fasting and prayer. Patient
returned to England at the Restoration. After a period helping the Pithay, Bristol, closed membership Calvinistic Baptists, he returned to
London where he began work once more as a colleague of William
Kiffin but died of the plague in 1666. Since Patient had been so
closely involved with Kiffin, and both men had contributed to King's
"Epistle Dedicatory" in which they highly commended the views set

forth in the book, it would have to be concluded that they all shared the same view of church government. The fact that Patient and Kiffin were co-pastors in the Devonshire Square church did not mean that they held to Keach's view of the eldership. Furthermore, the argument would have to be extended to Ireland, where Patient's influence was notable.

In the letter of exhortation to the churches in London, the Irish churches had included two documents, one of which contained the points of agreement of the churches for prayer and fasting, while the other contained details of the churches in Ireland. In the latter document, it was stated that Patient and the other leaders were constantly being moved about because they were army officers (White, Pt. 2: 119). Moreover, Patient had been called upon to baptize new believers, probably because he was one of the few, if not the only, ordained ministers there. The relevant portions of the document read as follows (White, Pt. 2: 119, 120):

> In Dublin. With whom are Brother Patience, brother Lamb, brother Vernon, brother Roberts, brother Smyth with several others through grace who walked comfortably togather [sic.] but most of the brethren besides brother Patient have relation to the army and therefore are subject to be called away, as occasion requires, to performe their duty in their places.

> In the north neere Carrick Fergus are severall lately receaved by brother Reade who were baptized heere by brother Patient whom wee understand are pretiouse but want some able brethren to establish them.

The esteem and influence of Thomas Patient in Ireland are not in doubt. Another man with whom Patient had close dealings in Ireland was Stephen Wade, a captain based in Waterford. Wade had shared in the debates about baptism with Hanserd Knollys in 1645, which led to their baptism. Later, after Henry Jessey's baptism, they rejoined his church. Wade signed as minister from Alcester (or Alchester) at the founding of the Midlands Association in 1655 (White, Pt. 2: 119, 123). Alcester was to have Bernard Foskett as pastor in the early 18th century, who then moved on to the Broadmead, Bristol, church which clearly held to the view of eldership advocated by Daniel King. Wade's close association with Thomas Patient in Ireland indicates that the two had held to the same view of eldership, which was that of King. It is, therefore, to be expected that the church in Alcester would in later days have Foskett as pastor, who held to the same view of the eldership. Foskett was later to ordain Benjamin Beddome as pastor, or "teaching elder", of another church in the Midlands, namely that at Bourton-on-the-Water, as has been seen above. All these relations provide support for the view that the churches in Ireland held to the same view of eldership, which was that of King.

4.3.9   Eldership in Northern England

The churches in the north of England were founded by the men who served in the Commonwealth troops, as well as by the deliberate missional efforts of the churches in London. Captains Paul Hobson and Thomas Gower (or Goare) had been the men who gathered the church at the Crutched Fryars in 1639, They both signed the 1644 and 1646 Confessions issued by the seven churches in London. By 1650, they were active leaders of the church founded in Newcastle. Numbered among the supporters were many other soldiers, including Captain John Turner, Captain Mason, Henry Hudson, and others. Because of the transfer of soldiers to other postings, the membership was subject to change.

Thomas Tillam was a volatile and charismatic figure who had become a member of Hanserd Knollys's church in Coleman Street, London, in 1651. The church commissioned Tillam as their messenger to the north to gather churches. Arriving in December 1651 in Hexham, he began undertaking evangelistic activities and engaged in preaching tours in Cheshire and in the North East in 1652 and 1653. His forceful and often impetuous personality was the cause of the dispute between the Hexham and the Newcastle congregations, lasting from 1653 until his departure from the area in early 1655 (Copson, 1991: 13-14).

At the first General Assembly of the Calvinistic Baptists in London in 1689, only the churches in Newcastle and Derwentwater sent messengers. The Assembly of 1690 recorded six churches in the Northern Association, namely Newcastle, Bitchburn, Egremont, Pontefract, Broughton and Torver-Hawkshead. The Derwentwater church, of which Bitchburn was its southern congregation, was active in reaching out and planting new causes (Copson, 1991: 19). The associated churches met at Bitchburn on the 6th of the 4th month of 1711, the record of which included the following (Copson, 1991: 102-103):

> Qu 4. Whether a Church of Christ being about to Call a Member to Office so as to take the Pastoral care and Charge over them and at the same time wanting Rule-ing Elders for the more orderly carrying on of the work Whether it may not be consistent with the Order of a Gospel Church to invite over an Elder of a Sister Church to assist in the Management of the work yea or nay?
> Answ. In the Affirmative as Tit 1.3,5. Acts 14.23.

Then, following the Association meeting at Bridlington in the County of York on 19th and 20th June 1723, a joint statement on the practical operation of the association was signed by representatives of the churches. The messengers of the church at Hampsterly and Cold Rowley in the County of Durham was represented by William Carr and Michael Wharton, each declaring himself, respectively, as "Pastor" and "Elder & Clerk to the Association". Carr was the pastor of the church, while Wharton was a ruling elder. Carr also wrote at length on the Christian ministry, answering the questions (Copson, 1991: 98-101):

> 1. Whether any man may or ought to take upon himself the Office of the Ministry in Preaching the Gospel & Administering the Ordinances of Baptism & the Lord's Supper (in an ordinary way) without being truely and orderly called thereunto?
> 2. Wherein doth a true and orderly Call to the Ministry consist what it is and how to be effected?

Carr's article (or "paper", as it would be called today) was discussed and accepted by the messengers. The call to the ministry of the word includes the call from God, and the call from the church. Carr's view of the call is consistent with Article 10 of Chapter 26, Article 2 of Chapter 28, and Article 3 of Chapter 30, of the 1689 Confession (Poh, 2000: 120-122).

It has been noted that the church at Broughton was a member of the Northern Association, the records of which were compiled by S. L. Copson for the years 1699 to 1732. The churches in the north had existed since the late 1640s. On the first page of the Church Book for the church meeting at Broughton and Porton, the following is found for the year 1669 (Broughton CB, 1669: 1): "This Booke is for ... that Church of Christ in Broughton ... whereof Mr. Gabrill Camelford is *Teaching Elder*" [emphasis added]. In the 1660s the Derwentwater church had three elders. In 1723, it had a pastor, elder and deacon.

The Hexham church had asked the Coleman Street church in London in March 1653 to have Thomas Tillam recommended as their pastor. By the end of 1654 they had ordained two elders and two deacons (Copson, 1991: 48).

A letter dated 29th December 1718 was sent from the church at Bridlington to the Cripplegate church in London, where a certain Braithwaite, a "gifted brother", had been baptized, mentioning that he had been "neither *elder* nor *pastor* at Torver-Hawkshead" [emphasis added]. The church at Torver-Hawkshead clearly differentiated between the pastor and the ruling elder.

From the survey of the churches in the north, it can be seen clearly that they had held to King's view of the eldership.

4.3.10   Eldership in the Western Association

The churches in the West Country were originally founded and greatly influenced by Thomas Collier. The Western Association in 1655 appointed and ordained him "General Superintendent and Messenger to all the Associated Churches". In 1659, eighteen churches were represented in the Association (White, Pt. 2: 75). In its meeting held from 24 to 27 of the 8th month of 1655, the following questions were asked and answered (White, Pt. 2: 60):

> Query 1. Whether the power of the keys spoken of in Mat. 16.19, John 20.23, Mat. 18.18, be given to the church or to the eldership in the church?
> Answer: the exercise of the power of Christ in a church having officers, in opening and shutting, in receiving in and casting out, belongs to the church with its eldership, Mat. 18.17f., I. Cor. 5.4f., III John 9ff., Acts 15. 4,22.
> Query 2. Whether a church of Christ in her election of elders are to invest the power of teaching and ruling in them all alike or to appoint some for teaching and some for ruling sutable [sic.] to their gift?
> Answer: it is the office of an elder both to teach and rule.

> The church, therefore, ordaining a person to that office do thereby invest him with a power both to teach and rule. Tit. 1.9ff., I.Tim. 3.2, Acts 20.17,28, Heb. 13.7,17, I. Peter 5.1f. Yet sutable to the gift are they to be most exercised, I.Tim. 5.17.

The answers do not state explicitly that there should be ruling elders. Before drawing too quick a conclusion to the contrary, it should be carefully noted that the answers are in line with that expressed by John Owen, Daniel King and the Association of South Wales. Church power is lodged *in* the church, *with* its elders. The membership of a church includes its elders, who have the authority and duty to execute the power given to it. The office of an elder includes both the duties to teach and to rule. Some focus more on teaching, while others focus more on ruling, as indicated in 1 Timothy 5:17, depending on their gifts, thus allowing for the possibility of both teaching elders and ruling elders. However, by not stating explicitly the validity of ruling elders, this explanation is still not satisfying. Confirmation has to be found from elsewhere.

Thomas Collier was first identified as a Particular Baptist in 1644 when he was involved in an evangelistic tour of Kent together with William Kiffin and Thomas Patient. As noted above, Kiffin and Patient were two of the men who a few years later strongly recommended Daniel King's book, "A Way to Sion". If this was indication that the two men were of the same view as King on the rulers of the church, as the present writer thinks it was, there is a high probability that Collier had held to the same view as well, since he was closely associated with the two. By 1674 Collier had gone astray from the Calvinistic position, publishing his "Body of Divinity" in which he stated that his belief now was that Christ died for all people. Collier's change of view caused much disagreement in the Western Association, resulting in those who agreed with him drifting away. By 1690 the Western Association was firmly in the Particular Baptist fold.

A notable member of the Association was the Broadmead Church in Bristol, whose pastor at the time was Thomas Vaux. The Broadmead Church held that the pastor was the "chief of the elders of the church", while the ruling elders shared with him the oversight (Underhill, 1847: 373). Scattered throughout the Church Record are mentions of ruling elders being appointed, chairing meetings in the absence of the pastor, and playing active roles in church discipline. An example is this: "Upon the sixth of the first month, anno 1666 [1667], according to the former conclusion, were these two brethren, Richard White and Edward Terrill, set apart by prayer and fasting to be ruling elders in this church" (Underhill, 1847: 91).

Bernard Foskett, the co-pastor of the Broadmead church in 1720 and sole pastor in 1724, was to initiate a new Western Baptist Association between 1732 and 1734, firmly basing it on the 1689 Confession. The Bristol Academy was reorganized by Foskett from 1720, and began in earnest to train men for the ministry from 1734. Seventy or more students were trained in the next twenty-five years, whose ministries had a tremendous impact in Wales and England. The doctrinal stance of the Western Association, led by the Broadmead church, kept both Arminianism and Unitarianism out of the churches, which in turn affected directly the work of other Associations in the Midlands, Wales, Ireland and the Northern Baptist Association (Hayden, 2006: 36). Would not the view on the eldership, upheld and practised so tenaciously in the Broadmead Church, have spread as well? The answer would seem to be in the affirmative. John Collett Ryland, a student of Foskett's, became the pastor of College Lane Baptist Church, Northampton, in October 1759 (Hayden, 2006: 72). This church clearly held to King's view of the eldership, as will be seen below.

One of the churches in the West Country was at Tiverton. The Tiverton church was represented by John Ball in the General Assembly of 1689 in London (Narrative, 1689: 19, 20, 24). John Ball was a founding member of a new church at Bampton, Devon, in 1690. The Bampton Church Book records that on the 23rd of the 9th month, 1690, John Ball was nominated to serve as a ruling elder (Bampton CB: 3, 5).

4.3.11 Eldership among the Open Communion Particular Baptist Churches

More would be said of the Calvinistic Baptist churches that were not members of regional associations in Chapter 6. Among the non-associated churches were various congregations that held to open communion, including those connected with Henry Jessey of London, John Bunyan of Bedfordshire, and John Tombes in Herefordshire in 1653. Henry Jessey's church spawned a number of the original Particular Baptist churches in London. Being a Separatist church that practised infant baptism, then moving to the open communion Baptist position when Jessey was pastor, it would be expected to have practised the eldership system of John Owen. Indeed, when he wrote a letter of protest to the New England Puritans for their harsh treatment "of some for being Anabaptists", Jessey had stated that such actions only hurt the cause of the "Gathered Churches called Independents" (Bell, 2000: 64).

Crosby reports that three men were trained up to be ministers by Tombes in his "society", one of whom was to become the eminent Particular Baptist pastor of the church in Bromsgrove, namely, John Eccles. Crosby records that "He was pastor of a congregation at Bromsgrove in the county of Worcester; and preached the gospel there and at Coventry, near sixty years" (Crosby, Vol. 3: 118). In the Bromsgrove Record Book, an entry for the 20th day of the 2nd month, 1692, reads (Bromsgrove CRB: 1): "Henry Hanson was ordained an elder by Brother Eckles and Brother Straford." With the appointment of Hanson, there would have been three elders, including Eccles. If Eccles was "the pastor", the other two men were most likely ruling elders. Crosby records that Eccles spent the latter part of his life at Coventry, where he died on 26th January, 1711, at age 76. The Bromsgrove Record Book shows that on 1696, "our beloved Brother William Peart [sic.] installed the Sole Pastor [sic.] of this Congregation". Presumably, Eccles had moved on from the church. It would be highly unlikely that the church had no other elders, since it had a history of having elders. Peart would have been the teaching elder. The link of the church to Tombes, through Eccles, would show that Tombes held to King's view of the eldership, although this cannot be said with certainty.

John Bunyan was known to have ministered regularly to some nine congregations in the Bedfordshire region, apart from the one in Bedford town (Howard, 1976: 187; Harrison, 1964: 144-145). He began to preach in 1656 and was ordained pastor of the church on 21st October, 1671. The full record of that meeting is produced below (Bunyan Meeting: 50-51):

> At a full assembly of the Church at Bedford the 21st of the 10th month [of 1671].
>
> After much seeking God by prayer, and sober conference formerly had, the Congregation did at this meeting with joyned consent (signifyed by solemne lifting up of their

hands) call forth and appoint our bro. John Bunyan to the pastorall office, or eldership; and he accepting thereof, gave up himself to serve Christ, and his church in that charge; And received of the elders the right hand of fellowship, after having preached 15 years. N.B. [S. F]enn the other elder continued in office.

The same time also, the Congregation had long experience of the faithfulnes of br. Joh: Fenne in his care for the poor, did after the same manner solemnely choose him to the honourable office of a deacon, and committed their care and purse to him; and he accepted thereof, and gave up himself to the Lord and them in that service.

Seven Brethren called to the work of the ministry
The same time; and after the same manner, the church did solemnly approve the gifts of, and called to the worke of the ministry, these brethren; John Fenne, Oliver Scott, Luke Ashwood, Thomas Cooper Edward Dent, Edward Haac[kix], Nehemiah Coxe for the furtherance of the worke of God, and carrying on thereof, in the meetings usually maintained by this congregation, as occasion and opportunity shall by providence be ministred to them.

And did further determine, that if any new place offer itself, or another people that we have not full knowledge of, or communion with, shall desire that any of these brethren should come to them, to be helpful to them, by the word, and doctrine, that then such brother so desired, shall first present the thing to the Congregation; who after due consideration will determine thereof; and according as they shall determine so shall such brother act, and doe.

The congregation did also determine to keep the 26th of this instant as a day of fasting and prayer, both here, and at homes, and at Gambinghay, solemnly to recommend to the grace of God bro. Bunyan, bro. Fenne, and the rest of the brethren; and to intreat his gracious assistance, and presence with them in their respective worke whereunto he hath called them.

Of interest to us is the note in the first paragraph of the entry indicating that another man, probably Samuel Fenn (also spelled Fenne) remained in office as "the other elder". (The elders from whom he received "the right hand of fellowship" could have included visiting pastors.) The next paragraph shows that another man, John Fenne, was appointed deacon. The subsequent paragraph shows that he was one of the seven recognized "ministers", a term similar to "gifted brethren", commonly used in those days. Three letters written by the church, recorded in the meetings at the beginning of the 4th month, on the 2nd day of the 8th month, and on the last day of the 9th month, were signed by John Bunyan, Samuel Fenne, John Fenne, and Nehemiah Coxe, among others, showing the existence of the two men surnamed Fenne. The last paragraph in the entry above seems to refer to the two elders of the church, namely John Bunyan and Samuel Fenne. Since Bunyan was the pastor, Samuel Fenne must have been the ruling elder.

Apart from the well-known Bunyan Meeting, there were other churches in the region of Bedfordshire and the border of Huntingdonshire, some of the church books of which have been transcribed by H. G. Tibbutt. A number of these churches show that they had pastors or elders. It is quite obvious that they had practised the system of eldership advocated by King and Owen because nearly all of them began as (paedobaptist) Independent churches which then became Baptist. Two churches, in particular, showed in their records that they were clearly of the King/Owen variety. One was the church at Kensworth which began in the 1650s as a "baptized congregation" and spawned many others. While waiting to appoint "a preaching brother", three men were appointed to temporarily officiate in the place of their deceased pastor, Thomas Hayward (Tibbutt, 1972: 16):

> November 1688. Imediatly after the desease of that laborious servant of Christ, Thomas Hayward, the whole church was assembled at Kinsworth to consider there scattered state, and there the church did elect Brother Finch, Brother Marsom and Brother Hardon jointly and equally to offitiate in the room of Brother Hayward in breaking bread, and other administeration of ordinances, and the church did at the same time agree to provide and mainetaine all, at there one charge, and did agree to give sufitient mainetaineance to a preaching brother to serve the

> church and to goe from meeting to meeting, and to every
> place the church shall apoint him within this congrega-
> tion. November 1688.
>
> Brother Harding aforesaid did except of the office of el-
> dership and did break bread with the church January
> 1688/9.

Another church was at Carlton, which seceded from the one at
Stevington. At first Independent, it later became Baptist, and in the
later years of the 19th century became Strict Baptist (that is, practising closed communion). Founded in 1688, the church "enchurch
anew" (or reconstituted) on 9th September, 1691, which probably
meant they became Baptist at that time. On 30th September, 1691,
two men were ordained ruling elders, and three were ordained deacons. On 15th October, John Greenwood was elected and ordained
pastor (Tibbutt, 1972: 47).

Another group of open communion Calvinistic Baptists was located in the Northamptonshire region. The formation and work of
the famed Northamptonshire Baptist Association, in connection with
William Carey's ministry in India, from 15 May 1765, is beyond the
purview of the present work. In the first half of the 18th century, a
number of Calvinistic Baptist churches were established and active
in this part of the country, one of which was the College Lane Church
in Lancaster. This church, founded in 1697, appointed one Samuel
Dunkley as ruling elder and two other men as deacons in 1733. On
1st September 1736, Samuel Haworth was called to the pastorate,
the ordination taking place on 9th June 1737 (Taylor, 1897: 20).
John Collett Ryland became the pastor in 1760 and was to continue
there for twenty years. His ordination took place on 18th September 1760, at which the ministers of two churches took part, together
with the elder of the church, Mr. William Lawrence (Taylor, 1897:
26).

4.3.12   The Predominant View of Eldership

This rather lengthy section on the eldership will now be summarized
in tabular form, based on the criteria that Owen's view of the eldership was practised if: (i) there was explicit mention of support to the
view; (ii) there was explicit belief in the teaching elder or the ruling
elder; (iii) the co-pastor was mentioned as an assistant to the pastor;

and (iv) the pastor was distinguished from the other elder, or elders, in the church. This "Rule of Explicit Mention" produces the following results:

	Person or Churches	Owen's view?
1	Daniel King	Yes
2	Hanserd Knollys	Yes
3	South Wales Association	Yes
4	Midlands Association	Yes
5	London Association	Probable
6	Abingdon Association	Yes
7	Irish Association	Probable
8	Northern Association	Yes
9	Western Association	Yes
10	Open Communion Churches	Yes

4.4   THE MANNER OF RULE

There are two aspects to the manner of ruling the church, namely, the authority of the elders to make decisions, and the responsibility of the congregation to consent to the elders' decisions. John Owen stated this as follows (Owen, 1976, Vol. 16: 40):

> ... all church-power ... hath a double exercise; – first, in the call or choosing of officers; secondly, in their voluntary acting with them and under them in all duties of rule. 1. All authority in the church is committed by Christ unto the officers or rulers of it, as unto all acts and duties whereunto office-power is required; and 2. Every individual person hath the liberty of his own judgement as unto his own consent or dissent in what he is himself concerned.

The first aspect of exercising rule is the taking of initiatives, the making of decisions, and the putting forth of the proposals to the congregation to get its consent. This is the basic meaning of ruling, which is the inherent duty of elders. Here, the extent of office power is not to be confused and confounded with the manner of executing that power, as has been done by some (e.g., Renihan, 1998, 128-176). Unlike the apostles' power, which was more extensive, the elders' power is limited to the local church (Owen, 1976, Vols. 15: 492-293; 4:439). The elders rule according to God's word, "with commands, and rules, for the due and right exerting, and executing of that power" (Confession, 1689: 7). "The rule and law of the exercise of power in the elders of the church is *the holy Scripture only*" (Owen, 1976, Vol. 16: 135). Daniel King described it like this:

> Now Elders in Scripture were taken, Sometimes for Officers among the Jews in their Church, Mark 8:31. Sometimes for Gospel-officers, Acts 11:30 and 14:23 Whose office was to feed, Acts 20:17 (i.e.) by preaching sound Doctrine, and suitable to the necessities of the Church, and leading them into various pastures for their welfare and fattening, and how they must do it is set down, 1 Pet. 5:1-3.
>
> 2. To consult in matters of controversy, Acts 5:2; 4:6, 22, 23. To set things in order in the Church, Acts 16:4. To advise for matter of doubt, Acts 21, 18, etc. To rule, oversee, and govern, 1 Tim. 5:17; it. 1:5; 1 Pet. 5:1, etc. To VISIT THE SICK, AND PRAY OVER THEM, BEING CALLED FOR, Jam. 5:14.

It can be seen that King's idea of the power and duties of elders consists in more than teaching God's word and the administration of the ordinances, which duties belong to the pastors, or teaching elders. The elders are also "to consult in controversy, to set things in order in the church, to advise in matters of doubt, to rule, oversee, and govern". The terms "to rule, oversee, and govern" are all-encompassing terms describing the authority and duties of the elders. All the elders have the authority and power over all these duties, while the duties are distributed generally into teaching and the accompanying administration of the ordinances, and ruling. The pastors, or teaching elders, both teach and rule, while the ruling elders only rule, although they are not barred from teaching as the occasion and personal gifts allow.

Consider what John Owen had to say on the two sorts of church power :

... authority to *teach* and administer the sacraments, which is commonly called the *power of order*; and also *ruling*, which is called a power of jurisdiction, corruptly ... (Owen, 1976, Vol. 16: 42).

Church-power, acted in its rule, is called "The keys of the kingdom of heaven," by an expression derived from the keys that were a sign of office-power in the families of the kings, Isa. xxii. 22; and it is used by our Saviour himself to denote the communication of church-power unto others, which is absolutely and universally vested in himself, under the name of "The key of David," Rev. iii. 7; Matt. xvi: 19.

These keys are usually referred under two heads, – namely, the one of *order*, the other of *jurisdiction*.

By the "key of order," the *spiritual right, power, and authority of bishops* or pastors to preach the word, to administer the sacraments, and doctrinally to bind and loose the consciences of men, are intended.

By 'jurisdiction,' *the rule, government, or discipline of the church is designed*; although it was never so called or esteemed in Scripture, or the primitive church until the whole nature of church rule or discipline was depraved and changed. ... that these keys do include the twofold distinct powers of teaching and rule, of doctrine and discipline, is freely granted (Owen, 1976, Vol. 16: 106-107).
[Emphasis original.]

Article 8, Chapter 26 of the 1689 Confession declares "the officers appointed and chosen by Christ ... for the peculiar administration of ordinances, and execution of power, or duty, which he instructs them with, or calls them to ... are bishops or elders and deacons". This would have to be understood in the light of what King and Owen wrote. Rule is not limited to some specific actions, such as teaching, the administration of the ordinances, and the declaration of admission and ejection of members, as claimed by Renihan (1998: 128-176).

The next aspect of ruling is obtaining the consent (or concurrence, or agreement) of the congregation before the execution of any decision pertaining to the welfare of the church. The 1689 Confession, Chapter 26, Article 9, states that the appointment of a bishop or elder to office is "by common suffrage of the church itself". Similarly, a deacon is to be chosen "by the like suffrage". The Shorter Oxford Dictionary (Onions, 1968) shows that the original meaning of the word "suffrage", as used from the 16th century, was: "A vote given by a member of a body, state, or society, in assent to a proposition or in favour of the election of a person; in the extended sense, a vote for or against any controverted question or nomination." Clearly, in the matter of the appointment of office-bearers, the Particular Baptists believed in the necessity of congregational consent.

To the Particular Baptists, the necessity of congregational consent extended to all other matters of church rule. Congregational consent is necessary for the appointment of the chief rulers of the church, namely the elders. It is necessary for the appointment of the lesser officers, namely the deacons. It should come as no surprise to us that consent is also needed in other lesser matters in the church. Isaac Watts (1674-1748) wrote:

> In church government [the Particular Baptists are] generally Independents. ... the generality of Independents follow rather Dr. Owen's notion; their tenets are such as these: 1st. That the power of church government resides in the pastors and elder of every particular church, and [2nd.] that it is the duty of the people to consent; and, nevertheless, because every act in a church is a church act, they never do any thing without the consent of the people, though they receive no new authority by the people's consenting (Milne, 1845: 193, 196).

Examples of congregational consent are not hard to find in the writings and church documents of the Particular Baptists. Here, some cases are presented, some of which merely make mention of the practice of congregational consent, while others more explicitly show the procedure involved. In the Bromsgrove Baptist Church the following records hold (Bromsgrove, CB: 39, 41):

> A day of fasting and prayer being solemnly kept the 10th day of the 9th month 1714 upon account of that sorrowful occasion of Samuel Bedford being fallen in the very great sins – effrontery, lying and uncleanness with an

adulterous woman; he was then by the whole consent of the congregation cast out of the Church.

At a General Church Meeting, and by solemn fasting and prayer, with a unanimous consent by all the members, our beloved Brother <u>William Peart</u> [sic.] installed the <u>Sole Pastor</u> [sic.] of this Congregation.

Another example of congregational consent in the appointment of an elder is found in the Bunyan Meeting which has been referred to (Bunyan Meeting: 50-51):

At a full assembly of the Church at Bedford the 21st of the 10th month [of 1671]
After much seeking God by prayer, and sober conference formerly had, the Congregation did at this meeting with joyned consent (signifyed by solemne lifting up of their hands) call forth and appoint our bro. John Bunyan to the pastorall office, or eldership; and he accepting thereof, gave up himself to serve Christ, and his church in that charge; And received of the elders the right hand of fellowship, after having preached 15 years. N.B. [S. F]enn the other elder continued in office.

Congregational consent shown in the appointment of elders and deacons was also known as election, to distinguish it from ordination, or the official installation of the persons into office. Said Owen, "The call of persons unto the pastoral office in the church consists of two parts, – first, *Election*; secondly, *Ordination*, as it is commonly called, or sacred separation by fasting and prayer" (Owen, 1976, Vol. 16: 54). Consent, whether in election to office or in other decisions taken, may be by the show of hands (Owen, 1976, Vol. 16: 63; Underhill, 1847: 383, 401, 405), or by some other means. In the Broadmead church, the manner of consent was shown on one particular occasion, at the appointment of two men to be ruling elders, as follows (Underhill, 1847: 91):

First, the pastor declaring to the congregation the work of the day, it was by him desired that the brethren, with the whole church, would signify their consent, if it were so their minds, by their silence; which they did. Afterwards the pastor declared to the whole church, if any, either brother or sister, were dissatisfied with either of the persons, or any particular in either, it was desired they should show their dissatisfaction by standing up; which none did. Then it was desired likewise by the pastor, that those two brethren elected would show their acceptance by their standing up; which, after some pause, they did.

A detailed account of the procedure adopted by the Bagnio-/Cripplegate church in decision-making has been wrongly interpreted by Renihan as supporting congregational democracy (Renihan, 1998: 163):

The church being assembled did unanimously agree that for the better carrying on of the work of God in it. That division might be prevented and peace preserved and purity and love maintained. That ten or twelve Brethren be desired to meet together to prepare matters for this church soe as that no materiall affaire be presented or transacted in the church till they have considered and agreed about it.

This was consented to with these limitations:
1. That none of the Brethren be excluded who shall be willing to be with them when they meet & to help in theire consultations.
2. That they shall determine nothing but only present theire consultations and agreement to the church for theire consideration, whose consent shall be the determination of it.
3. That when theire time or season of meeting is come any 5 or 7 of them shall be sufficient number to consider of such things as might be presented to them if the rest be absent.

Renihan makes much of the ten or twelve men appointed by the church as a "screening committee" for business brought to the church when, in reality, they were merely performing the functions of an eldership, since there were no other elders appointed yet at that time, apart from the pastor. Ten years later, when at least one other elder had been appointed apart from the pastor, the practice of having "12 brethren (not excluding others) appointed by ye church to prepare all matters for ye church" was kept up (Bagnio/Cripplegate CMB:

12). Common sense would have directed the church to have a number of men to join with the one pastor, or two or three elders, in decision-making before presenting the proposals to the congregation for its consent. This practice was by no means unique (Robinson, 1922: 116; White, 1996: 78), and is carried out even in churches today, in order that "nothing crude or indigested, nothing unsuited to the sense and duty of the church, will at any time be proposed therein, so as to give occasion unto contests or janglings, disputes contrary unto order or decency, but all things may be preserved in a due regard unto the gravity and authority of the rulers" (Owen, 1976, Vol. 16: 141).

John Owen considered the exceptional situation when the congregation refuses to give its consent (Owen, 1976, Vol. 15: 502):

> But if it be asked, "What, then, shall the elders do in case the church refuse to consent unto such acts as are indeed according to rule, and warranted by the institution of Christ?" it is answered, that they are, – 1. Diligently to *instruct* them from the word in their duty, making known the mind of Christ unto them in the matter under consideration; 2. To declare unto them the *danger* of their dissent in obstructing the edification of the body, to the dishonour of the Lord Christ and their own spiritual disadvantage; 3. To *wait patiently* for the concurrence of the grace of God with their ministry in giving light and obedience unto the church; and, 4. In case of the church's continuance in any failure of duty, to seek for advice and *counsel* from the elders and brethren of other churches .... [Emphasis original.]

An example of this procedure being put into practice occurred in the Wapping church, London, in 1684. When Hercules Collins, the pastor, was imprisoned, the congregation chose a "preaching brother" to administer the Lord's Supper. Collins, however, was convinced that it was "the privilege & duty of an Elder only" who had been duly ordained. When released, Collins informed the congregation that he would seek to persuade them of his viewpoint. If they were unconvinced, he would be willing to abide by the view of the majority. The members of the church maintained their position, and Collins kept to his word. Some in the congregation saw it as Collins's "lording it over God's heritage". Collins appears to have focussed upon teaching on the matter, instead of contending with the church, for it was his view that finally prevailed. After his death in 1702, the church requested Richard Adams, the pastor of Devonshire Square Baptist Church, to preside at the Lord's Supper (Kevan, 1933:66-67; MacDonald, 1982: 317-318, 339).

Hercules Collins was well-versed in John Owen's "A Brief Instruction in the Worship of God and Discipline of the Churches of the New Testament", as were other Particular Baptists of the 17th century. It has been noted that Owen's book, published in 1667, was very popular and came to be known as the "Independents' Catechism". In 1682, Collins published a book entitled "Some Reasons for Separation from the Church of England", in which an imaginary dialogue between a non-conforming Baptist and a Conformist took place. In the short tract of only 24 pages, the Baptist told the Conformist *seven times* to "See Doctor Owen's brief Instruction in the Worship of God". Although these references to Owen were not directly concerned with the composition of the eldership and the manner of ruling the congregation, the facts that it is the only book referred to, and that so frequently, show the book was indeed the definitive book of the Particular Baptists on church government at that time. The first reference to Owen's book was in regard to the definition of a gospel church, to which the Conformist commented (Collins, 1682: 4): "I think all the difference between us is, that the Doctors Definition s[peaks] a little of Independency and Churches Congregational, but we are for a [na]tional one." The Nonconformist in the dialogue, and therefore Collins himself, did not rebut or deny the identification of the Baptists with Independency. All seven occasions of reference to Owen's work cover the following points (Collins, 1682: 4, 10, 13, 14, 15, 21):

- The definition of the gospel church, which the Conformist did not hold to;

- The worship of God must be in accordance to His word, without addition, subtraction, or change – a point agreed to by the National Church, but contradicted by their practice with regard to the subject and method of baptism;

- The administration of the ordinances of baptism and the Lord's Supper are to be in accordance to apostolic practice, which the National Church did not adhere to;

- The power to appoint a Bishop, Elder or Presbyter, and a Deacon, lies with the particular church, and not with any Bishops or Elders of the Episcopal kind;

- Any Minister, Pastor, Elder or Bishop may take charge of only one church at a time, unlike the Episcopal system;

- Every congregation may choose its own Minister and maintain him, instead of having a Minister who may be transferred away and be maintained by others not of the congregation, as in the Episcopal system;

- No rites or ceremonies are to be introduced into the worship of God, contrary to His word, for "there is but one God, [and] there is but one way of worshipping him, the Rule of his Word: Yett [do] I affirm, That none should be compelled to worship God by a tempo[ral] Sword, but such as come willingly, and none can worship God to acc[ep]tance but such" (Collins, 1682: 20).

John Owen's other work, "The True nature of a Gospel Church and its Government", published in 1689, was to have a similar, if not greater, impact upon the Nonconformists. Another incident indicates this. A church in London which had been bereft of its pastor wrote persistently, in 1705, to the church at Bourton-on-the-Water in the Midlands, requesting that its pastor, Benjamin Beddome, be given to serve in the more influential metropolitan. The exchanges between the two churches show the intensity of feelings in the people involved, including Beddome himself. In Beddome's final letter, reasons were given for turning down the call to London, among which was an appeal to John Owen: "The judicious Dr Owen declares that such removals only are lawful, which are with the free consent of the churches concerned, and the advice of other churches or their elders with whom they walk in communion" (Brooks, 1861: 45). The lengthy quotation that followed was taken from the latter work of Owen (1976, Vol. 16: 94-95). Benjamin Keach was to publish "The Glory Of A True Church, And Its Discipline Display'd" in 1697, a book smaller than Owen's, focussing on church discipline, in which he said, "Many Reverend Divines of the Congregational way, have written most excellently (it is true) upon this Subject, I mean on Church-Discipline..." (Dever, 2001: 64). Keach was referring to

John Owen and Dr. Isaac Chauncy, whom he quoted in his book, at the same time acknowledging the widespread use of the more thorough books written by the Congregationalists. Despite the existence of Keach's book, Owen's book was appealed to by Beddome in 1705.

4.5 SUMMARY

By a "Rule of Explicit Mention", it has been shown from the Confessional statements, the ecclesiological literature, and the extant church books that, except for baptism, the Particular Baptists held to the same view of church government as John Owen. As far as the nature of church authority is concerned, they believed that the source of church power is Jesus Christ, and that the seat of power is the church, while the authority of executing that power lies with the elders. They believed that after the foundation of the church by the extraordinary officers, namely the apostles, prophets and evangelist, only the ordinary officers, namely elders and deacons, remain. Owen's view of the eldership was extensively upheld by the churches and individuals among the Particular Baptists, in which there are two sorts of elders, namely pastors or teaching elders, and ruling elders. All elders share the responsibility over the governance of the church, including teaching and ruling, although the ruling elders help the teaching elders primarily in the area of ruling. Practically, there are two aspects to the execution of the elders' authority in ruling, the first of which involves leading and making decisions, and the second involves getting the consent of the congregation before the execution of the decisions. A different view of the eldership began to be propagated by Benjamin Keach at the end of the 17th century. However, the influence of Bernard Foskett and the Bristol Academy resulted in the overwhelming influence of Owen's view of the eldership compared to that of Keach.

* * * * *

Five

THE BYWAYS

5.1   INTRODUCTION

In recent years there has been a spate of studies, both on the popular and scholarly levels, on some key Particular Baptist leaders of the 17th century (e.g. Haykin, 1996; Ramsbottom, 1989; Walker, 2004; Copeland, 2001; Brooks, 2006; Riker, 2009). Encouraging though this may be, there is plenty of scope still for expansion. D. B. Riker and J. C. Brooks have attempted to place Benjamin Keach in the perspective of the Reformation movement from the 16th century (Brooks, 2006; Riker, 2009). Although separated by 150 years, Keach must be seen as one among the many in the 17th century who were attempting to continue the work of reforming the church by recovering biblical primitivism. This entailed the purification of the church by the rejection of human traditions and wrong teachings, while recovering biblical doctrines and lost ordinances.

Benjamin Keach was a prolific writer among the Particular Baptists of the 17th century. He was the first among the Particular Baptists to write specifically on church government, although his book was deliberately short and focussed upon church discipline (Keach, 1697). Before him, others had written on various aspects of church government, but in the context of polemics against detractors.

It is seen in the previous chapter that Keach's view of the eldership was not exactly the same as the pervasive view held by other Particular Baptists of the time. There could have been a few men who held to his view before he wrote his book, but for want of definite indications of this, Keach's view would have to be considered an intrusion into the *status quo*. In this chapter, it will be shown how Keach's view developed away from the mainstream view of the Particular Baptists.

5.2   DEPARTURE IN THE 17TH CENTURY

The settled views of the Particular Baptists on church government are spelled out in the 1689 Confession. Chapter 26, Article 8 specifies the remaining offices of the church as "Bishops or Elders and Deacons", while Article 9 specifies that the calling of any person "fitted, and gifted by the Holy Spirit, unto the Office of Bishop, or Elder," is that he is chosen by "the common suffrage" of the church. Similarly, deacons are chosen by like suffrage of the church. The elders, however, not the deacons, are the officers chosen and set apart to rule the church.

Article 10 shows that pastors are to be supported financially to engage in full-time ministry of the Word and prayer. The "bishops or pastors", who preach the word "by way of office", mentioned in Article 11 are to be equated with the ministers of Chapter 28, Article 2, who administer the ordinances. This is indicated by the Scripture references used:

> 2. These holy appointments are to be administered by those only, who are qualified and thereunto called according (b) to the commission of Christ.
> (b) Mat.28.19. 1 Cor. 4.1.

Both Scripture references show that preachers specially called by Jesus Christ to the work of proclaiming His word are referred to. They are full-time ministers of the word who have received a special calling to the ministry of the Word. The necessity of a call to the ministry of the Word of God is a traditional Reformed doctrine, which the Particular Baptists upheld (Copson, 1991: 98-101; Collins, 1702: 52-53). Attention to the Scripture references used in the Confession at this most crucial point would have obviated the need to argue tortuously in denial of the ruling/teaching elder distinction, or of the necessity of the call to the ministry, as has been done by some (Waldron, *et al.*, 1997: 76-95, 127-132). It is a futile exercise, as the present writer has shown elsewhere (Poh, 2006). John Briggs has noted the importance of the Scripture references used in the Confessions of the Particular Baptists, saying (Briggs, 2004):

> ... the different points were decorated with copious scriptural references and you cannot doubt the force of the judgment of scripture on their thinking. Indeed, it is a kind of historical sin to reproduce such confessional statements without the scriptural references that tangibly demonstrate how saturated in scripture were those who penned them.

It has been noted that "bishop" and "elder" are interchangeable terms, while "pastor" is a reference to the elder or bishop who is set aside full-time to teach the word as well as to rule. There are other elders who assist the pastor in the work of ruling the church, but not in teaching on a regular basis. This view of the eldership, reflected in the writings of Daniel King and Hanserd Knollys, is the same as that of John Owen, who said, "The bishops or elders are of two sorts: – 1. Such as have authority to *teach* and administer the sacraments ... and, 2. Some have only *power for rule* ..." (Owen, 1976, Vol. 16: 42).

To Owen, all pastors are elders, but not all elders are pastors. Benjamin Keach, however, denied the validity of the office of ruling elder. To Keach, all pastors are elders, and all elders are pastors.

5.2.1 Benjamin Keach and Controversies

A brief biography of Benjamin Keach has been given in Chapter Two and will not be repeated here. The controversy associated with Keach advocating the laying on of hands upon baptized believers has been well noted in the literature (Parratt, 1966; White, 1996: 36-42). The controversy arising from Keach advocating the singing of hymns during worship also has been studied (MacDonald, 1982; Brooks, 2006). Studies on Keach all portray him as a conservative Particular Baptist in good standing, both doctrinally and socially, with the likes of William Kiffin and Knollys. Keach would not be classed together with the controversial Thomas Collier, who was finally condemned by the mainline Particular Baptists as a heretic. However, the fact that Keach was himself a controversial figure in the midst of the mainstream Particular Baptists has not been sufficiently noted. The two controversies already referred to were not the only occasions when he ruffled the other Particular Baptists.

It is to be remembered that Keach was a pastor among the General Baptists since the age of eighteen. He was described in a rather positive light by his son-in-law, the historian Thomas Crosby, who presented him as being involved in controversies all his life. Crosby, nevertheless, noted his quick temper which probably was connected with his constant ill-health (Crosby, Vol. 4). Another historian, W. T. Whitley, presented Keach as a significant leader among the London Baptists of the later 1660s whose regular biblical expositions were limited by his tendency to be involved in controversy. Whitley further criticized Keach as disinterested in working with others because cooperation threatened or limited his control, the hallmark of those who "prefer to withdraw and rule their small coterie" (Whitley, 1923: 178). J. B. Vaughn also characterizes Keach's life as marked by controversy to the extent that it "divided and disorganized" the London Particular Baptists (Vaughn, 1989: 139). Austin Walker presents Keach as a diligent and excellent preacher, yet challenged by a hot temper; a contemporary with John Bunyan and John Milton, though not as talented; and one who worked hard for unity, love, truth, and peace, both within and outside of his fellowship (Walker, 2004). Brooks noted that Keach remained "mixed" theologically, as he held positions of both the Particular and the General Baptists that were generally thought mutually exclusive, the example given being the laying on of hands after baptism, which was held by the General Baptists but not the Particular Baptists (Brooks, 2006: 24). These negative traits are listed here not with the intention of diminishing the positive contribution of the man, but simply to place his view of the eldership in perspective.

Keach stood shoulder-to-shoulder with the other Particular Baptists when he countered infant baptism and the federal theology of the Presbyterians, attacked the Quakers, and engaged with the Sabbatarians. However, he ruffled the other Particular Baptists by advocating the laying on of hands upon baptism, a practice apparently held by his predecessor, William Rider (Crosby, Vol. 4: 272). The Particular Baptists had settled this issue decades ago, when it was first fiercely controverted in the 1650s. William Kiffin had led the way by debating the General Baptist, Peter Chamberlen, on the issue. Kiffin had worked hard to keep the Particular Baptists separate from the General Baptists, and envisaged the danger of the two movements being associated together through the adoption of the laying on of hands (Bell, 2000: 171). Among those who had written on the subject was Daniel King. In his "A Postscript" (1656), King countered the practice of the laying on of hands on the newly baptized, and would admit of only two kinds of laying on of hands that continue in the church: the laying on of hands on officers of the church during ordination, and the expectation of suffering for Christ's sake when believers are laid hands on by their persecutors. When Keach resurrected the issue, he was stirring up the peace among the Particular Baptists. Among those who countered Keach was Henry Danvers, who published, "A Treatise of Laying on of Hands", in 1674. Keach was a late-comer, having definitely become a Calvinist only by 1672, the year he remarried after the death of his first wife. The church at Horsleydown, of which he was the pastor, and that of his son, Elias, in Ayles Street (Ivimey, III: 534), must have stood out among the Particular Baptist churches in London because of the practice of the laying on of hands, which they maintained all through their lives.

Benjamin Keach defended religious liberty, but in the process caused unease among the Particular Baptists. Stephen Copson perceptively noted the dilemma faced by the Baptists when toleration was in sight as William III and Mary II came to power (Copson, 1991: 6). Although William Kiffin led a deputation from the London congregations to welcome the new sovereigns in January 1689, the response of the Baptists to the new sovereigns was surprisingly unenthusiastic. It seemed that they had learned not to put too much trust in princes, after their recent experience with James and his pro-Catholic policies. Two prominent London Particular Baptists, Hanserd Knollys and Benjamin Keach, went into print in 1689, offering different responses to the new situation. Knollys expanded on his 1679 work which expounded on the eleventh chapter of the Apocalypse, "An Exposition of the Revelation". This time, he called the expanded work by the same name, and showed how persecution and toleration illustrate the battle between God and the forces of the Anti-Christ, as represented by the Church of Rome and the Turkish Empire. The frustration of one and the defeat of the other were tangible evidences of the truth of the interpretation (Knollys, 1689: 112, 136ff., 196ff.). William was not mentioned by name and his part in the overthrow of the Papist James was subsumed into the grand design of God. Keach, on the other hand, published "Distressed Sion Relieved", a poem in which events in the recent persecutions were seen as a campaign waged by the false church of Rome against the true church. Unlike the more cautious Knollys, Keach dedicated his poem to William and Mary in the "Epistle to the Reader", and cast them in the role of deliverers, lavishing praise upon them: "You have therefore an Account of the glorious Deliverance both of Church and State from Popery and Slavery by the hand of His now present Majesty" (Keach, 1689a). To Keach, the toleration that followed "opened a great door for the gospel and sent us blessed harvest weather" (Keach, 1689b: 102). The difference in the degree of enthusiasm over toleration between Knollys and Keach was indicative of the character and experience of Keach *vis-à-vis* the Particular Baptist leaders in London. It, in fact, shows the tension between Keach and the other Particular Baptist leaders – a point that has not been sufficiently noted in the literature.

The second-generation leaders among the Particular Baptists were deferential toward the first-generation leaders, a number of whom were still alive. Knollys and Kiffin were still in active ministry in London. John Spilsbury was still alive in Bromsgrove (Eccles, 1699). Thomas Collier, although denounced by the conservatives as a heretic in 1677, was still active in the West Country. Robert Steed, of the church in Dartmouth (White, 1971-7, Pt. 2: 107), collaborated with Kiffin in the hymn-singing controversy (Kiffin, 1692). Steed was also the assistant pastor to Knollys, despite being on different sides of the hymn-singing controversy. Not long before his own death in 1691, Knollys referred to him as "my reverend and beloved brother Steed", and urged the church to seek for a qualified pastor. Both these facts indicate that Steed was an old man at that time (Knollys, 1812: 59, 67). When Nehemiah Coxe was assigned to counter the teaching of Thomas Collier by writing the book "Vindiciae Veritatis", published in 1677, he could not have been more than forty years old. The year of his birth is unknown. In the brief epistle at the beginning of the book, signed by six well-respected and older Particular Baptist leaders, including Kiffin, Coxe's "inferiority in years" was mentioned. The London leaders stated that Coxe did not write the book out of a sense of personal ability, but at their request. They further said, "we hope, we may truly say, without particular respect to his Person, he hath behaved himself with that modesty of Spirit, joined with that fulness and clearness of answer and strength of argument, that we comfortably conceive (by God's blessing) it may prove a good and soveraign Antidote against the poison" (Coxe, 1677). Compared to

Coxe, Benjamin Keach could not have been much older. Born in 1640, he was 34 years old when he stirred up the controversy on the laying on of hands. He was 49 years old when he wrote his poem in praise of William and Mary, in 1689. Knollys was 90 years old.

Another controversy Keach was involved in concerned the responsibility of churches to support those employed in gospel ministry. For a long time, the clergy of the Established Church had been castigated for their pride and luxury, living off the tithe. The Dissenters were wary of whole-time support of their ministers, while the general poverty of the congregations prevented many from being able to support their ministers, even if they had wanted. Most of the Particular Baptist pastors were engaged in some forms of secular work to supplement their income, including leading men such as Knollys, Kiffin and Keach. Knollys supplemented his income by writing and teaching, and was introduced to investment in international trade by Kiffin. Kiffin built up quite a fortune through trading certain "commodities" in Holland (Bell, 2000: 131). Samuel Richardson was "a substantial London tradesman and was certainly one of the shrewdest and most influential of the Baptist leaders in the capital" (Underwood, 1947: 78). Keach supplemented his income by publishing and selling books. A member of Keach's church, Dr. John Roberts, was a physician who had concocted two effective medicines – one for "bloody flux and the gripes", the other a deworming medication for children – which he produced and sold, making a comfortable living out of this. When Dr. Roberts and his wife were too old to continue, they contracted the business out to one of Keach's daughters, who was required to pay for Dr. and Mrs. Roberts's living for the rest of their lives. Keach would have been helped financially by that business (Crosby, Vol. 3: 147). The Fifth Monarchists criticized the "gaping professors of those times" that sought to serve Mammon as well as God, attributing the changed social status of the Particular Baptist leaders to the temptation of "vast treasures got by the sweat of other men's brows". The Quakers criticized the Baptists for allowing their hearts to be "darkened" and their zeal quenched "and so much corrupted through places of honour". John Bunyan believed that Kiffin, in his wealth and position, disregarded him "because of my low descent among men, stigmatizing me for a person of that rank, that needed not be heeded". Other Baptists expressed similar frustrations towards the leaders (Bell, 2000:130-134).

When Keach advocated strongly for a supported ministry, in his book of 1688, "The Ministers Maintenance Vindicated", he requested the London leaders to write in support so that the book would be well-received by the Baptists in England and Wales. This the leaders in London did, the letter being signed by Hanserd Knollys, followed by William Kiffin, "and many others" (Crosby, Vol. 4: 295-296). In the General Assembly of the Particular Baptists in London the following year, it was agreed that Keach's book should be disseminated by the churches as widely as possible, and a general epistle was sent out urging all the churches to take heed to the responsibility of supporting their ministers. However, Keach was not aware that these older men had long ago recognized the need for a supported ministry. They had not been able to implement it because of various pressures, including: (a) the political turmoils coupled with persecution of the church; (b) the general poverty of the dissenting congregations; and (c) the stretched resources of the congregations as they actively engaged in evangelism and church planting. In the heat of a later controversy on hymn singing, Keach had written thus about the first churches in London (Keach, 1692):

> We ask you whether or no generally the same baptized Churches did not as unanimously conclude and declare it too, that for a Gospel-Minister to have a yearly Allowance or a competent Maintenance, was not an humane Invention, and Antichristian. We speak in part upon our own Knowledg, and by good Information we have had from others, that those Gospel-Duties (that is, Singing of Psalms, and the Ministers Maintenance) were equally decried, and we suppose you are not ignorant of it: Nay, and we hear some Churches, or Members of those Churches, are of the same Opinion still.

Upon being severely rebuked for expressing this opinion wrongly, in a book co-authored by William Kiffin, Robert Steed, George Barrett and Edward Man, Keach had had to retract his words, saying:

> Nor do I think it grievous to me to retract any Fault or Error this way; but contrariwise; since I have seen a Confession of Faith, put forth by several Brethren in the Year 1644, I am glad I have this to say for the clearing of the said baptized Churches in this great Case; though I de-

clare to you I knew nothing of that Confession till I was informed of it by the offended Brethren ...

Therefore with hearty sorrow ..., I do acknowledg my Error in this matter (though it was through Ignorance done) yet I ought to have inquired further about that Business before I published any such thing about it. As to what I speak of my Knowledg, all impartial Men must believe could not refer to those first baptized Churches in *London*, I being but about four Years old when that Confession of Faith was first printed, and but about eleven (as it appears) when it was the last time reprinted, but of some Churches in the Countrey of a later Date, and since it hath been received by the baptized Churches from their first being planted, *viz.* that they who preach the Gospel, should live of the Gospel. I hope all the Churches will accordingly to their utmost Abilities discharge their Duties to their Ministers herein, with all Faithfulness, and not expose them to the Cares and Incumbrances of the Affairs or the World, to get their own Bread.

The spat over the supported ministry occurred during the most serious controversy Keach was ever involved with. In 1691, Keach advocated the singing of hymns in the worship services of the church, believing it to be an ordinance of the Lord that needed to be recovered, just like believer's baptism. He was opposed in print by a member of his church, Isaac Marlow. Soon the controversy spilled over to the other churches, with the two elder statesmen of the Particular Baptists, Knollys and Kiffin, on opposing sides (MacDonald, 1982: 50-66). The General Assembly of 1692 appointed seven men to arbitrate on the matter, who examined four of the books. The committee unanimously concluded, "That those Persons who have been concern'd in this Controversy, have on both sides err'd in most of the Particulars that were laid before us." A three-pronged solution to the problem was proposed: first, "that God would make you all sensible of your Errors, humble you for them"; second, that the people involved no longer proceed in method or manner as before; and third, that the books be disposed of. The broader resolution for all the churches was that no member "buy, give, or disperse any of these Books aforesaid underwrit, nor any other that have those uncharitable Reflections in them against their Brethren; and that no Person do sell them, or give them to others" (Narrative, 1692: 11-13).

Both sides largely abided by the committee's admonition to cease publication on the subject. Keach published an apology, which on face value showed deep contrition on his part. Kiffin and the three co-authors published their response, acknowledging their wrong while indicating their disquiet that Keach had intimated he would reprint his book minus the offensive comments. Said Kiffin and his companions (Kiffin *et al.* 1692):

> But as for what we have Charged on Mr. *Keach* in our Book, we are not as yet conscious to our selves that any thing of it is untrue, as to the substance of it; although in our Answer there might be too much severity in Reflecting on Him, which we desire to own ...

> Whereas Mr. *Keach* in the Conclusion of his Printed Paper, doth intimate as if He would Reprint his Book which we have Answered, without Reflections, and with additions to the Argument: We shall only remember Him and others, That He in the last General Assembly of the Messengers, did of his own accord, without any one's perswading Him to it, (that we know of) openly declare and solemnly promise more than once, That he would write or meddle no more about the Argument concerning Singing ...

Keach did not write on this controversial matter after that, focusing instead on other issues. A reprint of his 1691 collection of three hundred hymns, "Spiritual Melody", appeared in 1692 as "Banqueting-House", with no mention of the controversy. In 1696, he published "A Feast of Fat Things", another collection of scripture songs and hymns, but it also contained no mention of the controversy (Brooks, 2006: 56). Isaac Marlow, however, who seems to have disagreed with the idea of settlement by the committee, continued publishing on the subject in the years following, ending with "The Controvesie of Singing Brought to an End" in 1696. In February 1692 (1693 by the new calendar), about twenty members of the Horsleydown congregation left, led by Marlow, to join with Knollys's congregation. In February of 1693 (1694 by the new calendar), the group left to form the Maze Pond church, which excluded congregational singing.

D. B. Riker evaluated Keach's controversy on baptism, and the related covenant theology and justification by faith, in the light of continuing the work of reforming the church. J. C. Brooks similarly placed Keach and his opponent in the hymn-singing controversy, Marlow, in the context of continuing the Reformation of the 16th century. M. R. Bell also saw these men, in all their controversies, as attempting to carry on the work of Reformation. The sincerity of the Particular Baptists in their attempt to be faithful to the Scripture need not be doubted, due to their submission to the headship of Christ. Their disagreements arose from this wider, shared, desire to understand Scripture correctly and to apply it in the work of reforming the church.

Some men each engaged in some controversies, but Keach was one man who engaged in all controversies. What Crosby wrote of Richard Baxter could be applied to Keach equally well – he was engaged "in almost every controversy on foot in his time" (Crosby, Vol. 4: 280). [The afore-mentioned quote was mistakenly applied to Keach in previous editions of this book. Despite Crosby's attempt to portray his father-in-law in a positive light, he said these of Keach (Crosby, Vol. 4: 290, 307): "This truly famous servant of Christ did not only stand up in defence of *believers baptism*, in opposition to that of *infants*, but also engaged in several controversies that were argued out among the Baptist themselves..." "The vivacity of his temper sometimes exposed him, to sharp and sudden fits of anger, which occasioned no small uneasiness to himself, as well as those who had given him any provocation; but those fits were but of a short continuance, and so the trouble occasioned by them was soon over."] From the way Benjamin Keach handled controversies, it can be seen that he was a prickly, rash, and independent-minded personality. Apart from his personality, the theological differences between Keach and the other Particular Baptist leaders did not endear him to them.

5.2.2   Knollys, Kiffin and Keach

In the literature of recent days, Benjamin Keach is portrayed as of the same stature as Hanserd Knollys and William Kiffin when, in reality, Keach was not as influential as the other two men. Keach was a second generation leader, much younger than the fathers of the faith, namely, Knollys and Kiffin.

In the hymn-singing controversy, Keach's view ultimately triumphed among the Particular Baptists. More and more Particular Baptist congregations adopted congregational hymn singing, to such an extent that those opposed to it became a minority in the 18th century. This, however, must not be attributed to Keach's role and writing alone. Other factors had been at work, which have not been noted sufficiently in studies on the subject. One factor was that the Particular Baptists had been more open to congregational singing than the General Baptists since the controversy first appeared in the 1650s. The General Baptists had largely followed John Smyth, who asserted that using a book of songs was an "invention of the man of synne" and that the structures of man's music, such as metre, rhythm, and tune, quenched the Holy Spirit (Brooks, 2006:100-101). The General Baptists' position on congregational singing in the 17th century was represented in the book "Christianismus Primitivus", written in 1678 by the influential Thomas Grantham (Grantham, 1678). The Particular Baptists, on the other hand, mostly followed Henry Ainsworth, pastor of the Separatist, Congregational, "Ancient Church" in Amsterdam. Ainsworth was dissatisfied that Smyth recognized singing as a gift of the Holy Spirit yet led a congregation that remained songless. Said he (Ainsworth, 1609: 22): "But it seemeth strange unto me that M. Sm. should now both allow of the scriptures to be sung in tunes in the Church; and also make the singing by gift of the spirit, a part of Gods proper worship in the new testament; and yet he & his disciples to use neither of these in their assemblies." While there were Particular Baptists, such as Edward Draper and Thomas Collier, who favoured spirit-guided singing more in the tradition of John Smyth, the majority seemed to have adopted the view of Ainsworth. William Kaye affirmed his support of metrical psalmody in his writing against the Quaker, John Whitehead (Kaye, 1654). Vavasor Powell (1617-1670), the influential Welsh preacher, declared that the "singing of Psalms (particularly Scripture-Psalms), Hymns, and Spiritual songs, is a continued Gospel-ordinance, and duty; and to be performed by all, but especially in the Churches" (Bagshaw, 1671: 41). The defining book of the Particular Baptists on congregational singing in the 17th century was the "Orthodox Catechism" of 1680, written by Hercules Collins. This document was essentially the Heidelberg Catechism of 1562 adjusted to the beliefs of Particular Baptists (Collins, 1680). At the end of the "Orthodox Catechism", Collins attached an appendix focused solely on the ordinance of singing, in which he approved of singing metrical psalms as well as hymns of human composition.

The second reason for the triumph of the singing of psalms and hymns among the Particular Baptists must be attributed to the stature and influence of Hanserd Knollys. In 1663, Knollys wrote an introduction to a collection of hymns written by Katherine Sutton, in which he maintained that the singing of "spiritual Songs and Hymnes" was "an ordinance of God's worship" (Sutton, 1663). In the hymn-singing controversy between Keach and Marlow, the issues included: (i) whether the psalms of the Old Testament should be sung; (ii) whether hymns of human composition should be sung; (iii) whether such songs should be put in metre and sung to melodies; (iv) whether the whole church, including unbelievers present, should sing together. William Kiffin, with Robert Steed, George Barrett and Edward Man wrote against such singing, rejecting even singing of the psalms, saying (Kiffin, *et. al.*, 1692: 57): "... How they dare to say, that Singing of Psalms in Meeter, with a tunable Voice, by the whole Church, and a mixt Multitude, is of Divine Institution, when not one Word of all they have written doth prove it?" In 1681, Knollys published his book, "The World that Now is; and the World that is to Come", ostensibly to expound on "several prophecies not yet fulfilled". It is, in fact, an exposition on the nature of the church, its government, and its discipline. In the chapter on the gospel ordinances, Knollys said (Knollys, 1681: 76):

> Singing is also a Gospel-Ordinance, which ought to be performed by the Church as part of God's Publick Worship, *Isa*. 52. 8. *With the Voice together shall they sing.* The Matter that we are to sing is the Word of God, *namely,* the Psalms, Hymns, and Spiritual Songs contained in the holy Scriptures, the Written Word of God, *Col*. 3. 16. *Let the Word of Christ dwell in you richly in all Wisdom, &c.* The Manner of Singing Psalms, Hymns, and Spiritual Songs, is to Sing in Meeter and Measure, with audible Voice, as our English manner is.
>
> The Psalms, Hymns, and Spiritual Songs in the Book of Psalms, were Sung in Meeter and Measure, [*As they that understand the Hebrew Tongue know well.*]
> [Emphasis original.]

Knollys asserted that humanly composed hymns and songs may

be sung in the church, but priority should be given to the singing of what are found in the Word of God. Ministers and members of the church "may Sing with the Spirit, and with understanding, unto Edification; but the *Psalms of David*, and of *Asaph*; and the *Song of Songs*, which is *Solomons*; and the *Hymns* of Jesus Christ and his Apostles, must have the Pre-eminence" (Knollys, 1681: 78). Hercules Collins held to the same view as Knollys, stating (Collins, 1680: 84):

> But yet also I do think, that we are at our liberty to compose other parts or portions of God's Word to that end; provided our Hymns are founded directly on God's Word, these very Hymns may be called the Word of God, or spiritual Hymns. For, as a learned Man saith, 'tis the sense and meaning is the Word of God, whether in prose, or in Meeter; and further saith, We may as well be said to sing God's Word, as to read it; it is only orderly composed and disposed for that action. Every Duty must be performed according to the Analogy of Faith, and founded on God's Word. All Prayer or Preaching, that doth not correspond with sacred Writ, notwithstanding any pretence or an extraordinary Inspiration, I am to explode out of God's Worship. And as Prayer and Preaching must correspond with the sacred Record, so must Singing; And as we count them the best Prayers and Sermons, that are fullest of Scripture, so those Hymns that are founded on the sacred Scriptures, can no more be denied to be of the Spirit, than a Man's Preaching or Prayer, which is full of the Word of God.

The third factor favouring the widespread practice of congregational singing among the Particular Baptists in the 18th century was the influence of the Independent minister, Isaac Watts. Watts's role in taking hymn-singing to the next level of acceptance, notably through his paraphrase of the Psalms, has been noted in the literature. However, insufficient attention has been given to the relationship between the Particular Baptists and the Independents from the end of the 17th century. The Presbyterians and Independents united in the "Happy Union" of 1691, but it abruptly ended within eight years. At the beginning of the 18th century, the Dissenters were again open to co-operation on account of the renewed tension and threatened persecution under Queen Anne. The hard trials they had experienced together, before William and Mary came into power, had provided them opportunities to discuss their church problems. In 1702, London ministers began a practice of presenting a Loyal Address, which was revived in 1727, with Baptists joining the Presbyterians and Independents in the General Body of the Three Denominations. In 1732, the first meeting of Protestant Dissenting Deputies was held, in which the ministers were joined by lay members of the three denominations (Brown, 1986: 54). Isaac Watts was actively involved in these ventures (Milner, 426-428). Watts's close interaction with, and known sympathy toward, the Calvinistic Baptists would have made his hymns acceptable to the latter (Milner, 485-486).

The focus here is on the "Knollys factor". While young Hercules Collins (1646/7-1702) had written definitively on hymn-singing in 1680, a year earlier than Knollys's "The World that Now is; and the World that is to Come", the older man was most influential among the Particular Baptists. Knollys was virtually the only Particular Baptist minister who had received a university training, and was well versed in the original languages of Scripture. Benjamin Cox, another former Anglican clergyman who was university trained, had died by 1664. William Kiffin described his long-time friend, Knollys, as "Learned Mr. *Knowles*, (who we believe understood the Greek tongue as well as *Beza* and others)" (Kiffin *et al.*, 1692: 49). In virtually every document issued by the Particular Baptists, Knollys's name appeared first in the list of signatories and, if not first, it was second, behind Kiffin's. Although the two men were on different sides of the hymn-singing controversy, they remained close friends to the end. When Knollys died in 1691, Kiffin wrote the preface to his autobiography which was republished. While taking a different view on congregational hymn-singing, Kiffin and his colleagues nevertheless referred to Knollys and Collins with great respect (Kiffin *et al.*, 1692: 10, 16, 49, 63). It is to be noted that Robert Steed, one of the four men who issued "A Serious Answer to a Late Book stiled, A Reply to Mr. Robert Steed's Epistle concerning Singing", was assistant pastor in Knollys's church. Both men could work together well despite holding to differing views on singing. Knollys's "Last Legacy to the Church" began with a plea to his colleague (Knollys, 1812: 59):

> First of all, I do humbly beseech my reverend and beloved brother Steed, for Christ's sake, that the fervent love to the church, and the watchful care over the particular

members of it, expressed and published in his little epistle touching singing, may be revived; and also that the brotherly love of the ministering brethren, and likewise of all my beloved brethren who are helps in government, may be stirred up to help, to assist, to provoke the rest unto good works, Gal. iv. 18.

In contrast, the relationship between Kiffin and Keach remained tense following the hymn-singing controversy. Keach has been portrayed in recent writings as a man with a catholic spirit. Riker has shown that although Keach wrote strongly in defence of believer's baptism, over against infant sprinkling, he nevertheless affirmed that paedobaptist congregations "are true churches, as well as we, they being godly Christians, tho I believe they are less compleat churches, than those who are baptised upon profession of faith, or not so orderly in their constitution" (Riker, 2009: 220). Haykin refers to Keach's invitation to the Seventh-Day Baptist, Joseph Stennett, to preach his funeral sermon in 1704 (Haykin, 1996: 103). Keach had preached and written against Sabbatarianism after losing fifteen members to Stennett's church, one of the fifteen being Keach's own daughter, Hannah. Stennett did not reply to the attack of Keach on his beliefs. Could it be that Keach was trying to make up with Stennett by inviting him to preach his funeral sermon? Regardless of these portrayals of Keach's big-heartedness, Kiffin and his three co-authors had this to say of him (Kiffin *et al.*, 1692: 61-62):

> As for Mr. *Keach*, who hath been the chief Instrument to raise up this Controversy, which may occasion more Contention than Edification in the Baptized Churches, we heartily desire he may for time to come labour after the things which make for Peace. We know, and he himself also, how long he hath maintained a Wall of Partition between him and the rest of the Baptized Churches, allowing no Church-Communion but such as can agree with him in his Opinion and Practice of Laying on of Hands upon the Members of the Church, both Men and Women, which Practice we find no where commanded by our Lord Jesus, nor his Apostles; yet we have not made it a Bone of Contention between him and us, neither concerned our selves for many Years, to make any publick Contest about it; but to say no more of that matter ...

Relationship between Keach and the other Particular Baptist leaders had obviously been strained for a long time. Referring to the book written by Keach and Whinnel, "A Reply to Mr. Robert Steed's Epistle concerning Singing", Kiffin and his co-authors said (Kiffin *et al.*, 1692: 6):

> But that their Book might pass with the greater Applause and Credit, it is in the beginning of it recommended by an Epistle as a very sober Answer, subscribed with several Names at the Conclusion of it: Some of those Persons, whose Names are there subscribed, are such as we have no Communion with, being such as are called Freewillers (or *Arminians*) holding a falling away from true Grace ...

Keach's combative personality and continuing interaction with the General Baptists irked the other Particular Baptists. His "mixed theology" vexed them as well. He was clearly Calvinistic in soteriology, and adhered strongly to believer's baptism, standing firmly with the other Particular Baptists on these issues. However, he clung on to the laying on of hands, and denied the validity of the office of ruling elder, which characterized the General Baptists. In the controversy on congregational singing, he had Knollys on his side, against the view of Kiffin. If not for the Knollys factor, it is unlikely that congregational singing would have spread among the Particular Baptists as quickly, and as pervasively, as it did. Keach was the most prolific writer among the Particular Baptists of the 17th century, publishing some 46 pieces of diverse writings. Knollys published some 13 books, roughly a quarter the number written by Keach. Knollys, however, was much more influential than Keach by virtue of his age, experience, and scholarly ability. An indication of this occurred in 1684, when Knollys was imprisoned for six months. He had been imprisoned before, following the Venner rebellion. While in prison the second time, a royal messenger was despatched to inquire whether he and the Particular Baptists would accept a royal gesture of toleration. Knollys, who was 84 years old, replied, "I am old, and know but few men's minds." Being further pressed for an answer, he said, "I am of opinion that no liberty but what came by act of parliament would be very acceptable, because that would be stable, firm, and certain." While Kiffin exerted an influence in high society (Ivimey, I: 336-338), including making a gift of 10,000 pounds to the king instead of giving a requested loan of 40,000 pounds (Ivimey, III: 4), although the veracity of this incident has been questioned (Kreitzer, 2010: 3), it was Knollys's opinion that was sought by the king concerning the Calvinistic Baptist community. Kiffin himself wrote some nine books, mostly apologia in defence of the Particular Baptists. While influential, he was more of an organizer – the executive officer and public relations man – among the London Particular Baptists, while Knollys was more of the theologian – the advisor and director. Putting it metaphorically, Kiffin was the Hermes, and Knollys the Zeus, of the Particular Baptist community. The three men – Knollys, Kiffin and Keach – were mighty men, but Knollys was chief of the three. In the light of this, Knollys's contribution to the ecclesiology of the Particular Baptists should be seen as pre-eminent.

5.2.3   Hanserd Knollys's True Stature

Surprisingly, Knollys's contribution to the ecclesiology of the Particular Baptists has been played down instead of being recognized. Why, and how, has that happened? Apart from the wrong impression of Keach's pre-eminence conveyed by the recent studies on him, Knollys has been portrayed as being at odds theologically with the mainstream Particular Baptists. The first area lies in his eschatology. Knollys was known to be sympathetic to the Fifth Monarchists of his time. In Chapter 3 it is noted that many of the Fifth Monarchists were members of the conservative Particular Baptist churches. Prominent leaders who held to Fifth Monarchist eschatology, but did not share in their belief in the use of force to achieve their ends, included Hanserd Knollys, Thomas Collier and Vavasor Powell. However, when Knollys's eschatology is seen in the perspective of church history, it becomes obvious that he was not the radical that he seemed to be. Knollys's eschatology, in fact, corresponds to the classical Pre-millennialism of the early church fathers, as distinct from modern Dispensational Pre-millennialism (Berkhof, 1949: 708-710). Knollys held that no one knows the exact time of Christ's second coming, but there are three general signs (Knollys, 1681b: 13-20):

- First, ungodliness will abound. "Christ told his Disciples, *Matth.* 24.12. *That Iniquity shall abound*, a little before his Second Coming, vers. 30. And it will be so with the Men and Women of these Cities, as it was with those Citizens of *Sodom* and *Gomorrah*, whose Cities were burned."

- Second, there will be great apostasy in doctrine and worship. "This sign of Christ's Second Coming, the Apostle *Paul* foretold, 2 *Thes*.2.1, 2, 3. ...An Apostasie *first* from the Doctrine of the Gospel, *especially*, Faith and Love, 1 Tim. 4.1, 2, 3." "As the Apostasie in Doctrine, so in Worship, is a sign of the Last Daies, and of the Second Coming of Christ. The Apostle *Paul* foretold thereof, 1 *Thes*. 2. 3, 4. & 2 *Tim*. 3. 1,5."

- Third, there will be severe persecution, "that great *Tribulation*, which our Saviour foretold his Disciples would be *immediately* before his Second Coming, and Appearance, *Matth*. 24. 21, 29, 30." "And the People of God (*especially his two Prophetical Witnesses, to wit, the separated Churches, and their faithful Ministers*) shall not be exempted from the Tribulation of those Daies; for they shall suffer Persecution, 2 *Tim*. 3.1,12."

According to Knollys, the resurrection of the dead will occur at the second coming of Christ (Knollys, 1681b: 30, 29, 28):

> After the Saints deceased are raised, and have lived and reigned with Christ a thousand years, shall be the general Resurrection, *Rev*. 20. 12, 13. *And I saw the Dead small and great stand before God*.
>
> But the rest of the Dead lived [n]ot again until the thousand years [w]ere finished, *Rev*. 20. 5, 6.
>
> And when the Kingdom of our LORD Jesus Christ is established on Earth, and all the Kingdoms of this world are become his; the thousand years of the Reign of Christ and his Saints being ended, (*Rev*. 20. 4, 5, 6, 7.) then Christ will Raise the Dead, and he will judge the Quick and the Dead; which being done, HE will deliver up the Kingdom to God, even the Father; *that God may be all in all*, 1 *Cor*. 15. 24-28.
> [Emphasis original.]

Connected with Knollys's eschatology is the impression given that he was somewhat of a mystic. His prediction of better days for the church from the year 1688 was fulfilled exactly, at least in Britain

169

(Bell, 2000: 85). His prayer life was unusual in that during the plague in London, there were sick persons healed even while he was praying for them (Crosby, I: 338). On an occasion of severe sickness on the part of Benjamin Keach, Knollys prayed for him to be given another fifteen years of life, as happened to Hezekiah in the Bible. He then said, "Brother Keach I shall be in heaven before you", before leaving quickly. Knollys died two years later, while Keach lived another fifteen years, dying in 1704 (Crosby, IV: 307-308). How should these unusual incidents be understood? Knollys's prediction of change in 1688 could be seen as coincidental or, rather, providential. Men with the unusual gift of prayer like that of Knollys are not unknown in history. The life of George Müller (1805-1898) is an example of this, as any good biography of this man will show. Instead of seeing this aspect of Knollys's personal life in a negative light, it should be considered a factor adding to his esteem among his peers.

The second area of alleged difference between Knollys and mainstream Particular Baptist teaching lies in his apparent disavowal of the church covenant. Charles Deweese, in his book "Baptist Church Covenants", helpfully differentiates between the purpose of the confession of faith compared to that of the church covenant (Deweese, 1990: 22): "Whereas confessions were designed to elicit a voluntary commitment to particular ways of believing, covenants were intended to produce a voluntary commitment to particular ways of practicing one's faith." Deweese showed that John Spilsbury, pastor of the first Particular Baptist church in London, held to the value of the church covenant. Deweese (1990: 24) made the claim that, in contrast,

> Hanserd Knollys, an important London pastor, opposed the use of church covenants. He noted that in some London Baptist churches, the only conditions which some preachers were propounding as essential for admission into their churches were "Faith, Repentance, and Baptisme; and none other." Further, these churches did not urge or make "any particular covenant with Members upon admittance." Finally, Knollys identified the following biblical passages as evidence that the use of church covenants was not a New Testament practice: Acts 8:12, 35-39; 16:30-33; 18:8.

This categorical claim of Deweese was based upon Knollys's book of 1645, entitled, "A Moderate Answer unto Dr. Bastwicks book; called Independency not God's Ordinance", and has been followed by subsequent writers, including Haykin (1994: 106), Hayden (2006: 146), and Renihan (1997: 97). This claim needs to be re-examined, in view of what Knollys later wrote in "The World that Now is" (Knollys, 1681a: 48-50):

> The Gospel-Form of a *particular* Church of God consists (*as we said*) in the *fitly* framing, compacting and joyning those sanctified Believers together into ONE Fellowship, Society and Gospel Brotherhood in a solemn Day of Prayer, with Fasting, wherein some Able Minister of the Gospel, having by Preaching the Word unto them, shewed them their Respective Duties in a Church relation, the Elders and Chief Brethren of some particular Churches of Saints being present, and assisting in the work of the Day (*if they may be obtained*) may in the Name and Authority of the LORD Jesus Christ (*by virtue of this Commission given to him*) constitute and make them a particular Visible Church of God; **they giving up themselves *professedly first* to the LORD, and *then* one to another,** *mutually* and *solemnly* with one accord engaging themselves to come together in ONE congregation, and to Assemble themselves together in some *one* Place every *first* Day of the week, to worship God *publickly* in all his holy Ordinances, with their *mutual* professed Subjection unto the Laws of God's House, and with a Professed Resolution to Continue in the Apostles Doctrine, and in Fellowship, and in Breaking of Bread, and Prayer, through the Help of God. All which being done, the same Minister ought to declare them to be a Church of Saints, and the Ministers and Brethren of other Churches being also present, ought to own and acknowledge them to be a Sister Church, by giving them the Right hand of Fellowship; and so to commend them by Prayer unto God, and to the Word of his Grace, who is able to build them up, and to give them an Inheritance among all them which are sanctified.
> [Italics original. Emphasis in bold added.]

This is a description of the constituting of a church, in which the

171

people involved bind themselves together by covenant, "they giving up themselves professedly first to the LORD, and then one to another". These words, from 2 Corinthians 8:5, have been incorporated into the 1689 Confession, Chapter 26, Article 6, and constitute virtually a formula for the church covenant. In an attempt to show that Knollys rejected the necessity of a formal covenant, Renihan selectively quoted from the above passage, but left out these crucial words of 2 Corinthians 8:5 (Renihan, 1998: 97-99). As seen in Chapter 2, it was the accepted practice of the Particular Baptists to adopt a written church covenant when constituting a church, an example of which was the church covenant produced by Benjamin Keach for his church. Had Knollys changed his view on the necessity of the church covenant between 1645 and 1681, or had he been misunderstood in his writing of 1645? In order to determine the answer, a reassessment of Knollys's 1645 work is needed.

Ordained a minister of the Church of England, Hanserd Knollys was writing as a Baptist in 1645 when he responded to the book written by the Presbyterian, Dr. Bastwick, called "Independencie not Gods Ordinance". It was a good ten years (1635 to 1645) since he broke with the Church of England and became a Separatist. In his book, "A Moderate Answer Unto Dr. Bastwicks Book", Knollys said (1645: 1):

> Passing by many things lesse considerable, because I intend brevity; In the 7th. page of the Doctors booke, *There is a twofold question betweene them called* PRESBYTERIANS *and their Brethren who are termed* INDEPENDENTS; *The first is, concerning the Government of the Church,* viz. *Whether it be* Presbyterian-Dependen [sic], *or* Presbyterian-Independent? *The second question is, concerning the Gathering of* CHURCHES.

The word "Presbyterian", used in this context, is a reference to the exercise of rule by presbyters, or elders, in both systems of church government. No one would be confused by its usage, just as none would be confused with the use of the word "Catholic" in Chapter 26, Article 1, of the 1689 Confession, which says, "THE Catholick or universal Church, which (with respect to the internal work of the Spirit, and truth of grace) may be called invisible." Throughout the book, Knollys spoke as an advocate of the Independent system of church government.

Dr. Bastwick's second question was concerned with the manner of gathering and admitting members and officers into the church. Knollys restated what he thought Dr. Bastwick had said (Knollys, 1645: 14):

> And now I come to the second question, which is concerning the manner of gathering of Churches, and admitting of Members and Officers pag. 98. which question the Dr. thus states, viz. 'Whether Ministers of the Gospell may, out of already gathered assemblies of Beleevers, select and chuse the most principle of them into a Church-fellowship peculiar unto themselves, and admit of uone [sic., none] into their society, but such as shall enter in by a private Covenant, and are allowed by the consent, and approbation of all the Congregation? And this question the Doctor brancheth into six queries pag. 98. 99. Wherein the judicious Reader may perceive the Doctor (through mis-information I conceive) hath mistaken the stating of the question, which he partly acknowledgeth pag. 100.

Knollys then rehashed Dr. Bastwick's arguments from Scripture and summarized them under three points: first, Christ has given a commission to His apostles to teach all nations and to baptise them; second, the condition or terms of admittance into the church were faith, repentance, and baptism; third, the apostles and all succeeding ministers of the gospel should admit whoever believed and were baptised to be members of the church and teach them to observe no other things but what Christ commanded them. According to Knollys, Dr. Bastwick said that this the apostles practised, without requiring them to take a private covenant, or enter into the church by way of a particular covenant (Knollys, 1645: 12-13). Knollys assured Dr. Bastwick that, based on his knowledge of the practice of some churches in London, "having walked with them", only those who professed faith in Jesus Christ, and had been baptised in the name of the Holy Trinity, were admitted members of the church. Such as did not believe, and would not be baptised, were not admitted into church communion. "This hath been the practice of some Churches of God in this City, without urging or making any particular covenant with Members upon admittance" (Knollys, 1645: 20).

On the basis of this statement, Deweese (1990: 24) drew the conclusion, followed by others, that Knollys was denying the need of a church covenant. In reality, Knollys was agreeing with Dr. Bastwick on the *conditions* for church membership, which are faith in Jesus Christ, repentance, and baptism in the name of the Holy Trinity. In this, Knollys agreed with Dr. Bastwick. Knollys was not discussing the *manner* by which a new church was constituted, which would have been by a covenanting service, in which a church covenant – whether rudimentary or more detailed – was adopted. Dr. Bastwick had mistakenly thought that the Independents required agreement to the church ("private", or extra-biblical) covenant on the part of the candidate, and congregational consent from the church, for admittance to church membership.

Knollys did not enter into discussion of what happened once a person was admitted into membership, let alone the *manner* by which a new church was to be constituted. He had declared from the start his intention to be brief (Knollys, 1645: 1): "Passing by many things lesse considerable, because I intend brevity." What might he have answered if he were asked, "What happens once a person is accepted into membership?" He would most probably have said what Keach said (Dever, 2001: 65): "And when admitted Members, before the church they must solemnly enter into a Covenant, to walk in the Fellowship of that particular Congregation." This would have involved a public declaration of acceptance into membership by the pastor and/or the signing of the membership book which included the church covenant, as seen in the many extant Church Records. Knollys *did* believe in a church being formed by a covenanting, or constituting, service. As noted already, he gave a detailed account of how such a service was to be conducted in his book, "The World that Now is" (Knollys, 1681a: 48-50).

The above re-assessment shows that Knollys was not rejecting the necessity of covenantal commitment in the constituting of a church – the view held across the board by all the Independents, including the Particular Baptists. There was disagreement on whether an explicit, written, covenant was needed, but there never was any disagreement on the need for voluntary consent and covenantal commitment, expressed at a constituting service. The Kiffin Manuscript (1641) states that on 11 January baptism "by dipping [the] Body" was carried out, "And then Manifesting (not by any formal Words a Covenant) which word was scrupled by some of them, but by mutual desires &

agreement each Testified." Fifty-three persons formed that church. In 1672 the church at Bromsgrove, Worcestershire, covenanted together according to the procedure laid down by Knollys, stating that the members had given themselves up "in a visible manner to ye Lord and to each other according to ye will of God" (Wortley, 1974: 5-10). The church in Bampton, Devonshire, was similarly constituted in 1690, "in the presence, and with the advice, of Elders of other Churches". Eighteen men and twenty-one women formed the membership, "assuming to themselves the name of a Church of Christ or their giving themselves one to another having first professedly in Baptism given themselves up to the Lord" (Bampton CB, 1). This congregation was viewed as an expression of Christ's mission in the world, who through the gospel, "many being called and separated from the world giving themselves up first unto the Lord and to one another by the will of God *by mutual contract* forming themselves into distinct communities or societies for the maintenance of the worship of God according to the institutions given them by Christ their Lord." [Emphasis added.]

The Particular Baptists would not repudiate a church that was formed with only a rudimentary church covenant. John Owen similarly would not invalidate a church that had an implicit covenant, but strongly advocated the value of an explicit one. Said Owen (1976, Vol. 16: 28):

> Now, whereas these things are, in themselves and for the substance of them, known gospel duties, which all believers are indispensably obliged unto, the *more express our engagement* is concerning them, the more do we glorify Christ in our profession, and the greater sense of our duty will abide on our consciences, and the greater encouragement be given unto the performance of mutual duties, as also the more evident will the warranty be for the exercise of church-power. Yet do I not deny the being of churches unto those societies wherein these things are virtually only observed, especially in churches of some continuance, wherein there is at least an implicit consent unto the first covenant constitution. [Emphasis original.]

A third area in which Knollys has been misrepresented as differing from the mainstream Particular Baptists was his assertion that there should be one church only in each city or locality, consisting of a number of separate congregations. Renihan described Knollys's view of church government as a "Modified Independency" (Renihan, 1998: 139). He detects "some modifications", one of which was that Knollys's view concerning the church in Jerusalem had changed. In 1645, Knollys had disagreed with Dr. Bastwick that the one church in Jerusalem consisted of several congregations but in 1681, he asserted that the one church in Jerusalem consisted of several congregations. While that is true, Knollys's main emphasis in 1645 is to be noted, namely, that the Independents denied that several assemblies were governed by "a Common councell, Consistory, College, or Court of Presbyters" of the Presbyterian kind (Knollys, 1645: 14 cf. 11). In 1681, Knollys asserted that the church in Jerusalem consisted of several distinct congregations, but they were one church (Knollys, 1681a: 44-45). Knollys further explained that "The Well-Being of a particular Church of Saints, doth principally consist in three things, viz. Oneness, Order, and Government." The oneness of the church requires first, "That there be but ONE Church in one City; and that all the Congregations of Saints in that City (called Churches) bear but one Name, to wit, the Church of God in that City, as in the Apostles daies, *Act.* 15.4. 22. I *Cor.* 1. 2." Secondly, "That this Church be of one Heart, and one Soul, *Act.* 4. 32." Thirdly, "That this one Church, and all the Congregations of Saints, that are Members thereof, walk by one and the same Rule *of the written Word of God*, being Ordered and Guided by their Bishops, Pastors, Teachers, Presbyters, or Elders" (Knollys, 1681a: 50-51).

Instead of seeing Knollys as practising a modified Independency, it would be more accurate to see him from the perspective of the Independents – including the Particular Baptists and the paedobaptist Congregationalists – who shared a common characteristic, namely, that they were extremely mission-minded to such an extent that each church normally spawned a number of satellite congregations, either by gathering or by splitting. In such a situation, many teaching elders and "gifted brethren" were needed, and also ruling elders or "helps in government". To the Independents, such multiple congregations would be regarded as constituting one church, until such time as they could, one by one, become autonomous. This situation is not to be confused with the plural church government of the Church of England, which all the Separatists disagreed with. Said Knollys (1681a: 45): "... the Churches of God under the Gospel, are not *National*, but *Political*, and *Congregational*." Also, it is not to be confused with the maintenance of long-term pastoral charge over a distant congregation. John Owen had addressed this, saying (Owen, 1976, Vol. 16: 90):

> It is manifest also from hence how inconsistent it is with this office, and the due discharge of it, for any one man to undertake the relation of a pastor unto more churches than one, especially if far distant from one another ... But one view of the duties incumbent on each pastor, and of whose diligent performance he is to give an account at the last day, will discard this practice from all approbation in the minds of them that are sober. However, it is as good to have ten churches at once, as, having but one, never to discharge the duty of a pastor towards it.

In connection with Knollys's multi-congregational church, Renihan (1998: 204-205) portrays him as unorthodox in his view of the eldership, in which there is one elder who is chosen by the presbytery to be pre-eminent among themselves. Said Renihan:

> This position is very unusual for Baptists, and I can find no evidence to demonstrate that it was ever put into practice among them. Knollys' view resembles the episcopalian structure of the National Church far more than the Independency with which the Baptists are commonly associated.

Renihan seems to have forgotten that, as early as 1645, Knollys was defending Independency from the attack of Dr. Bastwick. Could Knollys have changed his view so drastically in the intervening years? That is possible, but concrete evidence must be found to support it. It is shown in Chapter 4 that Knollys's view actually fitted the mainline Particular Baptists' view of the eldership, which was that of John Owen and Daniel King. Knollys declared, in his book of 1681, that "the Churches of God under the Gospel, are not *National*, but *Political*, and *Congregational*." The Shorter Oxford English Dictionary shows that in the 16th century, the word "political" means "having an organized government or polity". Benjamin Keach, quoting Dr. Chauncy, said that "The Political Power of Christ is in the Church, whereby it is exercised in the Name of Christ, having all lawful Rule and Government within itself" (Dever, 2001: 71). How could Knollys's view of the eldership resemble the episcopalian structure of the National Church? It has been noted that in his letter, "Last Legacy to the Church", he referred to "helps in government", a term which normally means ruling elders. In the records of his church, there were references to "elders" other than the pastor (shown in Chapter 4 of this present work). Owen actually held to the same view as Knollys on the set-up of the church in Jerusalem, saying (Owen, 1976, Vol. 16: 46-47, 59):

> The Scripture knows no more of an archbishop, such as all diocesan bishops are, nor of an archdeacon, than of an archapostle, or an archevangelist, or an archprophet. Howbeit it is evident that in all their assemblies they had one who did preside in the manner before described; which seems, among the apostles, to have been the prerogative of Peter.

> The brethren also of the church may be so multiplied as that the constant meeting of them all in one place may not be absolutely best for their edification; howbeit, that on all the solemn occasions of the church whereunto their consent was necessary, they did of old, and ought still, to meet in the same place, for advice, consultation, and consent ...

> That the church was greatly multiplied [at] that time, on the account of the conversion unto the faith recorded in the foregoing chapter [Acts 5]. It is probable, indeed, that many, yea, the most of them, were returned unto their own habitations; for the next year there were churches in all Judea, Galilee, and Samaria, chap. ix. 31.

Having dealt with the three ways by which Knollys has been portrayed misleadingly as out of line with his peers, it may be asserted that Knollys's ecclesiology was reflective of the view of the mainline Particular Baptists. Knollys's view of the eldership may be summarized with confidence as consisting of the following points: (i) a presbytery consisting of at least two elders rule in a church; (ii) they rule according to the word of God; (iii) the elders include teaching and ruling ones; and (iv) one of the elders, normally the pastor, is to be recognized as the leading elder. There are now three individuals, in three locations, who wrote fairly extensively on church government, spanning the 17th century: Daniel King, of Coventry in the Midlands, published "A Way to Sion" in 1650 and 1656; Hanserd Knollys, in London, published "The World that Now Is; and The World that is to Come" in 1681; and William Carr of Hamsterley, County of Durham, in northern England, wrote his paper on the call to the ministry by request of the Northern Association, in 1706. Added to these, there are John Owen's two books on ecclesiology, namely, "A Brief Instruction in the Worship of God and Discipline of the Churches of the New Testament" published in 1667, and "The True Nature Of A Gospel Church And Its Government" published in 1689. Little wonder that the vast majority of the Particular Baptists held to the same view of church government, as noted in the previous chapter.

5.2.4 Benjamin Keach on the Eldership

It is to be noted that Keach's ecclesiology did not differ much from the predominant view of John Owen in so far as the foundational principles were concerned, for example, in the matter and form of the church, the nature and seat of church power, the ordinary and continuing officers of the church, and the necessity of church discipline. However, there were points of difference in Keach's view which caused the whole system of church government to develop away from the Independency of the mainline Particular Baptists in those who held to them. What were those points of difference? They included:

  i the denial of the validity of ruling elders;

  ii the discouragement of multiple congregations in any one church;

  iii the confounding of duties of the two remaining offices of the church, namely, those of elders and deacons.

It has been noted how Keach categorically denied the validity of the ruling elders. Said Keach in his book of 1697, "The Glory of a True Church, and its Discipline Display'd" (Dever, 2001: 68-69):

> Query, *Are there no ruling Elders besides the Pastor?*
> *Answ.* There might be such in the Primitive Apostolical Church, but we see no ground to believe it an abiding Office to continue in the Church, but was only temporary.

1. Because we have none of the Qualifications of such Elders mention'd, or how to be chosen.
2. Because we read not particularly what their Work and Business is, or how distinct from preaching Elders; tho we see not but the Church may (if she sees meet) choose some able and discreet Brethren to be *Helps in Government*. We have the Qualifications of Bishops and Deacons directly laid down, and how to be chosen, and their Work declared, but no other Office or Officers in the Church, but these only.

In contrast, Owen declared thus in his book of 1689, "The True Nature of a Gospel Church and its Government" (Owen, 1976, Vol. 16: 42):

The bishops or elders are of two sorts: – 1. Such as have authority to *teach* and administer the sacraments, which is commonly called the *power of order*; and also of *ruling*, which is called a power of jurisdiction. corruptly: and, 2. Some have only *power for rule*; of which sort are some in all the churches in the world. [Emphasis original.]

In his book of 1667, "A Brief Instruction In the Worship of God and Discipline of the Churches", Owen wrote (15: 504):

Q. 31. *Are there appointed any elders in the church whose office and duty consist in rule and government only?*
A. Elders not called to teach ordinarily or administer the sacraments, but to assist and help in the rule and government of the church, are mentioned in the Scripture.– Rom. xii. 8; 1 Cor. xii. 28; 1 Tim. v. 17.

In the explication, Owen wrote (15: 504-505):

And it is in vain pretended that those words, "helps, governments," do denote gifts only, seeing the apostle expressly enumerates the persons in office, or officers, which the Lord Christ then used in the foundation and rule of the churches as then planted. He that *ruleth*, also, is distinguished from him that *teacheth* and him that *exhorteth*, Rom. xii. 8; and is prescribed diligence as his principal qualification in the discharge of his duty. And the words of the apostle to this purpose are expressed: 1 Tim. v. 17, "Let the elders that rule well be counted worthy of double honour, especially those who labour in word and doctrine." For the words expressly assign two sorts of elders, whereof some only attend unto rule; others, moreover, labour in the word and doctrine ...

The qualification of these elders, with the way of their call and setting apart unto their office, being the same with those of the teaching elders before insisted on, need not be here again repeated.
[Emphasis original.]

In his book of 1689, Owen devoted a whole chapter, consisting of 25 pages, to proving the validity of the ruling elders from Scripture. In view of Owen's extensive treatment of this matter, and the fact that Owen's writings were widely used by the Particular Baptists, it is unlikely that the majority of them were convinced by Keach's denial of the validity of ruling elders based on his arguments that (i) the qualifications of such elders, and how they are to be chosen, are not mentioned in Scripture; and (ii) their work and duties, as distinct from those of preaching elders, are not mentioned in Scripture.

The second point of difference in Keach's ecclesiology compared to that of Knollys lies in his discouragement of multiple congregations in any one church. Keach wrote (Dever, 2001: 64-65):

A Church of Christ, according to the Gospel-Institution, is a Congregation of Godly Christians, who as a Stated-Assembly (being baptized upon the Profession of Faith) do by mutual agreement and consent give themselves up to the Lord, and one to another, according to the Will of God; *and do ordinarily meet together in one Place*, for the Public Service and Worship of God; among whom the Word of God and Sacraments are duly administered, according to Christ's Institution. [Emphasis added.]

This point is also made in Keach's exposition of Matthew 24:45-51, in which he said (Keach, 1974: 635): "no steward of Christ is a steward or pastor of more than one church; they must meet, be fed, and worship God altogether." It is to be noted that Keach was not totally disallowing multiple congregations in one church, as encountered in the pioneering situations of the Particular Baptists in those days. He is emphasizing that, *ordinarily*, the one church should meet as one congregation. It would seem that there had been a tendency for Particular Baptist churches to continue meeting in different congregations, with no serious effort made for the preaching points to become churches in their own right. It also could be that some congregations were close enough to one another as to warrant combining them into one congregation. After all, there was a shortage of fully supported ministers, which Keach agitated for in the General Assembly of 1689. It is shown, in Chapter 4, that the Assembly urged small churches in close geographical proximity "to join together for the better and more comfortable support of their Ministry, and better edification of one another". Be that as it may, it is still significant that the point made by Keach was in direct contrast to what Knollys advocated in his book, "The World That Now Is". Knollys (1681a: 50) had stated:

> That there be but ONE Church in one City; and that all the Congregations of Saints in that City (called Churches) bear but one Name, to wit, the Church of God in that City, as in the Apostles daies, *Act*. 15. 4. 22. 1 *Cor*. 1. 2 ...

> That this one Church, and all the Congregations of Saints, that are Members thereof, walk by one and the same Rule *of the written Word of God*, being Ordered and Guided by their Bishops, Pastors, Teachers, Presbyters, or Elders, according to the Royal Laws of God's House ...
> [Emphasis original.]

This chapter attempts to understand Knollys's view in the light of the mission-mindedness of the Particular Baptists, and also of the paedobaptist Independents, of that time. Knollys was actively involved in planting churches in London and other areas of England and Wales. In December 1652 his church at Coleman Street, London, authorized Thomas Tillam to evangelize the north-east of the country. Thomas Collier, who was active in church planting in the West of England, also had close association with Knollys (Hayden, 2006: 5). The Independents – whether baptist or paedobaptist – were known for establishing satellite congregations which were regarded as parts of one church. Examples abound. The messengers of the Association of Churches in Northern England signed the conclusions of their meetings on behalf of their own churches, each consisting of two or three congregations. There were the "Messengers of the Church at Bridlington and Bainton in York", the "Messengers of the Church at Hampsterley & Cold Rowley in the County of Durham", etc. (Copson, 1991: 118-119). The church at Tiverton, Devon, had a branch in Bampton for many years before the latter was finally constituted as an independent church (Ivimey, Vol. II: 145). The first Church Book entries of the church at Stevington show that it had groups of members meeting in Bedfordshire and also in Northamptonshire (Tibbutt, 1972: 23, 30, 35). In Chapter 4, it is noted that John Bunyan's church consisted of a number of scattered congregations. This practice was pervasive, and it continued into the 18th century (Howard, 1976: 187, 213: Lovegrove, 2004). Shortly before Benjamin Beddome was appointed teaching elder of the church at Bourton-on-the-Water in 1743, the church at Stowe became one with the church at Bourton, but continued to meet as two congregations (Brooks, 1861: 27-28). In the light of Knollys's mission-mindedness and the common practice of the Independents of having satellite congregations, it can be seen that Knollys was addressing such situations in his book, "The World That Now Is". This may be seen from his words of qualification in advocating the priority of one elder above the others in the one church (Knollys, 1681a: 68):

> But I mean and intend any one of the Bishops, Pastors, Teachers, Presbyters, or Elders, who are, or shall by the Consent, Approbation and Choice of the rest be appointed, ordained, and set over them as Chief Bishop or Presbyter of the Church *in any City and Villages adjacent*, who for Order sake in Gospel-Government, hath Priority, Pre-eminence, and Authority above the rest of the Presbyters or Bishops of the same Church ... [Emphasis added.]

If any doubt still remains, Knollys's book of 1689, "An Exposition of the whole Book of the Revelation" should put this to rest. This concerns a similar situation of multiple congregations under one church, but arising from a single congregation splitting with numerical growth. Said Knollys concerning the seven churches in Asia (Knollys, 1689: 9):

> Although the Church in any City, at the beginning and first Planting of it, was but <u>one</u> congregation, and assembled themselves together in one place, ... yet when the

> number of the Disciples was multiplied, ... and multi-
> tudes both men and women were added to the Lord, and
> by the Lord to the Church, ... then the Church was ne-
> cessitated, for the edification of the Multitude, and great
> number of Members thereof, to assemble themselves to-
> gether in particular Congregations, and became distinct
> Companies, ... and each Company or Congregation had
> their Elders and Deacons, ... and the denomination of the
> Church, ... are called Churches.

The intention of gathering churches by having satellite congregations, or by a growing congregation splitting into multiple congregations, meant that the churches struggled to provide pastoral care
and preaching to the scattered congregations. The general poverty of
the churches, coupled with the political turmoils of the time, which
were often linked to persecution of the Dissenters, meant that few
churches could fully support their ministers. Ivimey (Vol. II: 549)
records that the indefatigable Andrew Gifford was unable to be supported by his people because "They had endured three severe persecutions, which prevented them from giving him support." Even in
London, the ministers were not supported fully by their congregations. Knollys was partially supported by his church, receiving "from
the Church always according to their Ability, most of the Members
being poor" (Kiffin et al., 1692: 63). He had to supplement his income from writing and teaching in a school (White, 1996: 130). The
need for preachers was alleviated by appointing "gifted brethren" or
"ministers" who were not elders, to preach. In Bunyan's church,
seven men were appointed in 1671 to be such ministers, including
Nehemiah Coxe (Bunyan Meeting, 50-51). It seems that the satellite
congregations remained satellites for longer than intended, so that
many churches ended up having multiple congregations almost per-
manently. It was to address such situations that Keach's words were
written: a church should "ordinarily meet together in one Place" (Dever, 2001: 65). Be that as it may, when the emphasis was placed on
the need to meet in one place, the tendency would arise of stifling
church planting. However, the mission-mindedness of the Particular
Baptists seemed none the worse affected because the majority did
not follow Keach's view. Keach's son, Elias, who held to his father's
view of the eldership, was to engage in planting two churches in
Pennsylvania, North America, before returning to become the pastor

of a church in Ayles Street, London. Instead, mission-mindedness was going to be stifled in a number of churches in the mid-18th century on account of the influence of the high Calvinism propagated by John Gill and John Brine (Oliver, 2006).

Wamble has similarly noted the practice of the Particular Baptists, calling it "the principle of division and amalgamation" (Wamble, 1955: 259-260). The principle was variously applied. In London large churches divided into two or more congregations or churches. The General Assembly of 1689 advised small labouring churches which lacked an adequate ministry to amalgamate when distance permitted. "Briefly stated, the principle of division and amalgamation was: distance permitting and ministerial needs demanding, small churches should unite; distance hindering and ministerial provisions permitting, large churches should divide."

The "meeting in one place" emphasis of Benjamin Keach was to have an effect in a different direction, namely, in the number of pastors needed in the church. As things stood, Keach did not believe in the validity of ruling elders. When there was only one congregation in one church, the need for more than one pastor was greatly minimized. This was heightened by the third area of difference in Keach's ecclesiology, namely, the confounding of duties of the elders and deacons. To be fair, it is to be noted that Keach did allow for the possibility of having more than one pastor in a church. In his book, "The Glory of a True Church, and its Discipline Display'd", he wrote (Dever, 2001: 65):

> A Church thus constituted ought forthwith to choose them a Pastor, Elder or Elders, and Deacons, (we reading of no other Officers, or Offices abiding in the Church) and what kind of Men they ought to be, and how qualified, is laid down by *Paul* to *Timothy*, and to *Titus*. Moreover, they are to take special care, that both Bishops, Overseers, or Elders, as well as the Deacons, have in some competent manner all those Qualifications ... Therefore such are very disorderly Churches who have no Pastor or Pastors ordained, they acting not according to the Rule of the Gospel, having something wanting.

As he proceeded in the book, Keach seemed to countenance a singular pastor or elder in a church, for he used expressions such as "Of the work of a Pastor, Bishop, or Overseer", "The work of a Pastor is

185

to preach the Word of Christ", "A Pastor is to visit his Flock", "Of the Duty of Church-Members to their Pastor", church members "ought to obey their Pastor or Elder", "the Elder and two or three more Persons may receive an account of his or her Faith" in the admittance of a new member, an offending brother to be admonished by "whether the Elder, or Member", and "the Elder solemnly proceeds and declares in the Name of the Lord Jesus" the excommunication (Dever, 2001: 66, 67, 68, 70, 72, 77). When Keach discussed the case of a sinning pastor who needed to be removed from office, he quoted from an unnamed source (probably Isaac Chauncy, who was quoted elsewhere in the book), and added (Dever, 2001: 77):

> Yet no doubt, the Church may Suspend him from Communion, & exercising of his Office presently, upon his being fully Convicted. But seeing in the multitude of Counsel there is safety, sure no Church would so proceed without the advice of the *Presbytery*, or of a Sister-*Church* at least.

This is where Keach's system fails. At least two other men would be needed to constitute the presbytery, to deal with the dismissal of the pastor, which would be quite impossible to find in a church that did not believe in having ruling elders. Keach, it must be remembered, believed that "ordinarily" the church should meet as one congregation in one place, a situation in which the need for more than one pastor is not so pressing. If there is only a single pastor, with no ruling elders, how is there going to be a presbytery?

If Keach was not stifled in his mission-mindedness but, instead, was active in church planting, how did he overcome the need for preachers to help him? He believed in the cultivation of "gifted brethren" and "teachers" in the church who were not elders. Keach considered a church amiss (Dever, 2001: 84):

> When Gifted Brethren are not duely encouraged: First privately to exercise their Gifts; and being in time approved, called forth to Preach or Exercise in the Church: And when encouragement is not given to bestow Learning also upon them, for their better Accomplishment. What will become of the Churches in time to come, if this be not prevented with speed?

It seems that these "gifted brethren" were the same as the "teachers" recognized in the church who, nevertheless, were not pastors or elders. Keach listed the first duty of church members to their pastor as (Dever, 2001: 67):

'Tis the Duty of every Member to pray for their Pastor and Teachers ... They that neglect this Duty seem not to care either for their Minister, or their own Souls, or whether Sinners be converted, and the Church edified or not. They pray for their daily Bread, and will they not pray to have the Bread of Life plentifully broken to them?

It is noticeable that Keach required members to pray for their "Pastor and Teachers", and then lapsed immediately into speaking of "their Minister" only. To Keach, the "teachers" are helpers of the pastor in teaching. Together, they are the "ministers" given by Christ to the church. The pastor teaches and rules by virtue of his gifts and office. The teachers only teach by virtue of their gifts, and gifts are to be used to the profit of the church and the good of sinners. The distinctions between the pastor and the teachers are delineated in detail in Keach's book, "An Exposition of the Parables, and Express Similitudes of Our Lord and Saviour Jesus Christ" (Keach, 1974: 634-642), and are referred to in various parts of that work (Keach, 1974: 267, 271, 470, 512, 513, etc.). In 1862, C. H. Spurgeon, a successor to the pulpit of Keach, looked over the history of the church and discovered that Keach had laboured under the title of Teacher during the pastorate of William Rider. In the pastorate of Keach, the church elected Benjamin Stinton to assist as a Teacher. On the removal of Keach, Stinton succeeded to the pastorate, and the church was spared the misery of long remaining without a pastor, or seeking some unknown person from abroad (Murray, Vol. 2, 1973: 77).

The main points of Keach's ecclesiology are summarized before proceeding further: (i) there should "ordinarily" be one congregation only in each church, meeting in one place; (ii) while allowing for the possibility of having more than one pastor, only one pastor is expected to be appointed, to teach and rule over the church; (iii) it is not biblically valid to have ruling elders; and (iv) "teachers" or "gifted brethren" should be tested and approved by the church to help the pastor in teaching. Of interest to us is the fact that Keach considered the deacons to be the "helps in government", in contrast to other Particular Baptists as well as John Owen (1976, Vol. 15:

505; Vol. 16: 111), who regarded these as ruling elders. Said Keach (1974: 513):

> Moreover, the deacons are to be helps in government. Some think Paul calls the deacons elders, when he speaks of "elders, that rule well," 1 Tim. v. 17, (as our annotators observe) though others judge he means ministers who are aged, and not able to preach the word, yet capable to help in ruling or governing the church; but some others think there were men ordained elders, that were not gifted to preach, but to be helpful in discipline, or in the government of the church; but we read neither of their qualifications, or how to be chosen (nor of their peculiar work, distinct from pastors, nor any such elders chosen in any particular church in the apostles' days) can see no ground for any such an office, or officers in the church.

It is seen here not only the denial of the validity of the ruling elder's office but also the affirmation of deacons performing the function of ruling, albeit doing it with, and under the direction of, the elders. This is in addition to their main tasks, which are (Keach, 1974: 512): "(1.) To see the Lord's table be provided for. (2.) To see the poor's table be provided for, and (3.) the minister or pastor's table also." This confutation of the work of ruling with the work of serving, that is, the confutation of the elder's function with those of the deacon's, was to lead to the situation of single-pastor-and-multiple-deacons seen in many Baptist churches in later days.

5.3 DEPARTURE IN THE 18TH CENTURY AND BEYOND

Benjamin Keach was not as influential among the Particular Baptists as he is portrayed to be today. His ecclesiology contained elements at variance with the Independency held by the vast majority of the Particular Baptists. These elements were to drive those who adopted his view to a position that resembled that of the General Baptists. In fact, it may be shown that Keach's ecclesiology constituted a major example (apart from the issue of the laying on of hands) of his "mix theology" which straddled the boundary that divided the Particular

Baptists and the General Baptists. Although the influence of Keach's ecclesiology in the Particular Baptist camp was small, it became quite significant from the mid-18th century because of the presence of the General Baptists alongside those who shared a similar view of church government with Keach. The influence was to gain momentum down the centuries to such an extent that, today, differences in ecclesiology among the Reformed Baptists constitute a bone of contention.

5.3.1 Benjamin Keach and the General Baptists

In Chapter 1, it is noted that the origin of the General Baptists may be traced to Thomas Helwys who separated from John Smyth. The cause of the separation was that Helwys believed their baptism, which arose from the self-baptism of Smyth, was valid, while Smyth had become convinced that he was too hasty in his self-baptism and now chose to be re-baptised by the Waterlander Mennonites. By the time Helwys led his congregation to return to England he had, together with Smyth, adopted the Arminianism of the Waterlanders. He had also adopted Smyth's view of the eldership, namely that pastors, teachers and elders were indistinguishable, and that every congregation should have a plurality of these officers (Haykin, 1996: 22-25). These had been the reasons for his separation from the Separatist congregation pastored by Francis Johnson in Amsterdam. The third cause of dispute with Johnson was the question of whether contributions could be made to the treasury of the church by non-members (Fiddes, 2010: 56).

During the 1650s, the General Baptists believed in a three-fold ministry consisting of messengers, elders or pastors, and deacons. The messenger was chosen by the churches and had a ministry beyond the local church and was the one who ordained the pastor chosen by the local congregation. In those days it was widely held that ministers ought to have an occupation that would, at least partly, provide for their material needs (White, 1996: 46). The General Baptist Confession of Faith of 1660 states this as follows (Lumpkin, 1969: 229-230):

> XV. That the Elders or Pastors which God hath appointed to oversee, and feed his Church (constituted as aforesaid) are such, who first being of the number of Disciples, shall in time appear to be *vigilant, sober, of good behaviour,*

*given to hospitality, apt to teach, &c. not greedy of filthy
lucre* (as too many National Ministers are) *but patient;
not a brawler, not covetous, &c.* and as such chose, and
ordained to office (according to the order of Scripture,
Acts 14.23.) who are to feed the flock with meat in due
season, and in much love to rule over them, with all care,
seeking after such as go astray; but as for all such who
labour to feed themselves with the fat, more than to feed
the flock, *Ezek.* 34. 2, 3. seeking more after theirs, than
them, expresly [sic.] contrary to the practise of the Ministers of old, who said, *we seek not yours, but you, 2 Cor.*
12. 14. All such we utterly deny, and hereby bear our
continued Testimony against, *Ezek.* 34.

XVI. That the Ministers of Christ, that have freely received from God, ought freely to Minister to others, *1
Cor.* 9. 17. and that such who have spiritual things,
freely Ministered unto them, ought freely to communicate necessary things to the Ministers, (upon the account
of their charge) *1 Cor.* 9. 11 *Gal.* 6.6. And as for Tyths,
or any forced Maintenance, we utterly deny to be the
Maintenance of Gospel Ministers.

In 1679, a group of General Baptists, led by Thomas Monk, put
out a Confession called the Orthodox Creed. Again, the officers of
the church are asserted as three, namely "Bishops, or Messengers;
and Elders, or Pastors; and Deacons, or Overseers of the poor". It
was now felt that the time for a tent-making ministry had passed
for, like the Particular Baptists, it was agreed that the pastors and
messengers should be supported fully (White, 1996: 121). This is
stated as follows in the Orthodox Creed (Lumpkin, 1969: 320):

... the bisops [sic.] and elders so chosen, and ordained,
to the work of God, ought to be enabled and capacitated
thereunto, by a sufficient and honourable maintenance
of the people that chose them, answerable to the dignity
of their places, and charge committed to them, without
which they cannot discharge their duty, as they ought to
do, in studying to divide the word of God aright ...

It is to be noted that, by this time, Benjamin Keach had turned
Calvinist and was actively involved in the life of the Particular Bap-

tists. Keach, however, had not cut off ties completely with the General Baptists. His commitment to the laying on of hands seemed to make him amenable to fellowship with General Baptist churches (White, 1996: 124). Keach's view of the eldership was virtually the same as that of the General Baptists, the only difference being that he considered the term "bishop" to be equivalent to "elder" and "pastor". Said Keach in his book "The Glory Of A True Church, And Its Discipline Display'd" (Dever, 2001: 65):

> A Church ... constituted ought ... to choose them a Pastor, Elder or Elders, and Deacons, (we reading of no other Officers, or Offices abiding in the Church) and what kind of Men they ought to be, and how qualified, is laid down by *Paul* to *Timothy*, and to *Titus*. Moreover, they are to take special care, that both Bishops, Overseers, or Elders, as well as the Deacons, have in some competent manner all those Qualifications; and after in a Day of solemn Prayer and Fasting, that they have elected them, (whether Pastor, &c., or Deacons) and they accepting the Office, must be ordained with Prayer, and laying on of Hands of the Eldership; being first prov'd, and found meet and fit Persons for so Sacred an Office ...

Keach did not discuss inter-church relationships in his book of 1697. He did not seem to have problems with the view of inter-church relationships propounded in the Chapter 26, Articles 14 and 15, of the 1689 Confession. He was one of the thirty-seven men who signed in assent of the Confession on behalf of the "upwards of, one hundred BAPTIZED Churches, in England and Wales" represented at the General Assembly of 1689. He, therefore, did not hold to the General Baptists' idea of the Messenger or Bishop who served a grouping of otherwise autonomous churches. Of interest is the fact that, in the Orthodox Creed, the deacon is referred to as an overseer – "*Bishops, or Messengers; and Elders, or Pastors; and Deacons, or Overseers of the poor" (Lumpkin, 1969: 319). The word "Bishop" is marked with an asterisk which pointed to the footnote, "Or overseer, or shepherd". The next mention of "bishop*" in the same article of the Creed is again marked with an asterisk, this time after the word. The Creed seems to indicate that, just as the Messenger or Bishop is the overseer or shepherd over the grouping of churches, so also the deacons were overseers or shepherds in their respective churches. It is obvious that one duty of deacons is to take care of the needs of the poor, but why call them "overseers of the poor"? Was this an indication that they were regarded as "helps in government" in the same way that Keach used the term for deacons? If so, this is another similarity between Keach and the General Baptists.

During the hymn-singing controversy, the Particular Baptist General Assembly of 1692 appointed seven men to arbitrate. Keach's main antagonist was Isaac Marlow, a member of his own church who had seceded with a number of others over the issue to form another church. More serious than the clash with Marlow was the fact that Keach had antagonized William Kiffin and three other leading men who were on the same side as Marlow in the controversy. In response to the findings of the seven-men committee, Kiffin *et al.* were willing to meet up with Keach for "a private Friendly Conference" with the view that "we might mutually have examined in a Spirit of Love and Meekness, where any weakness or miscarriage had lain on both sides, and in a Christian way made our Acknowledgments to each other." A summons came "from the Church whereof Mr. *Benjamin Keach* is Elder, delivered to us by two Messengers, with a Letter wherein we were expresly [sic.] required to appear before them, to make good our Reflections against Mr. *Keach*, Printed in our Reply to his Book." In response, Kiffin *et al.* sent a letter to these men, suggesting that they appointed four persons, and Kiffin *et al.* appointed four also, to meet at a convenient time agreed by both sides. These men would then examine both books written by the two sides, Kiffin *et al.* being willing to acknowledge any weakness and failing if shown, "hoping their Elder (Mr. *Benjamin Keach*) would do the like." Receiving no reply, a copy of the letter was sent again. This time, a response came "which was Signed by Four Persons, who called themselves Helps in Government; who therein did not only declare therewith that Churches absolute rejecting of our Proposal aforesaid, but also did therein reflect upon us" (Kiffin *et al.*, 1692).

A brief account of what transpired between the two sides has been given. The relevant passages quoted show that Keach was the sole elder of his church, and also that the four persons who called themselves "Helps in Government" could not be elders but were probably deacons. Keach, it must be remembered, did not believe in having ruling elders. Kiffin *et al.* appeared nonplussed with these men who called themselves "Helps in Government". They would be since they were themselves pastors who were now confronted by these "Helps in Government". Kiffin was the pastor of the Devonshire Square church, George Barrett was the pastor of the Mile End Green church, Robert Steed was the co-pastor with Hanserd Knollys in the Broken Wharf church, and Edward Man was the pastor of the Houndsditch church, all of whom had signed to affirm the 1689 Confession (Narrative, 1689). The difficulty faced by Keach in not having other elders to help him in a crisis like that is obvious.

How widespread was Keach's view of the eldership held by other Particular Baptists? In Chapter 4, the question has been answered by taking a bird's-eye view of the issue, and it is seen that the John Owen system was dominant among the Particular Baptists. When one tries to answer the same question from the particularistic viewpoint, one is hard-pressed to find individuals who definitely held to Keach's view. In Chapter 4, reference is made to the Bampton church, Devon, which appointed John Ball as the ruling elder in 1690. The Bampton Church Book also shows that in 1703, James Murch was ordained as pastor with the assistance of Andrew Gifford and Richard Sampson. After the ordination of Murch and two deacons, it was noted that (Bampton CB: 46):

> Diverse members of the neighbouring Churs being present
> the ordination of Bro: Frost a ruling Elder being proposed
> but both Bro: Gifford and Sampson declined it as having
> noe satisfaction in the thing so that it was concluded to
> be left as it was.

Renihan (1998: 203) takes this as showing that Gifford and Sampson were in disagreement with the host church on the validity of the ruling elder's office. Renihan also regards the South Wales Association, the Bampton church in Devon and the Broadmead church in Bristol as unusual in holding to the validity of ruling elders. He suggests that the relative geographic proximity indicates that the idea was more accepted in the west than in the rest of the country, although Andrew Gifford was the pastor of the other Particular Baptist church in Bristol and Sampson was pastor in Exeter, Devon – both also in the West.

Is Renihan's assessment right? It has been shown in Chapter 4 that Owen's view of the eldership was all-pervasive among the Particular Baptists throughout the country. According to Ivimey (II: 138ff.), Richard Sampson was sent from his church in Plymouth to be trained under a Mr. Thomas in Bristol, in 1689. Mr. Thomas was an ejected Nonconformist Baptist pastor who had been training men for the ministry. This was before the Bristol Academy began to operate under Bernard Foskett in 1720, based in the Broadmead open-communion church in Bristol. Sampson moved to Exeter in 1692 and would have been ordained pastor of the church there, for he attended the General Assembly in London as their minister in 1692. Andrew Gifford (1641-1679) was the older man of the two. He was a member of the Pithay closed-communion church in Bristol. Baptized in 1659, he began itinerant preaching for sixteen years before being appointed to be the pastor of the church in 1677 "by the laying on of hands of brother Dyk : and brother Nehemiah Cox, Elders in London, with fasting and prayer in the church". Gifford was active in the Western Association (Ivimey, II: 546). The West Country was the stronghold of the view of eldership spelled out in the meeting of the South Wales Association in August 1654, in which it was declared (White, 1971-7, Part I: 11), that "the ruling elder's, or helping office is, to oversee the lives and manners of men: to whom also double honour is due, 1 Tim. 5.17; Ro.12.8. He also must take care of God's house, Heb.13.17. 1 Tim. 3.5." The churches in Devon, including those at Tiverton and Bampton, all held to this view of eldership. The Broadmead church in Bristol also held to this view, and was to become greatly influential, having close fellowship with churches in South Wales as far back as the 1640s (Hayden, 2006: 92). It would be extremely odd that the two men, and their churches, held to a different view of eldership while interacting closely with the other Particular Baptist churches. When the ordination of Brother Frost, a ruling elder, was proposed, why did Gifford and Sampson have "noe satisfaction in the thing"? Was it because they did not agree with the office of ruling elder, or was it because they had some misgivings concerning the ordination of the proposed man on that day? If it is the former, Gifford and Sampson would be the only two men known definitely to hold to Keach's view of the eldership. There is the possibility, however, that Gifford and Sampson had "noe satisfaction in the thing" because the ordination of the ruling elder was suddenly raised, and not planned – it was "proposed" on the day itself. It was normal in those days for the ordination of church officers to be held considerably later after election into office. (For examples, see the Broadmead Church Book, Underhill, 1847: 197, 383, 499-500, and Collins, 1702: 58.) The decision made on the previous Lord's Day did not include the ordination of the ruling elder (Bampton CB: 46):

> After publique worship next thursday being appointed a
> day of fasting and prayer for the soleim ordination of
> Pastour and deacons aggreed that the Pastour should be
> publiquely ordained before the whole assembly [and] the
> deacons in the Church only.

Renihan engages in a species of "arguing from silence" to support his assertion that "The majority of the writers and churches did
not recognize a distinct office of ruling elder" (Renihan, 1998: 200).
In an ordination sermon, Coxe said this concerning the Elders, Bishops, Overseers, Pastors and Teachers: "it is evident the Holy Ghost
intends no distinction, or preeminence of Office among those that
bear these Characters, by any of these different Terms" (Coxe, 1681:
18). Coxe's exact words are to be noted; he said, "no distinction,
or preeminence *of Office*" [emphasis added]. This was the view of
John Owen. In so far as the office is concerned, and therefore the
power and authority connected with it, all elders are equal. A priority or preeminence of one elder among the elders in a church is
not to be confused with a difference in office power. Arguing against
Episcopacy, Owen said (16: 45-46):

> Those whose names are the same, equally common and
> applicable unto them all, whose function is the same,
> whose qualifications and characters are the same, whose
> duties, account, and reward are the same, concerning
> whom there is in no one place of Scripture the least men-
> tion of inequality, disparity, or preference in office among
> them, they are essentially and every way the same. That
> thus it is with the elders and bishops in the Scripture can-
> not modestly be denied.
>
> I do acknowledge, that where a church is greatly increased,
> so as that there is a necessity of *many elders* in it for its
> instruction and rule, decency and order do require that
> one of them do, in the management of all church-affairs,
> preside, to guide and direct the way and manner thereof
> ...
>
> I shall never oppose this *order*, but rather desire to see
> it in practice, – namely, that particular churches were
> of such an extent as necessarily to require *many elders*,
> both teaching and ruling, for their instruction and gov-

ernment; for the better observation of order and decency in the public assemblies ... that among these elders one should be chosen by themselves, with the consent of the church, not into a new order, not into a degree of authority above his brethren, but only unto his part of the common work in a peculiar manner, which requires some kind of precedency. ... only the work and duty of it is cast into such an order as the very light of nature doth require.

But there is not any intimation in the Scripture of the least imparity or inequality, in order, degree, or authority, among officers of the same sort, whether extraordinary or ordinary. The apostles were all equal; so were the evangelists, so were elders or bishops, and so were deacons also .... Howbeit it is evident that in all their assemblies they had one who did preside in the manner before described; which seems, among the apostles, to have been the prerogative of Peter.
[Emphasis original.]

Nehemiah Coxe was expressing precisely Owen's view. One would have wished that Coxe had said something about ruling elders, so that all controversies about what he meant were put to rest. Coxe, however, had not said anything about ruling elders, but expressed those points that coincided with Owen's view of the eldership: the office is one, all who occupy that office are equal. Since he did not explicitly deny the validity of ruling elders, it is hazardous to claim that he held to Keach's view of the eldership. It is to be noted that Coxe was preaching at the ordination of one elder and two or more deacons, as the title of the published sermon shows. That elder happened to be a teaching one, called the Pastor, who preaches regularly: "Remember that your Pastor is *the Minister of Christ,* one that dispenseth the Mysteries of God to you in his Name" (Coxe, 1681: 63).

Renihan (1998: 200-201) makes much of the fact that Nehemiah Coxe and William Collins "were solemnly ordained pastors or elders in this church." Similarly, in the Devonshire Square church, London, Richard Adams was ordained into "sayd worke & office of an elder amongst them, in conjunction wth Bro. Wm Kiffin." Likewise, in 1706, when Mark Key was ordained into office with him, Adams was instructed to say "...my Bro: Mark Key is by this church appointed or ordained a joynt elder Pastor or overseer wth my self over her." These three instances constitute one single argument, namely, that they were co-pastors, with no pre-eminence of one over the other and, by inference from silence, this was a denial of the validity of ruling elders. It has been noted that being co-pastors did not mean a denial of the validity of ruling elders, nor any contradiction with the view of Owen that all the elders are equal in power in the same office. In the case of Knollys, there is an explicit declaration of belief in the priority of one elder over the others without in any way contradicting the equality in office-power, just as in Owen. It has been noted that in Knollys's church, he was "the Pastor" while Robert Steed was his co-pastor. In the "Last Legacy to the Church", Knollys began with the words, "To the Church whereof I am Pastor", and referred to himself as "your very aged Pastor". In the same letter, he referred to Steed as "my reverend and beloved brother Steed" and "our honoured and beloved Elder". There were others in the church who were "ministering brethren who are helps in government" (Knollys, 1812: 59, 66). Steed and Knollys both signed their names and indicated themselves as "Pastor" of the Broken Wharf church, to affirm the 1689 Confession at the General Assembly of that year (Narrative, 1689). Thus, it can be seen that Steed was a pastor and, therefore, an elder of the church, while Knollys was clearly the leading elder. There were other men called "helps in government" who were elders, as shown in the church records (as has been shown in the previous chapter).

Most churches had only one pastor, or teaching elder, as they were unable to support more than one. As noted repeatedly, even the single pastor had often to supplement his income by other work. At a time when there was controversy over whether men called to the ministry should receive formal training or simply rely on the gifts of the Spirit, Hercules Collins was particularly concerned about the recognition, training, and ordination of pastors, saying (Collins, 1702: 13):

> Suppose that God should take away but a few Ministers out of some Churches in the City of London, **where there is but one Gift in a Church ordinarily in Exercise,** what a loss might such be at in an Eye of Reason? Therefore it is greatly desired, and would be a very glorious Work, if all the Elders of the Church in every City in England would

not only be concern'd in their own particular Congregation
for a future Ministry, but that the several Elders would set
apart some time every Week for the instructing young Men,
Members of Churches, inclin'd to Divine Studies; and so
in the Country where two or three Churches are not far
asunder, that all their Elders would agree to meet once a
Month, or oftner, to hear the Gifts that God hath given
their Churches.
[Italics original. Emphasis in bold added.]

As in the "Ordination Sermon" of Nehemiah Coxe referred to above, the absence of mention of ruling elders does not necessarily imply the denial of the validity of ruling elders. In the case of Knollys's church where there were ruling elders, Knollys did not refer to them in his exposition on the "Gospel-Ministry" (Knollys, 1681: 55-69). Hercules Collins was saying that, "ordinarily", there was only one pastor in the church. He was expounding on the call to the ministry of the Word, not on the government of the church. Keeping to the "Rule of Explicit Mention", it would not be possible to say whether or not Collins believed in having ruling elders. That he did was highly likely because of his heavy reliance on Owen's book, "A Brief Instruction in the Worship of God and Discipline of the Churches of the New Testament", in his short tract, "Some Reasons for Separation from the Communion of the Church of England". This has been seen in Chapter 4 of the present work. Further support for the presence of ruling elders in Collins's church is found in E. F. Kevan's book, "London's Oldest Baptist Church" (1933). (This writer has no access to the church books, and would not claim proof here.) Writing from the perspective of the 20th century, when the church had settled into the single-pastor-and-multiple-deacons situation, Kevan emphasized the offices of the pastor and the deacons and played down the existence of the ruling elders. He recorded the ordination of deacons (Kevan, 1933: 92-93), but not that of elders. He listed "deacons" in the Index (Kevan, 1933: 190), but not "elders". He praised the decisions, and magnified the ministry, of the deacons (Kevan, 1933: 50, 82, 94, 106, 109, 111, 122, 144, 168, 185), but made a passing reference to a member who removed to America and became a "ruling elder" in the church there (Kevan, 1933: 58). Definite mentions of the existence of elders other than the pastor are found in connection with the church dividing its members according to four districts for the purpose of monthly visitation by the elders. Said Kevan (1933: 83, 147): "This custom and system of visitation of members by elders continued without break [from 1663] right on to the time of removal from Commercial Street to Walthamstow 1909-1914." When Collins indicated that "ordinarily" there was one pastor in each church, he was referring to the "teaching elder" or "pastor", in the Owenian sense. Owen countenanced only one pastor, or teaching elder, in a church ordinarily. Said Owen (1976, Vol. 16: 105, 141):

> It is certain that the order very early observed in the church was one pastor ... with many elders assisting in rule and teaching, and deacons ministering in the things of this life ...

> Whereas there may be, and ofttimes is, but one teaching-elder, pastor, or teacher in a church, upon his death or removal it is the work and duty of these [ruling] elders *to preserve the church in peace and unity*, to take care of the continuation of its assemblies, to prevent irregularities in any persons or parties among them, and to go before, to direct and guide the church in the call and choice of some other meet person or persons in the room of the deceased or removed.
> [Emphasis original.]

Not only was one pastor *ordinarily* expected in one church, there were ruling elders whose duties included "to go before, to direct and guide the church in the call and choice" of a replacement pastor. The elders truly ruled, or governed, the church. No democratic congregationalism was hinted at.

Renihan is mistaken in assuming that being co-pastors in the same church necessarily meant a rejection of the validity of ruling elders. Renihan is mistaken also in assuming that having an equality of office-power necessarily rules out the possibility of pre-eminence or leadership in one of the elders. Renihan includes an incident in Kensworth, Bedfordshire, in 1688, in which three men were chosen "jointly and equally to offitiate in the room of [deceased pastor] Brother Hayward in breaking bread, and other administration of ordinances, and the church did at the same time agree to provide and mainetaine all, at there one charge" (Renihan, 1998: 201). These words were quoted to support the idea of equality among the elders.

However, the situation was not quite like that, for Renihan had left out the words that followed those already quoted. Given below is the fuller account of the records (Tibbutt, 1972:16):

> ... jointly and equally to offitiate in the room of [deceased pastor] Brother Hayward in breaking bread, and other administration of ordinances, and the church did at the same time agree to provide and mainetaine all, at there one charge, and did agree to give a sufficient maine-taineance to a preaching brother to serve the church and to goe from meeting to meeting, and to every place the church shall apoint him within this congregation. November 1688.

> Brother Harding aforesaid did accept of the office of eldership and did break bread with the church January 1688/9 and desire the church to chuse others to officiat in his office of a decon.

From this, it can be seen that the preaching elder who was supported full-time, namely, Brother Harding, had the pre-eminence in that he took over the administration of the ordinances and the preaching in the different meeting places, from the other three elders. He replaced the deceased Brother Hayward as pastor. By 1694, two of the elders had died or ceased to be elders, leaving only Brother Finch and Brother Harding as the elders remaining. By May of that year, Brother Finch died. The church records say (Tibbutt, 1972: 17):

> After the death of our dear Brother Finch, one of the elders of this our congregation of the church of Kinsworth, our dear brother Harding being onely left alone in the office of the eldershead, he did desire some brother or brethren as the church should think fit, should bee chosen to asist him, because the largnes of the congregation and the great distance of meeting caused the work to ly heavy upon him. The church ... did elect and charge Brother Britaine to asist Brother Harding ...

> Brother Britaine hath excepted of the office of eldership and did break bread with the church as an elder, and hath aminerstred other ordinances to the great satisfaction of the church, 1694.

It can be seen from this that Brother Harding remained the supported elder, while Brother Britaine was appointed an elder to assist him, whose main task was to administer the Lord's Supper, although also administering "other ordinances", which were, presumably, baptism and preaching the word of God. Far from supporting the type of "equality" in the eldership claimed by Renihan, the practice of the Kensworth church was an example of the outworking of the Owen-type eldership.

Concluding this section, it is to be noted that no hard evidence has been found of anyone outside Keach's church who held to his view of the eldership. It is an unfounded claim that "the majority of the writers and churches did not recognize a distinct office of ruling elder", and that "the majority of the Particular Baptists were committed to a plurality and parity of elders in their churches" (Renihan, 1998: 200, 205). It is a gross understatement to claim that "a small number of the churches made a distinction between teaching and ruling elders" (Renihan, 1998: 203, 238). Keach was a virtual loner who carried his "mixed theology" of the laying on of hands and the single-pastor-and-multiple-deacons system of church government from his General Baptist background into his new-found Particular Baptist home.

5.3.2 Particular Baptist Ecclesiology after Keach

By the time of Benjamin Keach's death in 1704, at the age of sixty-eight, Owen's ecclesiology (minus infant baptism) was held across-the-board by the Particular Baptists. This is confirmed by the reliable observation of Isaac Watts (1674-1748). It has been noted, above, that Watts was actively involved in the General Body of the Three Denominations, begun in 1727. The overall testimony to the competency and reliability of Watts's personal knowledge of the general condition of the churches and the practice of the Particular Baptists is unassailable. Renihan (1998: 134-135), however, has chosen to question the reliability of Watts's testimony. Said Renihan about Watts, "While he may have been intimately acquainted with the practices of the Baptists, he may also have been merely a casual observer." Having been alerted to the testimony of Watts, Renihan missed the opportunity of following up on the lead. In contrast, Milner's assessment of Watts is as follows (Milner, 1845: 439):

Dr. Watts was an attentive observer of the signs of the times; not only did the spiritual prosperity of his own people lie near his heart, but his expansive charity led to a lively concern for the improvement of others; and he could not witness symptoms of degeneracy, without attempting to correct the evil and avert the calamity.

Watts was not only competent in his own right, but had first hand knowledge of the Particular Baptists. It was even rumoured that a certain Dr. Gibbons had claimed Dr. Watts as saying, before his death, "that he wished infant baptism was laid aside". That seemed to convey the impression that Watts had dropped infant baptism and had perhaps embraced the Baptist position. To correct that wrong impression, Dr. Gibbons wrote to explain the actual situation "with the strictest regard to truth, and without the least tincture of partiality". Dr. Gibbons continued (Milner, 1845: 485):

The doctor and myself were one day, perhaps two or three years before his decease, in a free converse together, when (I cannot recollect how the subject was introduced) he expressed himself to this purpose: that he had sometimes thought of a compromise with our Baptist brethren, by their giving up their mode of baptism, immersion, on the one side, and our giving up the baptism of infants on the other, as he had not observed any benefit arising from the administration of the ordinance to them. This was the whole, from what I remember, the doctor said upon the point; which in my opinion, falls much short of a declaration from him, that he wished ["]infant baptism to be laid aside." It would be highly desirable, for the sake of peace and the manifestation of Christian charity, if the Baptists and Independents were to merge into one body, as there is no difference between them as to doctrine or discipline, but upon the one point of baptism: Dr. Watts would, it appears, have conceded the baptism of *infants,* if the other party would have given up the *immersion* of adults ...

It can be seen here Dr. Gibbons saying that Watts thought it highly desirable "if the Baptists and Independents were to merge into one body, as there is no difference between them as to doctrine or discipline, but upon the one point of baptism". This was "two or three years before his decease", which would be in 1745 or 1746. That Watts himself – not just what Dr. Gibbons thought of him – saw no difference between the Baptists and Independents "as to doctrine and discipline", baptism excepted, may be seen from the letter he wrote to his brother Enoch, some time in 1702. The letter was undated, but Milner placed it at the end of a number of letters which were dated and arranged chronologically at about that time. Concerning the Anabaptists "this day in England" Watts said (Milner, 1845: 186, 193):

> They differ not from Calvinists in their doctrine, unless in the article of infant baptism. They generally deny any children to be in the covenant of grace, and so deny the seal of the covenant to them. They deny baptism by sprinkling to be real and true baptism. In church government [they are] generally Independents.

According to Isaac Watts, the Particular Baptists were "generally Independents". The Particular Baptists were clearly distinguished from the General Baptists who, by the 1740s, were characterized by heterodoxy (Milner, 1845: 658). What were the characteristics of Independency? According to Watts (Milner, 1845: 196-197):

> [T]he generality of Independents follow rather Dr. Owen's notions; their tenets are such as these: 1st, That the power of church government resides in the pastors and elders of every particular church, and that it is the duty of the people to consent; and, [2nd,] nevertheless, because every act in a church is a church act, they never do any thing without the consent of the people, though they receive no new authority by the people's consenting. 3d, They generally think a minister not to be ordained but to a particular church, though many of them now think that, by virtue of communion of churches, he may preach authoritatively, and administer the ordinances to other churches upon extraordinary occasions. 4th, That it is not absolutely necessary that a minister be ordained by the imposition of hands of other ministers, but only requisite that other ministers should be there present as advisers and assistants when he is ordained by the church;

that is, set apart by their choice, his acceptance, mutual fasting and prayer. 5th, They generally hold more to the doctrine of Calvin than Presbyterians do. 6th, They think it not sufficient ground to be admitted a member, if the person be only examined as to his doctrinal knowledge and sobriety of conversation; but they require with all some hints, or means, or evidences of the work of grace on their souls, to be professed by them, and that not only to the minister but to the elders also, who are joint rulers in the church. Though this profession of some of their experience is generally made first to the minister, either by word or writing, but the elders always hear it, and are satisfied before the person is admitted a member. 7th, These relations, which the Independents require, are not (as some think) of the word or scripture, or time, or place, or sermon, by which they were converted; for very few can tell this ; but only they discourse and examine them a little of the way of their conviction of sin, of their being brought to know Christ; or at least ask them what evidences they can give why they hope they are true believers, and try to search whether there be sincerity in the heart, as much as may be found by outward profession, that they may, as much as in them lies, exclude hypocrites.

Thus it is seen that John Owen's view of church government was clearly the dominant one among the Particular Baptists up to at least the middle of the 18th century, when Watts expressed to Dr. Gibbons his wish that "infant baptism be laid aside". Benjamin Keach's son, Elias, was about the only person known to definitely hold to his father's view of church government. Elias went to America in 1686 and settled at Pennepek, or Pennepack (Jones, HG, 1869; Ivimey, II: 467-469). He arrived as a wild youth of nineteen, and for sport dressed like a minister of that time. Soon, invitations to preach came to him. While attempting to preach, conviction seized him. To those gathered he confessed his imposture. Converted on that occasion, he sought baptism. He later went forth as an evangelist and was known to have planted two churches in Pennsylvania. He married the daughter of Chief Justice Moore of Pennsylvania, before returning to London in 1692, and assumed the pastorate of the Tallow

Chandler's Hall Church. In 1697, he concurred with his father to publish a set of articles of faith in the name of his church. These articles were almost exactly the 1689 Confession, with the addition of articles on hymn-singing and the laying on of hands upon baptized believers (Lumpkin, 1969: 348). Elias Keach died in October 27, 1699, at the age of thirty-four (Ivimey, III: 534). (The year of death is stated as 1701 in Ivimey, II: 470, the precise date not being mentioned.)

A hundred and fifty copies of the history of the Pennepek Baptist Church in Pennsylvania were published by Horatio Gates Jones in 1869. This published history of the church is of great interest for a number of reasons. First, it is seen that Elias Keach followed the pattern set by the Particular Baptists and Congregational Independents of England in establishing a number of congregations which were governed by the Pennepek church (Jones, HG, 1869: 6-7). The more than seven congregations of Pennsylvania and New Jersey "were regarded as general members of this Church", which were visited in circuit. During the absence of the pastor from any congregation, meetings for prayer and exhortation, called "meetings for conference", were held (Jones, HG, 1869: 8-9). It was at such "meetings for conference" that gifted brethren were discovered and trained up to help in preaching. Two "General Meetings" were appointed in a year at which all were expected to attend to hear the word preached and to partake of the Lord's table. In the spring it was held at Salem, and in the fall at Dublin or Burlington. At such General Meetings, ordinary church business was transacted. The record says, "As the number of baptized believers increased in places at a distance from Pennepek, it was considered best to form separate Churches." Second, it is seen that Elias Keach left the church he founded, after two years as its pastor, because of disagreement over the laying on of hands upon those newly baptized, as well as other doctrinal issues. The rite of laying on of hands was regarded as a matter of indifference by the church, and hence discontinued (Jones, HG, 1869: 10, 11). The Welsh Baptists in Pennsylvania, however, held tenaciously to the rite. Third, it is seen that ruling elders were appointed in the Pennepek church – "a species of officers which most of the early Baptist Churches of Pennsylvania, New Jersey, and Delaware had among them, as the early records show" (Jones, HG, 1869: 12). The overwhelming number of Baptists who had come from Wales seems to have influenced the Pennepek church, such that Elias Keach's denial of the office of the ruling elder did not hold sway (Jones, HG, 1869: 4, 12; Jones, HM, 1995). H. G. Jones went on to say:

> When this office was discontinued does not appear; but it is certain that it was not used in 1770. The latest mention of such is in a manuscript List of Members, for 1763, when William Marshall is named as the Ruling Elder.

In 1724 the Philadelphia Association, in a statement concerning the Sabbath, referred to "the Confession of Faith, set forth by the elders and brethren met in London, 1689, and owned by us". [In 1728, in response to a query on what course to take in choosing a ruling elder in the church, the answer was:

> We answer, that a church wanting ruling elders or deacons, as in other cases, should set a day apart, and by fasting and prayer, seek the guidance and direction of God, and then unanimously pitch upon one or more of their brethren to act upon trial in the office of ruling elder or deacon; and our judgment is, that persons called upon trial in the said offices, may act by authority of the church, with as full power as if completely qualified; but not so teaching elders or ministers of the word and ordinances.

In 1738, there was a query, "Whether a person, ordained by laying on of hands, for a ruling elder, who should afterwards be called by the church, by reason of his gifts, to the word and doctrine, must be again ordained by imposition of hands?" The answer given was in the affirmative. (Baptist History Homepage, last accessed Sep. 2025.)]

In 1742, the Association formally adopted a slightly modified version of the Confession, calling it the "Philadelphia Confession", which included two articles from Keach's Confession. One of these concerned the singing of Psalms, hymns, and spiritual songs as of "divine institution", and the other considered the imposition of hands upon baptized believers as "an ordinance of Christ". The Association omitted the Appendix of the original edition of the 1677 Confession, replacing it with "A Short Treatise Concerning a True and Orderly Gospel Church" in 1743, written by Benjamin Griffith. In this Appendix by Griffith, the validity of ruling elders is clearly affirmed (Dever, 2001: 98):

> Ruling elders are such persons as are endued with gifts
> to assist the pastor or teacher in the government of the
> church; it was a statute in Israel, Exo. 18. Deut. 1:9-
> 13. The works of teaching and ruling belong both to the
> pastor; but in case he be unable; or the work of ruling too
> great for him, God hath provided such for his assistance,
> and they are called ruling elders, 1 Tim. 5:17. helps, 1
> Cor. 12:28. governments, or he that ruleth, Rom. 12:8.

Returning to the situation in Britain, it is to be noted that upon
the death of Benjamin Keach in 1704, Benjamin Stinton, who had
married one of his daughters, became the pastor. During his tenure
as pastor, the church had quite settled into the single-pastor-and-
multiple-deacons situation, in which the deacons were the "helps in
government". When Stinton died, the church was divided over the
call of John Gill to be the pastor. Ninety members, including one
deacon, left with Gill, while one hundred and twenty-two members,
including six deacons, remained in the Goat Street premises (Ivimey,
Vol. III: 418). In May 1723, a number of those who had left returned
to join with Gill's church. John Gill (1697-1771) was a leading Particular Baptist in his day. He strongly rejected the suggestion of having a co-pastor to assist him, claiming (Ivimey, Vol. III: 451):

> That Christ gives *pastors* to churches is certain, but that
> he gives *co-pastors* is not so certain. A co-pastor is an
> officer the Scripture is entirely silent about, and which is
> much the same thing as if a woman should marry another
> man, while she is under the law, dominion, and power of
> her former husband ... I should not like a co-pastor to
> hang about my neck, nor an assistant to be dangling at
> my heels! [Italics original.]

John Gill was succeeded by John Rippon (1750-1836), and then
by C. H. Spurgeon (1834-1892). Spurgeon, serving as pastor at
the Metropolitan Tabernacle during a period of mighty revival, convinced his church of the biblical validity of the ruling elder's office.
The number of ruling elders appointed to meet the needs of the time
was about twenty-five! Spurgeon next convinced the church to have
his younger brother, James, appointed as assistant or co-pastor (Murray, Vol. 2, 1973: 75, 77). Spurgeon's valiant effort at restoring
the John Owen view of eldership was significant for, by that time,

many Particular Baptist churches had lapsed into the single-pastor-and-multiple-deacons situation. The factors leading to the lapse of many churches to the single-pastor-and-multiple deacons situation from the mid-18th century on will be discussed in Chapter 7. The influence of Keach's view was one of those factors. The development of this view of eldership has been traced up to the time of Spurgeon only because he was a successor of the pastorate in the same church. It is to be noted that Spurgeon ministered in the 19th century, which is far beyond the purview of the present work.

It has been noted that at least up to the mid-18th century, the Owen view of the eldership was predominant among the Particular Baptists. It has been noted also that in America, the Pennepek church founded by Elias Keach held to the validity of ruling elders, contrary to the view of its founder, right up to at least 1763. The Bristol Academy also exerted a tremendous influence upon the Particular Baptists throughout England and Wales in the 18th century, through its graduates who upheld the view of eldership of their *alma mater*, which was none other than that of John Owen. This has been noted in the previous chapter.

5.4   SUMMARY

Benjamin Keach was not as influential among the Particular Baptists as has been portrayed in recent literature. He was the most prolific writer among his peers, but his relationship with others was hampered by an irritable temper, probably brought about by ill-health. His combative personality and continuing interaction with the General Baptists irked the other Particular Baptists. His "mixed theology" vexed them as well. He was involved in all the controversies of his time, of which the most damaging – to himself and the Particular Baptist cause – was the hymn-singing controversy.

Keach's view on hymn-singing was to prevail among the Particular Baptists, not just because of the effort he expended in promulgating the practice, but also because Hanserd Knollys held to the same view in the controversy. William Kiffin was more influential than Keach in his days, while Knollys was the most influential of them all on account of his age, experience, and learning. While Keach's stature and influence have been magnified beyond reality in the recent literature, Knollys's true stature and influence have been unwittingly downplayed. Knollys's ecclesiology was the same as that of John Owen, in which preeminence is given to the pastor, or one of them if plural, in a presbytery which included ruling elders, who together occupy the same office of rule.

Benjamin Keach's view of church government, although similar to Owen's view in the fundamental principles, differed in the following points: (i) the denial of the validity of ruling elders; (ii) the discouragement of multiple congregations in any one church; (iii) the confounding of duties of the two remaining offices of the church, namely, those of elders and deacons. Keach's view was to lead to the single-pastor-and-multiple-deacons situation encountered in Baptist churches in later days.

Benjamin Keach's formative years were spent among the General Baptists. He continued to have close interaction with them even after becoming strongly Calvinistic. His "mixed theology" included not only the laying on of hands on the newly baptized, but also an ecclesiology similar to that of the General Baptists. No hard evidence has been found of anyone outside Keach's church who held to his view of the eldership.

Isaac Watts, who interacted closely and widely with the Particular Baptists, testified to the fact that the vast majority of the Particular Baptists held to Owen's ecclesiology, at least up to the mid-18th century. The departure of many churches to the single-pastor-and-multiple-deacons situation, seen in the 19th century, was due to various factors, of which the influence of Keach's view is one.

※ ※ ※ ※ ※

Six

THE COMMUNION OF CHURCHES

6.1 INTRODUCTION

The Church of England had its monolithic church structure where-by church power was exercised by the hierarchy of clergy fanning down from the top. The Presbyterians had their own version of church hierarchy, consisting of committees of individuals whose power of government fanned down to the individual congregations. The Congregationalists (or paedobaptist Independents) held strongly to the autonomy of the local church, although there was recourse for the redress of injustice, and mutual edification between churches, through the messengers meeting in a "synod" or council. The synod may only give advice, and has no power "to exercise any censures, either over any churches or persons, or to impose their determinations on the churches or officers" (Savoy Platform, 1658: XXVI). The Particular Baptists, who shared a similar form of church government with the Congregationalists, infant baptism excepted, held to the same idea of inter-church fellowship, but avoided the use of the word "synod". Instead, the terms used were "general meeting", "assembly", "meeting", etc. The term "association" did not become popular until after 1689 (Wamble, 1955: 312).

The associational life of the Particular Baptists was, to some degree, affected by the parallel experiences of the General Baptists and the Congregationalists. While much study has been done of the par-

211

allel developments of the Particular Baptists and the General Baptists, including their respective associational lives, much less attention has been given to parallel developments with the Congregationalists. The focus in this chapter will be on the development of the associational life of the Particular Baptists, with passing reference to similar developments among the General Baptists and the Congregationalists.

6.2 CONNECTIONALISM IN THE 17TH CENTURY

The period of concern extends from 1650 to 1750. To facilitate this study, the three periods in the 17th century encountered in Chapters 2 and 3 of the present thesis will be used. These are not arbitrary periods but discernible ones in which the ecclesiology of the Particular Baptists developed. Here, the three periods are recalled, covering the development of the principles of local church autonomy and the headship of Christ, with the additional principle of inter-church connectionalism (or connexionalism):

Period	Autonomy	Christ's Headship	Connectionalism
1640-1660	Baptism w.r.t. church membership	Headship w.r.t. violent radicalism	Beginning of associations
1660-1680	Baptism w.r.t. Lord's Supper	Headship w.r.t. passive radicalism	Consolidation of associations
1680-1700	Baptism w.r.t. covenant of grace	Headship w.r.t. persecution	Failures of national assemblies

6.2.1 The Beginning of Associations (1640-1660)

Wamble (1955) made a study of inter-church relationships of the Baptists in the 17th century, with equal emphases given to the General and the Particular Baptists. He discerned a period of informal fellowship between the churches before 1650, after which formal associations began to be formed. Since the first churches in London were founded in the 1630s, leading to the formalization of Baptist connectionalism in the publication of the 1644 Confession, it seems better to consider the beginning of formal associations from 1640 rather than from 1650.

For ease of reference, the seven churches in London that issued the 1644 Confession are listed:

i The church at Wapping was gathered by John Spilsbury in 1633. Samuel Eaton, one of the ministers, was imprisoned in the mid-1630s during the "Reign of Terror" of Archbishop Laud. Eaton died mysteriously while in prison. The signers of the 1644 Confession for this church were John Spilsbury, George Tipping, and Samuel Richardson.

ii The church at Devonshire Square was gathered by William Kiffin in 1638. Kiffin and Thomas Patient signed the 1644 and the 1646 Confessions, before the latter went to Ireland as a military officer.

iii The church at Crutched Fryars was gathered by Paul Hobson and Thomas Gower (or Goare) in 1639. They signed the 1644 and 1646 Confessions.

iv The church at the Glasshouse was gathered by Thomas Gunne and John Mabbatt between 1640 and 1642. This church sponsored the Thomas Proud and John Myles missions effort in Wales.

v The church at Southwark was gathered by Thomas Skippard and Thomas Munday (or Munden) between 1640 to 1642, arising from the Blunt (or Blount) Mission to the Netherlands (see Chapter 2).

vi The church at Petty France was gathered by Thomas Kilcop and John Webb between 1640 and 1642, also arising from the Blunt Mission.

vii The seventh church was gathered by Joseph Phelpes and Edward Heath between 1640 and 1642, probably also arising from the Blunt mission. Nothing is known of these men or their church, apart from the fact that they signed the 1644 Confession (Lumpkin, 1969: 143-171).

The publication of the Confession in 1644, and its subsequent editions, galvanized the association of the seven churches in London.

White calculated that five of the signatories in 1644 had had experience of the Congregational life that revolved around the Henry Jacob church, and noted that it was from this background in English Independency that Particular Baptist associations grew (White, 1968: 586). The Confession was probably drawn up by John Spilsbury, with the assistance of William Kiffin and Samuel Richardson (Lumpkin, 1969: 146). It has been noted in Chapter 1 that this Confession was revised in 1646, after criticisms by their opponents. Three more editions followed, in 1651, 1652, and 1653, and an edition was also printed in Scotland in 1653 (Underhill, 1854: x; Lumpkin, 1969: 152). Throughout this period, the Particular Baptists were busily planting churches. The Glaziers' Hall church sent John Miles and Thomas Proud to South Wales in 1649. By 1652, five churches had been gathered. The church led by Hanserd Knollys, meeting at Swan Alley, Coleman Street, sent Thomas Tillam to Northumberland in 1651. Within a year, a church was established at Hexham. From this church, others were spawned in Scotland and in Yorkshire. Between 1644 and 1646, Thomas Patient was involved with William Kiffin in an unsuccessful mission to Kent where the converts were taken over by the General Baptists. Patient seemed to have joined the English invasion of Ireland in early 1650. There he played a prominent role in building Baptist congregations. Other Baptists in the army were also establishing congregations wherever they were stationed. Paul Hobson and Thomas Gower founded a closed communion Particular Baptist church at Newcastle, which clashed with Thomas Tillam of Hexham, twenty miles away, who were beginning to be influenced to the open communion view by John Tombes. Hobson and Gower were from the same church in London and had signed the London Confession in 1644 and 1646 (White, 1966). The churches founded in each locality by an individual would naturally share much in common. The informal fellowship between them quickly formalized into regional associations, much in the same way as the seven churches in London were associated.

Several other churches were gathered in London after 1644. The 1652 edition of the Confession was signed by "several churches in or about London". Hanserd Knollys, who signed the 1646 edition of the Confession, gathered the church of sixteen individuals at Broken Wharf which soon grew to nearly a thousand people. This church was to play a prominent role in the gathering of churches during the period of toleration under Oliver Cromwell. Benjamin Cox published

"An appendix to a confession of faith" (1646) in which he explicated the practice of closed communion in contrast to the open communion of the likes of Henry Jessey and John Tombes. Cox explained that a disciple stirred up by the Spirit within to preach the gospel "is a man authorized by Christ". Such a man not only has the right to administer baptism and the Lord's Supper "but may also call upon the churches, and advise them to choose fit men for officers, and may settle such officers so chosen by a church, in places of offices to which they are chosen, by imposition of hands and prayer". A number of men sent out by the London churches were to play key roles not only in gathering churches, but also in organizing them into associations. They included Benjamin Cox, John Miles, Thomas Patient, Thomas Collier, Daniel King and Nathaniel Strange (White, 1966). All these churches held to the principle of closed communion.

Formal associations developed out of the attempt to maintain fellowship and to preserve denominational integrity, in the face of attacks from the Anglicans and the Presbyterians on the one hand, and the radical sectaries on the other. The doctrine of the universal church undergirded their experiment at connectionalism. General Baptists held to the doctrine of the universal church as well, although they did not emphasize it in their confessions. The Particular Baptists emphasized the doctrine of the universal church in the 1644 Confession, stating (Lumpkin, 1969: 168-169):

> And although the particular Congregations be distinct and severall Bodies, every one a compact and knit Citie in it selfe; yet are they all to walk by one and the same Rule, and by all meanes convenient to have counsell and help one of another in all needfull affaires of the Church, as members of one body in the common faith under Christ their onely head.
> 1 Cor. 4.17, & 14.33, 36 & 16.1. Matth. 28.20. 1 Tim. 3.15. & 6.13, 14. Rev. 22.18, 19. Col. 2.6, 19, & 4.16.

This article was taken from the 1596 Confession of the Separatists, but with more proof texts added. The "one and the same Rule" was a reference to the Bible (White, 1968: 583-584).

Because of their belief in the universal church, fellowship between the churches was expressed practically in the formation of associations. The justification for the existence of an association of churches was stated in the records of the first General Meeting of the Abingdon Association held in 1652 (White, 1971-7: Pt. 3: 126):

> ... there is the same relation betwixt the perticular churches each towards other as there is betwixt perticular members of one church. For the churches of Christ doe all make up one body or church in generall under Christ their head as Eph 1.22f; Col 1.24; Eph 5.23ff; 2 Cor 12.13f ... Wherefor we conclude that every church ought to manifest its care over other churches as fellow members of the same body of Christ in generall do rejoice and mourne with them according to the law of theire nere relation in Christ.

This was followed by five practical purposes: (i) to keep each other pure, which cannot be done unless "orderly walking churches be owned orderly and disorderly churches be orderly disowned"; (ii) to show forth the love between churches; (iii) to more efficiently carry out God's work "by a combination of prayers and endeavors"; (iv) to encourage one another when lukewarm, to help when in want, to assist in counsel in doubtful matters, and prevent prejudices against one another; (v) to convince the world that we are the true churches of Christ.

6.2.2   The Consolidation of Associations (1660-1680)

In South Wales, the first General Meeting, held on 6th to 7th November 1650, consisted of three churches. In the sixth General Meeting, held on 30th to 31st August 1654, there were five churches represented (White, 1971-7: Pt. 1: 4, 13). The first General Meeting of the churches in the Midlands was held on 2nd May 1655, which was closely followed by the second General Meeting on 26th June 1655, at which seven churches were represented. The number of churches remained the same in 1657, although messengers from other associations were present at some of the meetings. By the eighth General Meeting, held on 15th to 17th September 1657, the records were already using the word "associations" in reference to such groupings of churches (White, 1971-7: Pt. 1: 20, 33). The churches of the West Country first met on 8th to 9th of the 9th month of 1653. The fourth General Meeting was held on 17th to 19th of the second month of 1655, at which eighteen churches were represented

(White, 1971-7: Pt. 2: 58, 72, 75). In 1653, in the months before the failure of the Barebone's Parliament and the inauguration
of Oliver Cromwell as Lord Protector, the Calvinistic Baptists of Ireland wrote to the churches of London urging a synchronized time of
prayer every first Wednesday of the month. The London churches received this exhortation with favour, believing that it was "to awake to
righteousness, to remember our first love, to rend our hearts and not
our garments and to turne to the Lord with our whole hearts", "to
bring to remembrance all the deadnes, wantonness, unfruitfullnes,
want of love and unsuitablenes of spirit which have to[o] much prevailed". The letter received by the London churches gave details of
ten "churches of Christ in Ireland walking together in the faith and
order of the Gospell" (White, 1971-7: Pt. 2: 110-111, 119). The
first General Meeting of the Abingdon Association met on the 8th
day of the 8th month of 1652 at which three churches were represented. The twenty-third General Meeting met on 19th to 20th of the
4th month of 1660, at which eleven churches were represented, together with Benjamin Cox who represented "the association in Bedfordshire and Hertfordshire etc." (White, 1971-7: Pt. 3: 126, 203).
The word "association" was used at this time. Other regional associations of churches were formed after 1660, not all of which have
extant records. In the period of persecution from 1660 to 1685, few
meetings were held and few written records were left as evidence.

The Northern Association was formed by the work of the London
ministers in the 17th century, and was reconstituted in 1691 after the
1689 Assembly. Records of the Northern Association starting from
1699 to 1732 have been transcribed by S. L. Copson. Representatives
of three churches were meeting together when they were arrested for
complicity in the "Muggleswick Conspiracy" of 1663 (Copson, 1991:
32). Only two churches, namely Newcastle and Derwentwater, sent
messengers to the General Assembly in London in 1689. The General
Assembly that met in London in 1689 was represented by messengers
"for upwards of 100 congregations in England and Wales", while the
one which met in 1692 was represented by 107 churches (Crosby,
Vol. III: 258, 264).

The above data may be presented in tabular form:

The number of churches in each association tended to stabilize after the initial spurt of expansion. In Wales, for example, the number
of churches associated was five in 1654, and six in 1690 (Wamble,
1955: 257). Another example is seen in the Northern Association.

Place	No. of churches	Year
South Wales	5	1654
Midlands	7	1657
West Country	18	1655
Ireland	10	1653
Abingdon	11	1660
Northern England	3	1663
General Assembly	100+	1689
General Assembly	107	1692

The third General Assembly of 1691 listed six churches in the Northern Association (Ivimey, Vol. I: 516). The Association records for the meeting of 10th June 1724 also listed six churches, comprising eleven congregations (Copson, 1991: 19, 119). It is to be remembered that churches tended to consist of multiple congregations at the time. There was no increase in the number of churches.

Of interest to us is the fact that the number of churches in the six known regional associations totals up to 55. Although it is known that existing associations continued to meet, albeit less frequently, during the period of persecution from 1660 to 1685 (Copson, 1991: 4), it is hardly likely that too many new associations were formed in that time. Allowing for the existence of two or three more regional associations whose records are lost, the total number of associated churches could not have added up to the more than 100 churches that met at the first General Assembly in London, or the 107 churches that met at the Assembly of 1692. It would seem that many of those churches represented at the General Assemblies of 1689 to 1692 were not members of any regional associations. There are indications from the extant association records of the existence of churches that were not associated, either because of geographical distance or because they were not convinced of the necessity of associating. At a General Meeting of the Abingdon Association in 1657, a letter was received from the churches in London urging the churches to contribute toward the support of full-time ministers. It was agreed at that meeting that the letter from London should be copied by the respective churches and presented "to the adjacent churches who are not in association with them" (White, 1971-7: Pt. 3: 175). In the same year, the churches of Kensworth, Eversholt, Pirton and Hempsteed requested the Abingdon Association, of which they were members, to allow them to form a separate association. Distance was cited as a reason. The other reason was that there were several churches near them which might join in the new association, which were not willing "for severall considerable reasons, to joyne in the present association" (White, 1971-7: Pt. 3: 180). White noted a number of churches in the Midlands which were not members of the Association (White, 1971-7: Pt. 1: 42). In 1653, "the Church of Christ, usually meeting at Leith and Edingburgh" published an edition of the 1644 Confession (Lumpkin, 1969: 152). Not much is known of the group of churches which sprang up in Scotland among the English garrisons in the early 1600s. They were not represented in the General Assemblies in London.

In addition, there were the open communion churches like those of Henry Jessey, John Tombes and John Bunyan. The letter from the churches in Ireland to those in London, urging closer fellowship and suggesting a monthly day of prayer and fasting, triggered off a similar letter among the open communion churches. In 1653, Henry Jessey of Swan Alley, London, and an unidentified messenger of Great All-hallows visited thirty Independent and Baptist churches in Essex, Suffolk, and Norfolk. In 1655, Jessey visited at least thirteen churches in West Anglia. There is no indication of any associational setup. Instead, these visits had the objective of preserving fellowship and unity through formal correspondence and visitations (Wamble, 1955: 320-321). The open communion Particular Baptist churches tend-ed to interact more with the Congregationalists. A number of them were to be absorbed into their fold, as happened to John Bunyan's congregation in Bedford.

There were also the Fifth Monarchists such as Vavasor Powell, John Simpson, and John Canne who were Calvinistic Baptists of the open communion kind. Vavasor Powell was a radical itinerant evangelist in Wales who was influential in the development of a number of Baptist congregations. He was closely associated with Henry Jessey and was ejected as a licensed Baptist in Wales (Bell, 2000: 172). These churches were all not joined in formal associations. When the more radical elements of Fifth Monarchism died out, the churches continued as unassociated churches. Considered together, the unassociated churches – including those of closed communion conviction, the open communion churches, and the Fifth Monarchists – must have been very numerous, perhaps outnumbering the mainline, closed communion, Particular Baptists, before 1689. This point has not been noted in the literature to date.

It remains for us to briefly consider the Congregationalists, with whom the seven original churches in London had much interaction. The Congregationalists were to develop their idea of connectionalism in tandem with that of the Particular Baptists. A few months before the publication of the 1644 Confession, John Cotton's book "The Keys of the Kingdom of Heaven" appeared in London with a preface from Thomas Goodwin and Philip Nye, two of the five "Dissenting Brethren" at the Westminster Assembly. The book considered "an association or communion of Churches, sending their Elders and Messengers into a Synod" to be an ordinance of Christ. White considered the influence of the Congregationalists upon the connectional life of the Particular Baptists more significant than has been noticed. He critiqued the theory that the origin of the "associations" of the Particular Baptists lay in military associations of the Civil Wars (White, 1968). It has been shown that the Congregational church gathered at Axminster in 1660 practised a definite connectionalism of the kind representative of Independent church polity (Howard, 1976: 259-261). Although not exactly the same as the regional associationalism of the Particular Baptists, they seem to have pursued connectionalism widely (Nuttall, 1957).

The Congregational view on the communion of churches had been expressed in the Savoy Platform of 1658. This was further elaborated by John Owen in his posthumous work, "The True Nature of a Gospel Church and its Government", published in 1689. Owen defined the communion of churches as "their joint actings in the same gospel duties towards God in Christ, with their mutual actings towards each other with respect unto the end of their institution and being, which is the glory of Christ in the edification of the whole catholic church" (Owen, 1976, Vol. 16: 191). Owen warned against churches that operated independently without reference to the welfare of the church catholic, saying (Owen, 1976, Vol. 16: 196):

> No church, therefore, is so independent as that it can always and in all cases observe the duties it owes unto the Lord Christ and the church catholic, by all those powers which it is able to act in itself distinctly, without conjunction with others. And the church that confines its duty unto acts of its own assemblies cuts itself off from the external communion of the church catholic; nor will it be

safe for any man to commit the conduct of his soul to such a church.

As with the Particular Baptists, the doctrine of the universal church is the basis of the communion of churches. This gives expression practically in the local association of churches, which Owen called "synods", at which messengers of the churches meet. The messengers should be elders of the churches, plus other men, if any, who are approved by the churches. Said Owen (1976, Vol. 16: 204-205):

> Of these delegates and messengers of the churches, the elders or officers of them, or some of them at least, ought to be the principal; for there is a peculiar care of *public edification* incumbent on them, which they are to exercise on all just occasions. They are justly presumed to know best the state of their own churches, and to be best able to judge of matters under consideration; and they do better represent the churches from whom they are sent than any private brethren can do, and so receive that respect and reverence which is due to the churches themselves; as also, they are most meet to report and recommend the synodical determinations unto their churches; and a contrary practice would quickly introduce confusion.

> But yet it is not necessary that they alone should be so sent or delegated by the churches, but [they] may have others joined with them, and had so until prelatical usurpation overturned their liberties. So there were others besides Paul and Barnabas sent from Antioch to Jerusalem; and the brethren of that church, whatever is impudently pretended to the contrary, concurred in the decree and the determination there made.
> [Emphasis original.]

It can be seen, thus, a similar theoretical and practical outworking of the communion of churches among the Particular Baptists and the Congregationalists. The parallel development between them in church communion is indicative of closer resemblance in other aspects of their respective ecclesiologies.

6.2.3   The Failure of the National Assemblies (1680-1700)

It has been noted that the London churches drew up their second Confession of Faith in 1677. When toleration came, the Particular Baptists were quick to act. A letter of invitation, signed by leading London ministers including Hanserd Knollys and William Kiffin, was despatched to most of the Particular Baptist churches known to them, to meet in London. The first General Assembly met in September 1689 for ten days. The General Baptists had similarly met in London three months earlier. For the Particular Baptists, this was to be the first of four Assemblies, held each year until 1692. The Assemblies were careful to disclaim "all manner of superiority and superintendence over the churches" while acknowledging "no power to prescribe or impose any thing upon the faith or practice of any of the churches of Christ" (Ivimey, Vol. I: 489). Raymond Brown has noted three characteristics about these Assemblies (Brown, 1986: 37-38). First, they were nominated by London. The London ministers took the initiative to call for the Assembly, the ministerial fund collections agreed upon in the first assembly were to be sent to London, and appointed London ministers were to interview ministerial candidates. While administratively expedient, it created the impression of dominance by a metropolitan elite.

Second, there was preoccupation with ministry. Interaction with the Presbyterians and Congregationalists had led to the awareness of ministerial deficiency among the Particular Baptists. The combined accusation of an untrained ministry and engagement in secular work was a sore point with them. The assemblies were to be preoccupied with the issue of ministerial training for the next few years, such that the hymn-singing controversy of later years had undertones of unhappiness over ministerial authority. Third, the controversy over hymn-singing came to a head in 1691, such that the 1692 Assembly devoted much time to dealing with it. In the Assembly of 1692, it was thought best to divide the churches into two groupings. The official reason given was difficulties arising from distance and funding of travels. In each year, one group would meet in London, the other in Bristol. The London and Bristol assemblies would each send two representatives to each other's meetings. The one in Bristol was to continue actively as "the Western Association", while the one in London ceased to meet because of division among the London ministers caused by the bitter controversy over hymn-singing, which dragged on for ten years.

From the first General Assembly, the theoretical basis underlying the regional associations of churches was applied to the national gatherings. The 1677 Confession was adopted by the over 100 churches represented in the 1689 Assembly, giving rise to its moniker, "the 1689 London Baptist Confession of Faith". The parallel articles of the Savoy Confession had been incorporated as Articles 14 and 15 of Chapter 26 in the 1677 Confession:

> 14. As each *Church*, and all the Members of it are bound to (d) pray continually, for the good and prosperity of all the *Churches* of *Christ*, in all places; and upon all occasions to further it (every one within the bounds of their places, and callings, in the Exercise of their Gifts and Graces) so the *Churches* (when planted by the providence of God so as they may injoy opportunity and advantage for it) ought to hold (e) communion amongst themselves for their peace, increase of love,and [sic.] mutual edification.
> (d) Eph. 6.18. Ps. 122.6. (e) Rom. 16. 1, 2. 3 Joh. 8, 9, 10.

> 15. In cases of difficulties, or differences, either in point of Doctrine, or Administration; wherein either the Churches in general are concerned, or any one Church in their peace, union, and edification; or any member, or members, of any Church are injured, in or by any proceedings in censures not agreeable to truth, and order: it is according to the mind of Christ, that many Churches holding communion together, do by their messengers meet to consider, (f) and give their advice, in or about that matter in difference, to be reported to all the Churches concerned; howbeit these messengers assembled are not entrusted with any Church-power properly so called; or with any jurisdiction over the Churches themselves, to exercise any censures either over any Churches, or Persons: or (g) to impose their determination on the Churches, or Officers.
> (f) Act. 15. 2, 4, 6. & 22, 23.25. (g) 2 Cor. 1.24. 1 Joh. 4.1.

The theoretical basis of connectionalism had worked well for the regional associations founded from the 1650s. London's failure to meet in Assembly after 1692 left the western branch plodding on heroically. However, in 1694 it broke down, partly because of conflicts around the theology of the deceased Thomas Collier and his views on predestination. The twelve associations listed in the 1691 Assembly continued to function into the 18th century and beyond (Ivimey, Vol. I: 514-517). It is likely that many of these associations were organized, or re-organized, as a result of the 1689 General Assembly, as happened to the Northern Association. Whitley has argued that the Calvinistic Baptists were reluctant to organize themselves adequately to face the future after the accession of William and Mary (Whitley, 1923: 174). Copson attributes the collapse of the London Assemblies to the schemes undertaken being too elaborate and beyond the financial and administrative capabilities at that time, although the controversy over hymn-singing was a contributory factor (Copson, 1991: 9). Be that as it may, the attempt to express unity on a national scale had failed dismally.

6.3   ASSOCIATIONALISM IN THE 18TH CENTURY

The final decade of the 17th century was a watershed for Particular Baptists in the nation. The London churches were divided and unable to recover their leading role. The Western Association began to take the lead through the first half of the 18th century.

6.3.1   The Aftermath of the London Assemblies

Wamble sees the extensive project of ministerial aid, education, and itineration undertaken by the 1689 Assembly as manifesting vitality and optimism. However, the project was not completed because of ministerial elevation, strict Calvinism, and general religious indifference. Wamble also sees the amicable division of the General Assembly into two meetings in 1692 as a positive attempt at decentralization. In 1700 the Welsh Association separated from the Western Assembly amicably, again for purposes of efficiency and convenience (Wamble, 1955: 330, 337; Hayden, 2006: 40-41). This contrasted with the General Baptists who became over-centralized, in which the messenger of a regional association of churches had a ministry beyond the local church. It was unanimously held that the local church is superior to any member, including the minister. The Orthodox Creed of 1678, although not representative of the General Baptists, claimed for the association a plenary authority over constituent churches. Practically, however, General Baptists proceeded upon the premise and attempted to enforce "advice", "agreement" and "counsel". When these attempts were seen as abridgments of local church authority, separation was frequently the result (Wamble, 1955: 331-332). These observations by Wamble preempt the assessment, in the closing chapter of this thesis, of the tendencies seen in the ecclesiology of Reformed Baptists today.

What happened to the London churches after the breakup of the Assembly in 1692? In 1704, an attempt was made by thirteen churches to revive the London Assembly, consisting of churches in London and the home counties. However, divisive factors were still present. The inclusion of the Barbican church, which received both Calvinists and Arminians into its fellowship, was deemed unacceptable to some. The inclusion of the Pinners' Hall church, with its Seventh Day convictions, was a stumbling-block to others. Five churches withdrew, and within two or three years this newly revived Assembly ceased to function (Brown, 1986: 40-41).

The failed attempt of the General Assemblies of the late 17th century to provide funding for the training of ministers was not lost upon the London Particular Baptists. In 1717, the Particular Baptist Fund was started to provide educational support for prospective ministers as well as poorly paid men already engaged in pastoral ministry. Benjamin Keach was the driving force behind this fund. One of the beneficiaries of this fund was John Gill, a candidate for the ministry gifted in the classical languages. In January 1723/24, a ministers' fraternal, called the Baptist Board, was formed. Although initially a small group, the Board's influence was to extend far beyond London, as advice was sought from them on various issues. The Board was functioning like an association of churches, except that the meetings were limited to ministers.

As the years rolled on, London's most influential Particular Baptist ministers were to adopt a heightened and intensified form of Calvinism. Two of the most influential men were John Gill (1697-1771) and John Brine (1703-1765). Gill became the successor to the pastorate of Benjamin Keach's church after the death of Benjamin Stinton. Brine became the pastor of the Currier's Hall, Cripplegate, church in 1730. He succeeded John Skepp, whose book

"Divine Energy", published in 1722, sparked off the controversy over high Calvinism. The ministries of John Gill and John Brine, through their voluminous writings, were used to preserve orthodox teaching at a time when rationalism was damaging many churches. Unfortunately, they at the same time encouraged many Particular Baptists into engaging in abstruse debates over high Calvinism. The propriety of inviting the unconverted to trust in Christ was becoming a divisive issue within paedobaptist as well as Particular Baptist circles. White described this period thus (Grell, Israel, & Tyacke: 1991: 325): "It was twilight for the Calvinistic Baptists in a special sense: The heroic age of the persecution was over and instead had come the time of half-hearted institutionalization and internal doctrinal dispute." As noted in Chapter 5, Gill played no small role in the propagation of the single-pastor-and-multiple-deacons system of church government popularly practised among the General Baptists.

6.3.2   The Influence of the Western Baptist Association

The openness of interaction between Dissenters after the Toleration Act of 1689 led to more frequent meetings between General and Particular Baptist leaders. The Western Association had encompassed both General Baptists and Particular Baptists since Thomas Collier abandoned Calvinism in 1674, when he published his "Body of Divinity". Among the thirty-six men who signed to adopt the 1689 Confession at the Assembly in London that year, no fewer than twelve were from the Western Association. The General Assembly of 1689, which was made up largely of closed membership churches, had invited the open communion Broadmead church in Bristol to attend.

Bernard Foskett (1685-1758) succeeded as pastor of the Broadmead church in 1720. Doctrinal tensions had weakened the Western Association, and came to a head in 1719, after the famous Salters' Hall Conference. The Conference had been called to resolve a dispute about Trinitarian belief that had arisen among Presbyterians in Exeter, which attracted the attention of Baptists and Congregationalists. This controversy was to infect some men in the Western Association. The Western Association had no accepted statement of faith. Foskett and his assistant, Hugh Evans, called for the formation of a new Western Baptist Association in 1732. When the new Association was formed the following year, it settled upon the 1689 Confession as the doctrinal basis. Inevitably, the General Baptists were excluded.

This doctrinal stance also directly affected the work of other Associations in the Midlands, Wales, Ireland and the Northern Baptist Association. Once the doctrinal matters were resolved, Foskett turned his attention to the training of an educated Baptist ministry under the provisions of Edward Terrill's bequest at Broadmead. Terrill had been an elder and the church historian who was concerned about the lack of trained ministry among the Particular Baptists. The Bristol Academy started functioning in 1734, with Foskett training the majority of the over seventy students, in equal numbers from Wales and England, in the next twenty-five years (Hayden, 2006: 30-36). The graduates of the Academy were to exert a positive influence upon the Particular Baptists throughout the nation, including London. Not only was the tide of high Calvinism (encouraged by the writings of Gill and Brine) impeded, but also the influence of Benjamin Keach's system of church government. How did this happen?

There were two Baptist churches in Bristol before 1650. The Pithay church, representative of the majority of the Particular Baptist churches of the 17th century, was a closed communion church from the beginning. The Broadmead church evolved from an Independent congregation to being predominantly Baptist in the 1650s. Some members of the church had been with Henry Jessey's open communion church in London as refugees during the Civil War in the 1640s. In 1652 Thomas Munday, perhaps the same person who signed the Confession of 1644, protested against the impropriety of infant baptism. His request to the Broadmead church to join Pithay was finally granted. In 1653 Timothy Cattle desired believer's baptism, but the Broadmead church established the rule that members may receive baptism provided they "keep their places in the church, and not leave their communion". Cattle was sent to London for baptism, at the hands of Henry Jessey. In 1653, the pastor, Mr. Ewins, and the ruling elder, Mr. Purnell, similarly went down to London to be baptized by Jessey. The Broadmead church was now a Baptist church that practised open membership and open communion. The Congregationalists in their midst became a declining minority. Of the last forty-five members received before the membership list was prepared in November 1679, only two were received without believer's baptism (Underhill, 1847: 417-418). In 1757 the Congregationalists formed a small congregation which met elsewhere in the building simultaneously with the Baptists. It became known as the "little church" within the predominantly Baptist church. They united with the Baptists in calling ministers, and relations between the two groups were good (Wamble, 1955: 388). To be noted is the fact that the Broadmead church was moving increasingly closer to the theological and ecclesiological position of the mainstream Particular Baptists. The church was invited to attend the General Assembly of 1689 in London. It had adopted the 1689 Confession, and was now coming to a virtually closed membership position. Bearing in mind the Independent, that is, Congregational, beginning of the church and its practice of open membership, the wisdom and charity in the gradual shift of position are obvious.

Changes were taking place among the mainline Particular Baptists nationwide. Those who organized the nationwide Particular Baptist network of associations in the 1650s were all convinced of closed membership and closed communion. Their strength was increased by Congregational churches becoming Baptist ones. The closed communion of the Congregational churches arose directly from the gathered church principle, which they held in common with the Baptists (Howard, 1976:231-261). Many Congregationalists felt the contradiction between infant baptism and the gathered church principle, for how could the indispensable requisites of holiness, separation, and voluntary consent be asked of infants? It is no wonder that many Congregational churches became Baptist. The churches at Keysoe Brook End, Stevington, and Carlton in the Bedfordshire region all became Baptist at differing times of their history (Tibbutt, 1972). A Presbyterian, Adam Steuart, made the following observation (Friend, 1644:10):

> The Anabaptists here in London, for the most part, agree with the Independents in all things, save only in delaying of Baptisme till the time that the parties to be baptized be of age sufficient to give an account of their faith, and in rebaptizing such as are baptized in all other Churches .... Sundry of the Independents also hold them for very good men, as they declare to the people in their sermons ... Many of them also hold the Anabaptists errors very tolerable, which is the cause so many daily fall away from Independency to Anabaptisme, and that not without just cause. For, if the Independents stand to their owne principles, and hold no men to be members of Christs Church, or visible Christians till they be able to give an account

of their faith and motion of grace that they feele, what neede they to christen those that are not visible Christians?

The flow was not in one direction, for many open communion Particular Baptist churches, because of isolation by the closed communion ones, consorted with the Congregationalists and were ultimately absorbed by them. Reference has been made to Vavasor Powell who founded open communion churches in Wales. Of the twenty churches founded by Powell in the Montgomeryshire area, nineteen became Congregational by 1668. However, despite claims to the contrary, it has been demonstrated conclusively that the open communion churches were in a minority in the 17th century throughout the country, and certainly in Wales (Wamble, 1955: 389; White, 1996: 10-11). Meanwhile, after the serious pamphlet war with the open communionists like John Bunyan, and the friendship forged with Congregationalists and Presbyterians following the periods of persecution, the Particular Baptists were increasingly tolerant of open communion churches while holding tenaciously to closed communion. The 1677 Confession had a long appendix expounding the covenant theology and baptism of the Particular Baptists, which declared that there were "some things wherein we (as well as others) are not at a full accord among our selves" (Appendix, 1677: 137). An example of the "some things" they were not fully agreed about was the degree of fellowship each church had with other non-closed communion churches. Those who issued the Confession "purposely omitted the mention of things of that nature". When the 1677 Confession was adopted by the churches present at the General Assembly of 1689, the Appendix was not included. The Assembly had also invited the open communion Broadmead church to attend. The mainstream Particular Baptists were adopting a more tolerant approach toward peripheral differences while upholding and propagating what they held dear to.

It can be seen that the changes among the Particular Baptists were in two directions. The mainstream closed communion churches were becoming tolerant of differences on issues such as the laying on of hands, congregational hymn-singing, and relationship with open communion churches. The open communion churches, like that at Broadmead, Bristol, were tightening on their theology and ecclesiology by adopting the 1689 Confession of Faith and moving towards

229

closed membership while maintaining open communion. Those that refused to change, like the Bunyan Meeting, were to draw nearer to the Congregationalists and be absorbed by them. The London churches had emphasized a trained ministry in which the learning of Hebrew and Greek was included, while the western churches had emphasized the importance of giftedness by the Holy Spirit in order to be in ministry. Apart from differences in emphasis, the need for a trained ministry was recognized by all after the 1689 General Assembly (Hayden, 2006: 17-18). These changes among the Particular Baptists were significant in view of the fact that the Broadmead church was to wield tremendous influence in the 18th century. The Bristol Academy, which was based in the church, had equal numbers of the students drawn from Wales and England and were trained by Bernard Foskett. By 1757, when the "little church" was gathered separately in the Broadmead church, the graduates of Bristol Academy were going forth throughout the nation leavening the theology and ecclesiology of the Particular Baptists. The Broadmead church, it must be remembered, held to the John Owen view of the eldership.

6.3.3   Associations beyond 1750

The positive influence of Bristol Academy was to extend beyond the mid-1750s. However, high Calvinism was also spreading, while rationalism was affecting many preachers and theologians. The spiritual revival that accompanied the preaching of George Whitefield and the Wesley brothers, John and Charles, were not welcomed by many of the Particular Baptists. Jonathan Edwards had published his account of the revival that was sweeping New England in "A Faithful Narrative of the Surprising Work of God" in 1737. The book was circulated in England by Isaac Watts and John Guyse, but it did not elicit enthusiasm from the Particular Baptists. Not all the Particular Baptists, however, were opposed to the revival. Notable among those who were thankful for the revival were Andrew Gifford (1700-1784), and the graduates of the Bristol Academy. The graduates of the Bristol Academy were known for their devotional hymnology, passion for associating, and evangelistic initiatives which helped to divert many churches from high Calvinism. Following the practice initiated by the Western Baptist Association, the various regional associations were to circulate letters among the churches (Brown, 1986: 71-95). These letters were to become a rich source of information about their associational life.

Older Associations continued to function, and newer ones were formed, beyond 1750. On 14th August 1765, the Midlands Association met at Bourton on the occasion of the opening of the new church building there. Fourteen churches were in the Association, but there was twice the number of ministers present for the occasion (Brooks, 1861: 53). There had been a two-fold increase in the number of churches since 1657, probably as a result of the various satellite congregations becoming autonomous churches. In 1764 a new association of churches was formed in Kettering, calling itself the Northamptonshire Association. The men connected with this association were to be responsible for the formation of the Baptist Missionary Society in 1792, which sent William Carey and others to India (Haykin, 1994). The high Calvinists, on the other hand, became increasingly suspicious of associating, questioning its biblical warrant (Brown, 1986: 92; Oliver, 2006: 312-336). Together with the open communion churches that had not been organized into associations since the 17th century, the number of unassociated churches must have remained high. The 1689 Confession of Faith, however, seemed to be generally accepted by all shades of Particular Baptist churches from after the meeting of the first General Assembly.

General Baptists and Particular Baptists had remained separate in the 17th century. Their difference in origin and soteriology had kept them apart. In the first half of the 18th century, there were still no significant interactions between the two groupings. The General Baptists drifted more and more into Unitarianism, just as a number of Particular Baptists drifted into high Calvinism. There were those among the General Baptists who responded positively to the revival and the evangelistic preaching of George Whitefield and the Wesley brothers. A new grouping of General Baptist churches came into existence in 1770, calling itself the New Connexion. Under the charismatic leadership of Dan Taylor, the New Connexion was drawn into closer interaction with Andrew Fuller and other Particular Baptist preachers. The closing decades of the 18th century saw the rise not only of missionary societies, but also of medical, religious, moral and educational charities, including the Sunday School movement. In the early 19th century, churches of the General and Particular Baptist persuasions were drawn closer together through their common commitment to overseas missions (Brown, 1986: 115-141). The closer interaction between the two denominations would mean the willing and unwitting downplaying of differences and the emphasis of commonalities. Influences would have flowed both ways, but Keach's ecclesiology, which shared closer resemblance to that of the General Baptists, would gain more adherence among the Particular Baptists, what with the influence of theological giants like John Gill. Increasingly, Particular Baptists began to embrace the Congregationalism of the General Baptists, characterized by the single-pastor-and-multiple-deacons system of church officers, and ruling by congregational democracy.

6.4   SUMMARY

Informal fellowship between the Particular Baptist churches in London before 1640 formalized into an organized association with the publication of the 1644 Confession of Faith. The London churches sent out men to plant churches in other parts of the country in the period 1640-1660. The churches that were planted were consciously organized into associations by the men sent out. The word "association" became popular only after 1689, although it was beginning to be used in the 1650s. The associations met in General Meetings at which representatives of the churches were the minister and a member approved by the respective churches. The doctrine of the universal church undergirded the practice of the communion between the churches.

The Associations consolidated during the period 1660-1680. The number of churches in each Association settled quickly, although there were churches known not to have participated. Despite persecution, the churches continued to meet, although less frequently. The open communion Particular Baptist churches did not associate formally, but engaged in loose fellowship involving visitation and exchange of letters. Excluded by the closed communion churches, they interacted more with the Congregationalists. The churches that were formerly Fifth Monarchist were also open communion, and did not engage in formal connectionalism. The total number of unassociated churches must have been large, probably outnumbering the associated ones in the years before 1689.

When Toleration came, the Particular Baptists met in General Assembly once a year in London, from 1689 to 1692. In 1692, it was decided that future Assemblies should split into two – one meeting in London and the other in Bristol. The branch in London failed to meet because of the continuing controversy over congregational hymn-singing among the prominent leaders. The branch meeting in Bristol was faced with doctrinal controversies, which came to a head in 1694. It was reorganized as the Western Baptist Association in 1733, by the initiative of Bernard Foskett. The 1689 Confession was made its doctrinal basis. Foskett, who was based in the open communion Broadmead church, also spearheaded the Bristol Academy, which trained men for the ministry. These men were to be instrumental in impeding the spread of high Calvinism and Keach's ecclesiology, for they were characterized by a lively evangelical Calvinism and held to Owen's view of church government.

Various reasons have been advanced for the dismal failure of the national Assemblies. These included geographical distance, the general poverty of the congregations (1689 Assembly), ministerial elevation, strict Calvinism, and general religious indifference (Wamble), reluctance to organize themselves in view of change in the political climate (Whitley), the enormity of the projects for the time (Copson), ministerial elevation and doctrinal controversies (Brown). However, some good came out of the experiment with national connectionalism. The achievements of the Assemblies included encouraging the unassociated churches to be organized into regional Associations, emphasizing the need for a trained and full-time ministry, deemphasizing differences over church communion while encouraging unity around the fundamental doctrines of the 1689 Confession of Faith. The regional Associations thrived, notably the Western Baptist Association, which was able to implement much of what the General Assemblies failed to do. The unassociated churches, including those of closed communion conviction, the open communion churches, and the Fifth Monarchists, must have been very numerous. The 1689 Confession of Faith, however, came to be generally accepted by all Particular Baptists.

Associationalism continued beyond 1750. Many Particular Baptists at first did not welcome the Evangelical Revival. Others, including the graduates of Bristol Academy, embraced it enthusiastically. The Baptist Missionary Society was formed in 1792 and sent William Carey and his friends to India. The high Calvinists became increasingly suspicious of associating, questioning the biblical warrant for it. At the turn of the century, the New Connexion of General Baptists was interacting more closely with the Particular Baptists because

233

of their common interest in overseas missions. The closer interaction would explain the swing of many Particular Baptist churches to the single-pastor-and-multiple-deacons view of church government in which rule is effected by congregational democracy.

* * * * *

Seven

CONCLUSION

7.1 INTRODUCTION

The spiritual heirs of the Particular Baptists are known generally today as Reformed Baptists. In this last chapter, the issues related to ecclesiology over which the Reformed Baptists are disagreed will be considered. Some recommendations toward resolving these differences, based on the ecclesiology of the Particular Baptists in the 17th and 18th centuries, will then be offered.

7.2 UNSETTLED ISSUES OF THE REFORMED BAPTISTS

In the 1960s there arose a renewed interest in Reformed theology in Britain and North America. This Reformed movement spread worldwide at a time when the charismatic movement was spreading like wild fire. The churches that benefited from the renewed interest in Reformed theology included the Presbyterians and Baptists, as well as churches of other communions. The Reformed books of earlier generations were republished, ministers' conferences were held, and new churches were established. The newer Calvinistic Baptist churches merged with the revived older Baptist churches which had their roots in the 17th and 18th centuries, forging the stream of Reformed Baptist churches that uphold the 1689 Confession of Faith. The Reformed Baptists discovered a closer affinity with the Presbyterians than with the General Baptists, with their shared thankfulness for the Reformation of the 16th century, their common Calvinistic soteriology, and their equal insistence on the Bible as the sole authority in all matters of faith and practice. The desire to be faithful to the Bible inevitably led them to examine their ecclesiology.

7.2.1 Biblicism and Historical Precedence

It is fair to say that Reformed Baptists desire their doctrine and practice to be based on the Bible. There is also the recognition that the Spirit of God has guided men of the past who were equally committed to the principle of *sola scriptura* (Scripture alone). By seeking to understand the Bible with the guidance of the Holy Spirit today, and seeking to know how the Spirit has guided men in the past in the understanding of the Bible, confident conclusions may be drawn concerning the *jus divinum* (divinely ordained) form of church government.

Comprehensive books on ecclesiology written by Calvinistic Baptists are notoriously scarce, if any. Smaller treatises covering church discipline, like Benjamin Keach's "The Glory of a True Church", have been produced through the centuries. Even so, these have become readily available only in recent years (Dever, 2001). Baptists have traditionally relied on the more extensive writings of Congregationalists on church government. Two books written by John Owen that were relied upon by the Particular Baptists of the 17th and 18th centuries have been mentioned, namely, "A Brief Instruction in the Worship of God and Discipline of the Churches of the New Testament" (1667) and "The True Nature of a Gospel Church and its Government" (1689). In the 19th century the Particular Baptists had again to rely on a Congregationalist, Ralph Wardlaw (1779-1853), who wrote "Congregational Independency" (Wardlaw, 1864). C. H. Spurgeon made mention of him (Murray, 1973: 46), and William Williams, professor in the Southern Baptist Theological Seminary, South Carolina, referred to him favourably in his book "Apostolical Church Polity" (Dever, 2001: 535).

Wardlaw's was probably the only significant work in the 19th century expounding Congregationalism since John Owen's post-humous work, "The True Nature of a Gospel Church". However, the positions of the two men were different. Wardlaw denied the validity of ruling elders. While admitting that the evidence for the plurality of elders seems to be strong in the Bible, he nevertheless would accept the situation of one elder as long as the ends of the office are met (Wardlaw, 1864: 218). He accepted the criticism of the Presbyterians that the Congregationalists had been inconsistent in believing in a plurality of elders but lapsing into a single elder situation. How this happened was described by the Presbyterian critic thus (Wardlaw, 1864: 212): "[T]hey think all elders must be teaching elders; and, since the pulpit can be supplied as well by one as by a dozen, and the support of more than one minister is burdensome, or impossible, they content themselves with one such elder for a church, as equal to its necessity." The explanation given by the Presbyterian critic was not countered by Wardlaw, and seemed to find confirmation in the experience of the Baptists.

The Particular Baptists who followed Keach's view of the eldership, in which all pastors are elders and all elders are pastors, found difficulty in maintaining more than one pastor. John Gill, a successor to the pastorate in Keach's church, was opposed to having a co-pastor. If the validity of ruling elders is denied, and a co-pastor is not appointed, what have we but the single-pastor-and-multiple-deacons situation? John Owen, who was a contemporary of Benjamin Keach, although much older in age, had written against the tendency towards the one-elder rule, saying (Owen, 1976, Vol. 16: 113):

> And some there are who begin to maintain that there is no need of any more but *one pastor, bishop, or elder* in a particular church, which hath its rule in itself, other elders for rule being unnecessary. This is a novel opinion, contradictory to the sense and practice of the church in all ages. [Emphasis original.]

The General Baptists had been practising the single-pastor-and-multiple-deacons system from the 17th century. The closer interaction between the two communions from the late 18th century onwards constituted another factor that caused the Particular Baptists to slide into that system. It took the courageous and capable C. H. Spurgeon to restore a plural eldership in his church, in which he was clearly the pastor (Murray, 1973: 75, 77).

It is of interest to note the same phenomenon in America. In 1846 W. B. Johnson who laboured in South Carolina, produced "The Gospel Developed through the Government and Order of the Churches of Jesus Christ", in which "the plurality and equality of elders" is expressed as follows (Dever, 2001: 192): "It is worthy of particular attention, that each church had a plurality of elders, and that although there was a difference in their respective department of service, there was a perfect equality of rank among them." Johnson, however, recognized the difficulty faced by churches in appointing more than one such elder. He proposed that the church prays to the Head of the churches for such men, and that the members must be willing to liberally support them. He then, in effect, justified the single-pastor-and-multiple-deacons situation practised by the churches at that time, saying (Dever, 2001: 194):

> Whilst a plurality of bishops is required for each church, the number is not fixed, for the obvious reason, that circumstances must necessarily determine what that number shall be. In a church where more than one cannot be obtained, that one may be appointed upon the principle, that as soon as another can be procured there shall be a plurality. And when, from the poverty and fewness of the members, it may be impractical for them to afford a support to the ruler or rulers they may have, let the members faithfully do what they can, and let the rulers imitate the example of Paul, who "ministered with his hands to his necessities, and then to them that were with him."

In 1995 the present writer's book "The Keys of the Kingdom" was published, in which the Independent form of church government is expounded on the basis of Scripture, and supported by references to the 1689 and 1644/6 Confessions and to John Owen's writings. The present writer interacts with the writings of the 19th century and 20th century Presbyterian writings, which have been readily available and relied upon heavily by Reformed Baptists who advocate the Absolute Equality view of the eldership. Those who advocate the Absolute Equality view of eldership were quick to engage with the said book (Waldron et al., 1997). Strong feelings were expressed, and misrepresentation of the present writer's position was put forward, probably unintentionally. The present writer had, finally, to respond to their criticism (Poh, 2006). Another attempt to interact with the book came from James Renihan, through his PhD thesis (Renihan, 1998). Renihan takes issue with its heavy reliance on Owen, and attempts to show that the ecclesiology of the Particular Baptists moved away from that of the paedobaptist Independents, despite their historical links. At some points Renihan makes it appear that the present writer argues for "extensive rule" of the elders in the sense that they may go beyond the teaching of Scripture in their work of ruling the church (e.g., Renihan, 1998: 158, 175, 176). Whether this is deliberate or otherwise is hard to say.

The present work is a supplement to "The Keys of the Kingdom", in that it provides historical support from primary sources. As expected, the present writer's research shows that the Particular Baptists did hold to John Owen's system of Independency, infant baptism excepted. In the first place, this expectation was based on the important pointer provided in Isaac Watts's writings, and the fact that the Particular Baptists had their beginnings in the Puritan-Separatist movement, and not directly in Anabaptism. The 1644 Confession was based on the 1596 Confession of the English Separatists in Amsterdam, while the chapter on the church in the 1689 Confession was based on the Savoy Platform of the Congregationalists. The Particular Baptists were no mindless imitators of others. Instead, they modified their confessions to suit their understanding of the teaching of Scripture. B. R. White has shown that the 1644 Confession moved to the left of the Separatist Confession at three vital points: first, baptism was advocated instead of infant baptism; second, the authority of the ministry in the congregation was weakened; third, there was a rejection of any link with the State (White, 1968: 590). J. Briggs has pointed out that the Particular Baptists reverted to an emphasis similar to that of earlier Separatists, namely that ministry was the essence of the church (Briggs, 2004). These differences aside, affinity with English Independency was strong. White calculated that five of the signatories in the 1644 had come from the Independent church of Henry Jacob (White, 1968: 586). It has been noted in the preceding chapters how Congregational churches became Baptist ones, and vice versa, throughout the 17th century, indicating that there was great similarity in church polity between them, apart from the issue of baptism.

Of necessity, the present writer has to interact directly with Renihan's PhD thesis. This has been done to some extent in the earlier chapters, but more needs to be said in the present one. Such work is fraught with the potential risks of being taken personally, of losing friends, and of causing polarization. If taken in the right spirit, it will be seen that such interactions are intended to elucidate truth, to sharpen perceptions, and to edify the church. Renihan's is strictly a historical study based on the Confessional statements, the ecclesiological literature, and the extant church books. His study has not established a clearly defined form of church government. The present study is based similarly on the Confessional statements, the ecclesiological literature, and extant church books, but is aimed at defining the form of church government practised by the Particular Baptists. These two works intersect at two crucial areas which affect the church polity of Reformed Baptists today, namely the nature and constituent members of the eldership, and the manner of executing rule in the church. Apart from the historical affinity between the Particular Baptists and the Congregationalists, the basic meanings of elders "ruling" and the congregation giving "consent" would have alerted one to the great likelihood of the Particular Baptists practising the Independency of the John Owen variety. Renihan, however, was insistent on embarking on the hazardous task of proving otherwise.

7.2.2   The Rulers of the Church

In the book "The Keys of the Kingdom", the three views of the Presbyterians on the eldership, arising from the controversies they have encountered since the days of the Westminster Assembly in 1643, are delineated (Poh, 2000: 139-162). One is the Presbyterian view, in which the minister of the gospel holds an office that is different from the ruling elders. The ruling elders are not strictly "presbyters" in the biblical sense but lay representatives in the presbytery. The second is the Independent view, corresponding to the view of John Owen, in which the minister shares the same office as the ruling elders, but has the priority over the other elders. The third is the Absolute Equality view, in which all elders are pastors and all pastors are elders. This corresponds to Benjamin Keach's view of the eldership. Today, a whole constituency of Reformed Baptist churches in the United States of America, as well as a smattering of churches throughout the world, have come to embrace the Absolute Equality view. This view has been propagated mainly through preaching and the distribution of messages on cassette tapes and, in recent days, on compact discs and via the internet. About the only written work on the subject has come from the pen of Samuel Waldron *et al.*, who produced "In Defense of Parity" (Waldron *et al.*, 1997) as a critique of the book, "The Keys of the Kingdom". It is to be noted that "The

Keys of the Kingdom" was first published in 1995. Since the book "In Defense of Parity" has been responded to in detail in another book "Against Parity" (Poh, 2006), the arguments of both sides will not be reproduced here.

James Renihan has attempted to counter the Independent form of church government that was advocated in "The Keys of the Kingdom", in his PhD thesis (Renihan, 1998). He does so in two ways. In Chapter 3 of his thesis, he deals with the manner of rule practised by the Particular Baptists. In Chapter 4 of his thesis, he attempts to show that "the majority of the writers and churches did not recognize a distinct office of ruling elder", "the majority of the Particular Baptists were committed to a plurality and parity of elders in their churches", and that "there were, however, a few churches that made a distinction between ruling and teaching elders" (Renihan, 1998: 200, 205, 238). A careful scrutiny of Renihan's work will reveal that he makes assertions without proof, draws general conclusions from minimal data, and overlooks or misinterprets other data. In Chapter 4 of the present thesis, it is shown that John Owen's view of the eldership was prevalent among the Particular Baptists. The record of the Bunyan Meeting for 21st October, 1671 includes the following as the first paragraph (Bunyan Meeting: 50-51):

> After much seeking God by prayer, and sober conference formerly had, the Congregation did at this meeting with joyned consent (signifyed by solemne lifting up of their hands) call forth and appoint our bro. John Bunyan to the pastorall office, or eldership; and he accepting thereof, gave up himself to serve Christ, and his church in that charge; And received of the elders the right hand of fellowship, after having preached 15 years. N.B. [S. F]enn the other elder continued in office.

Samuel Fenn was "the other elder" in the church when Bunyan was appointed to the pastoral office. Since Bunyan was the pastor of the church, Fenn must have been a ruling elder. Renihan quotes the subsequent paragraphs of this entry to show that Nehemiah Coxe was one of the seven men chosen on that occasion as a "gifted brother" (Renihan, 1998: 223). Despite being aware of this entry in the Bunyan Meeting, Renihan chooses not to reveal the first paragraph when discussing the rulers of the church, as it would not be to his favour.

Another example is an entry in the Bampton Church Book which Renihan quotes in support of his contention that the majority of the Particular Baptists did not believe in the validity of ruling elders (Renihan, 1998: 203). In 1703, James Murch was ordained as pastor with the assistance of Andrew Gifford and Richard Sampson. After the ordination of Murch and two deacons, it was noted that (Bampton CB: 46):

> Diverse members of the neighbouring Churs being present the ordination of Bro: Frost a ruling Elder being proposed but both Bro: Gifford and Sampson declined it as having noe satisfaction in the thing so that it was concluded to be left as it was.

On the same page of the Church Book was an entry for the previous Lord's Day in which the ordination of the ruling elder was not part of the decision made (Bampton CB: 46):

> After publique worship next thursday being appointed a day of fasting and prayer for the soleim ordination of Pastour and deacons aggreed that the Pastour should be publiquely ordained before the whole assembly [and] the deacons in the Church only.

It was normal in those days for the ordination of church officers to be held considerably later after election into office. Hercules Collins lamented thus (Collins, 1702: 58):

> Be exhorted ever more to maintain, and not lose that blessed Ordinance of Ordination, and calling those to Office who are fit for it: Some have been Probationers all their days; and it is matter of Lamentation, that some Churches have imploy'd Persons in Preaching and administring Ordinances ten or twenty years, tho fitly qualified, and yet never call'd them to Office.

In Chapter 5 of this thesis, it has been suggested that Gifford and Sampson had "noe satisfaction in the thing" because the ordination of the ruling elder was suddenly raised, and not planned – it was "proposed" on the day itself. This is a possible, and perhaps better, explanation for the incident recorded of the following Lord's Day.

Renihan has chosen not to reveal the entry of the previous Lord's Day.

One would like to think that the instances mentioned here, and below, are genuine oversights by Renihan. The necessity of correcting misleading conclusions from historical data is underlined when it is noted that they are easily picked up by others and propagated (Newton, 2005: 26). The misleading conclusions of Renihan seem to have hampered Dever and Newton from explicating the nature of the pastoral ministry in the plural *episkopos, vis-à-vis* the roles of the other elders, more explicitly (Dever, 2004; Dever and Alexander, 2005; Newton, 2005). While it may be argued that the traditional terms "teaching elders" and "ruling elders" of Independency are extra-biblical, it is to be noted that they express the biblical truths embodied in those terms. One is reminded of the term "Trinity" that is widely used in theology. The unambiguous delineation of the nature and roles of the two categories of elders occupying the one office of rule, as found in Independency, is necessary in the face of the aggressive propagation of the Absolute Equality view among Reformed Baptists in recent years. Both views hold to the plurality of elders, sharing the same power and authority of rule, but the two views do not share the same understanding of the nature of the pastoral ministry and the roles of the other elders. The Absolute Equality view is similar to Keach's view of the eldership, in which all pastors are elders, and all elders are pastors. It has the immediate effect of undermining the ministry of the Word, and the long term effect of undermining the office of ruling elders. With the historical precedent of what happened to the Particular Baptists in the 19th century, in which the single-pastor-and-multiple-deacons system prevailed, Reformed Baptists today should be wary of the Absolute Equality view of the eldership.

7.2.3 The Manner of Rule

In the book "The Keys of the Kingdom" the present writer puts forward the view that Congregationalism, as understood today, should be distinguished from Independency (Poh, 2000: 3-31). From the early 17th century, the terms "Congregationalism" and "Independency" were used interchangeably to refer to the same system of church government that stood in contrast to Episcopacy and Presbyterianism. No fourth system of church government was conceived apart from these three. Churches that practised popular democracy were regarded merely as extreme Congregationalists. The Congregationalism of today is actually a descendant of the extreme Congregationalism of the past, which was also known as Brownism (after Robert Brown, 1550-1633). It would have helped everyone, proponents and detractors alike, if four systems of church government had been conceived of from the beginning, namely, Episcopacy, Presbyterianism, Independency, and Congregationalism. The term "Congregational" was used originally to mean that the visible church of Jesus Christ on earth consists of local congregations made up of called-out saints, in contrast to the hierarchical structuralism of Presbyterianism or the national church concept of the Episcopalians. The term "Independent" was used to indicate that the local church is autonomous, with no external authority allowed to interfere with its governance.

That the terms "Congregationalism" and "Independency" were used interchangeably is not difficult to prove. Nuttall has shown that Congregationalism had many weighty advocates who were referred to by Matthias Maurice as follows (Nuttall, 1957: 42):

> In Church Discipline he [Richard Davies] was of the same Judgement with the blessed Hooker, Cotton, Owen, Goodwin, Chauncy, and other eminent and faithful Servants of Christ in the Congregational Way; which the Doctor [Calamy] calls Independency.

Hercules Collins, in his tract "Some Reasons for Separation from the Communion of the Church of England", put these words to the mouth of the Conformist (Collins, 1682: 4):

> I think all the difference between us is, that the Doctors Definitions a little of Independency and Churches Congregational, but we are for a [n]ational one.

That the Baptists were practising Independency, infant baptism excepted, may also be easily proved. In 1644, the Presbyterian, Adam Steuart, made the following observation (Friend, 1644:10):

> The Anabaptists here in London, for the most part, agree with the Independents in all things, save only in delaying of Baptisme till the time that the parties to be baptized

be of age sufficient to give an account of their faith, and in rebaptizing such as are baptized in all other Churches.

In 1645, Hanserd Knollys responded to attacks against the Independents in his book, "A Moderate Answer unto Dr. Bastwicks Book; Called Independencie not God's Ordinance". In 1682 Hercules Collins, in the above-mentioned tract, defended Independency through the mouth of the Nonconformist. The Nonconformist was obviously a Baptist, as indicated in the full title of the tract. Seven times in the tract, the Nonconformist urged the Conformist to refer to John Owen's book, "A Brief Instruction in the Worship of God and Discipline of the Churches of the New Testament", with the relevant pages mentioned. It has been shown, in Chapter 5 of this thesis, that Isaac Watts wrote to his brother Enoch in about 1702 describing the Anabaptists (i.e., the Baptists) thus (Milner, 1845: 186, 193):

> They differ not from Calvinists in their doctrine, unless in the article of infant baptism. They generally deny any children to be in the covenant of grace, and so deny the seal of the covenant to them. They deny baptism by sprinkling to be real and true baptism. In church government [they are] generally Independents.

That there was an extreme variety of Congregationalism may also be easily proved. John Owen described the extreme Congregationalism of his day as follows (Owen, 1976, Vol. 16: 112):

> The government of the church, in the judgment and practice of some, is absolutely *democratical or popular*. They judge that all church power or authority is seated and settled in the community of the brethren, or body of the people; and they look on elders or ministers only as servants of the church, not only materially in the duties they perform, and finally for their edification, serving for the good of the church in the things of the church, but formally also, as acting the authority of the church by a mere delegation. [Emphasis original.]

Isaac Watts, in the same letter referred to above, said (Milner, 1845: 196-197):

> There are some of the Independents heretofore called
> Brownists, some of whom were very irregular in the man-
> agement of church affairs, but they are not to be found
> now: the tenets of rigid Independent are; 1st, That every
> church hath all the power of governing itself in itself, and
> that every thing done in a church must be by the majority
> of the votes of the brethren. 2d, That every church has its
> minister ordained to itself, and that he cannot adminis-
> ter the ordinances to any other people, and if he preaches
> among others it is but as a gifted brother.

Whether the "rigid Independents" are to be equated with the Brownists is hard to say. It would seem that the Brownists, who were not
to be found by that time, were even more "extreme" than the "rigid
Independents". The characteristics of the "rigid Independents" certainty fit the description of those who practised "absolutely demo-
cratical or popular" government in Owen's days. They certainly survived into the 19th century and up to today. They are the modern
Congregationalists, represented by nearly all General Baptist churches
and other free churches, as well as some Particular Baptist ones.
They believe strongly that all the necessary power and authority to
rule has been vested by Christ in the local church. In this, they are
similar to the Independents. However, they insist that the pastor, elders (if any), and deacons are all servants of the church who carry
out what is decided by the congregation through a process of democratic voting. The church members raise issues, discuss the issues,
and arrive at a consensus of opinion by voting. The pastor is only the
facilitator, or chairman of the meeting. If the pastor does not chair
the meeting, it is the "chairman" of the "executive committee" of the
church who does so. Although not all churches that practise Congregationalism today are necessarily unruly, unruliness in the members'
meetings is not unknown (Newton, 2005: 114, 150). Modern Congregationalism, tracing its history back to the "extreme Congregationalism" of the early 17th century, should have been distinguished
from Independency. This unfortunately has not been done.

That only three basic forms of church government have been
countenanced in the literature may be easily shown. Isaac Watts
wrote as follows (Milner, 1845: 195):

> The several opinions about religion are ... in respect
> of discipline and order. The three chief in England at

present are called by the names of Episcopacy, Presbytery, and Independency.

Reference has been made to Ralph Wardlaw, who expounded Congregationalism over against Episcopacy and Presbyterianism. The full title of the book was "Congregational Independency in Contradistinction to Episcopacy and Presbyterianism: the Church Polity of the New Testament" (Wardlaw, 1864). No fourth category of church government was considered.

The concern here is with the manner of rule in the church. In Chapter 4 of this thesis, it is shown that the process of ruling consists of two aspects. The first aspect of exercising rule is the taking of initiatives, the making of decisions, and the putting forth of the proposals to the congregation to get its consent. This is the basic meaning of ruling, which is the inherent duty of elders. Here, the extent of office power is not to be confused and confounded with the manner of executing that power, as has been done by some (e.g., Renihan, 1998, 128-176). The next aspect of ruling is obtaining the consent (or concurrence, or agreement) of the congregation before the execution of any decision pertaining to the welfare of the church. The decisions made by the elders in their meeting together are to be submitted to the meeting of members of the church for its consideration, at which questions and comments are received and handled by the elders, after which agreement is given by a show of hands or some other means. If an insufficient number of votes, as agreed upon in the written constitution or rules of the church, is secured, the decision of the elders cannot be executed as it is not regarded as a decision of the church.

This procedure has been described in detail in the book, "The Keys of the Kingdom" (Poh, 2000: 251-256). Hanserd Knollys alluded to this procedure when he said, "It is not denied by the Brethren [the Independents], that the Presbyters in all Churches were the men in the Government of the Churches in which they are Elders" (Knollys, 1645: 11), while maintaining, at the same time, that the whole congregation has power to judge and admonish in matters of discipline, "the whole church, the multitude ... were present" and approved of the decisions recorded in Acts 15, and "the Brethren" of the church have a right to participate in the admission of members (Knollys, 1645: 7, 13, 16). Renihan tried to make this out as a case of elders making the decisions in some matters, and the congregation

247

making decisions in others, when it is obvious that Knollys was describing "rule by elders, with congregational consent". Knollys was countering Dr. Bastwick's claim that the Scripture proves the admission of members to the church by the authority of the presbyters alone. Said Knollys (1645: 17), "How can the Doctor make good, that 'The Presbyters alone *without the consent of Brethren* may admit members, and cast out members, and that the Brethren or the congregation hath nothing to doe to hinder any such ...". [Emphasis added.]

Renihan continues to nullify Knollys's teaching on "elders rule, with congregational consent" in the latter's book, "The World that Now Is, and The World That is to Come", by a process of misinterpretation. In the first chapter of his book, Knollys explained in detail the doctrine of salvation and the matter and form of the church in a manner consistent with Independency, ending with church discipline which consists of three steps, namely, admonition, suspension, and excommunication (Knollys, 1681: 54). In the next chapter of his book, Knollys covered the "Gospel-Ministry" in which he said (Knollys, 1681: 56):

> The Office of a *Pastor, Bishop,* and *Presbyter,* or *Elder* in the Church of God, is to take the Charge, Oversight, and Care of those Souls which the Lord Jesus Christ hath committed to them, to feed the Flock of God; to watch for their Souls, to Rule, Guide and Govern them (*by virtue of their Commission, and Authority received from Christ, Mat. 28. 18, 19, 20 & Titus 2. 15.*) according to the Laws, Constitutions and Ordinances of the Gospel. [Emphasis original.]

The all-encompassing extent of the elders' authority in the church, obvious in these words, is artificially and wrongly limited by Renihan to the three steps of church discipline in the earlier chapter of Knollys's book, namely, admonition, suspension, and excommunication. Renihan (1998: 145) concludes from this that, "The rule of elders is specifically defined and carried out in certain spheres. It is not an absolute rule, but a limited rule, circumscribed by Christ's command."

That the authority of the elders is circumscribed by Christ's command is not the issue controverted, for Knollys asserted that clearly in the above-quoted passage: "according to the Laws, Constitutions and Ordinances of the Gospel". John Owen said, "The rule and law of the exercise of power in the elders of the church is *the holy Scripture only* [emphasis original]" (Owen, 1976, Vol. 16: 135). The claim that "the rule of elders is specifically defined and carried out in certain spheres" is another matter – one of Renihan's invention. Renihan, in his resolute intent to defend "democratic congregationalism" in which is "a high level of congregational participation in the decision making process" (Renihan, 1998: 160, 270), has confused and confounded the extent over which rule is exercised by the elders with the extent of the elders' power. Owen's view is that the elders' sphere of authority extends to all areas of church life, while the extent of their power is limited to, and by, the teaching of the Bible. Renihan also has confused and confounded the manner by which rule is exercised in the church with the manner by which a decision is arrived at in the church. Owen's view is that the authority to rule is never executed or wielded by the congregation, but by the elders who are the rulers. In the process of executing that rule, decisions have to be made by the elders which are presented to the congregation for discussion, comments and, finally, for its consent or otherwise. The decision of the elders becomes the decision of the church only upon obtaining the latter's consent. In Owen's (and Knollys's) Independency, there is a high level of congregational participation, but not of the kind envisaged by Renihan.

Ample evidence has been provided in Chapter 4 of this thesis to show that the practice of the Particular Baptists was that of John Owen's, in which elders rule, but with congregational consent. Here, it is shown that Renihan has had to engage in misinterpretation and selective use of data in order to make out a case for the limited extent of the elders' authority and the expanded extent of congregational authority. Two examples have been given above with regard to how Renihan handles Knollys's works. Another example is in his handling of Benjamin Keach, whom he quotes selectively to show that one of the limited areas in which the pastor exercises his authority is in the pronouncement of the sentence of excommunication (Renihan, 1998: 152-153). Renihan explains:

> Keach provides further detail with regard to discipline. If the process of reconciliation commanded in Matthew 18 does not produce the desired response, then the church must act. The elder presents the case to the church, and

they deliberate and determine that the offender is "incorrigible" and so must be cast out of the assembly. When
the decision has been reached, [the quote from Keach
follows].

To be noted is that Renihan explains a portion of Keach's writing, and
then quotes the words following. It is of interest to us to consider the
correctness of Renihan's explanation of the unquoted part of Keach's
writing, namely (Dever, 2001: 73):

But if he will not hear them after all due Means and Ad-
monitions used, then it must be brought to the Church;
and if he will not hear the Church, he must be cast out:
The Elder is to put the Question, whether the offending Brother be in their Judgements incorrigible, and refuseth to hear the Church; which passing in the Affirmative by the Vote of the Congregation, or the Majority of
the Brethren by the lifting up of their Hands, or by their
Silence; [the quote from Keach follows].

Does Renihan do justice to this passage from Keach, in his explanation? The Elder is to "put the Question, whether the offending
Brother be in their Judgements incorrigible, and refuseth to hear the
Church". The members do not "deliberate and determine that the
offender is incorrigible", until "the decision has been reached", as
claimed by Renihan. The decision is brought by the Elder to the congregation to consider in their own minds, not to be debated. The
congregation then gives its consent to have the offending brother
excommunicated. Questions might have been asked, and comments
made, which is different from debating the issue and coming to a
decision on the matter through that process.

Another example of the dubious way Renihan garners support
for a limited sphere of the elders' authority, and an expanded sphere
of the congregation's authority, in decision making, is seen in his interpretation of the 1689 Confession. Renihan sees the term "power"
used in a succession of paragraphs in Chapter 26 of the Confession.
In paragraph 4, Christ is said to have received power for the origin, order and government of the church in a supreme and sovereign
fashion. In paragraph 5, Christ expresses His power by calling people to salvation and commanding them to walk together as churches.
Paragraph 6 does not use the word "power" but expresses the convic-

tion that these converted church members are to submit to Christ in the "ordinances of the Gospel". Paragraph 7 shows that each church has been "given all the power and authority, which is in any way needful for their carrying on that order in worship and discipline". Paragraph 8 shows that officers, namely "bishops or elders or deacons", are to be "chosen and set apart" for the "execution of power, or duty, which he entrusts them with, or calls them to". Renihan sees a logical and theological progression in the definition of power described here. Christ has supreme power. The church, as His institution, derives power from Him for worship and discipline. Within the church there are some who hold office, and to them is granted a specific execution of power. There is a diminishing sphere of the exercise of power in these statements. Christ's power is all-encompassing. The church's power, received from Him, extends to its proper functions of worship and discipline. It does not extend to other spheres. The elders' power is "peculiar" or specific in its expression as well.

This writer does not see the "logical and theological progression in the definition of power" that Renihan sees. What he sees is a logical and theological progression in the development of the doctrine of the church. Church power and its expression is only incidental. If it were a primary element, it would be mentioned in all the paragraphs, and there would be no gap in its mention, as in paragraph 6. Paragraphs 4 to 8 of the 1689 Confession are derived from the Savoy Platform of 1658, using mostly identical words (Renihan, 2004). Unless there is explicit indication of departure, the meaning of the 1689 Confession must coincide with that of the Savoy Platform. It has been shown in Chapter 4 of this thesis that even the oft-quoted difference in the continuing officers of the church does not constitute difference in substance, but only in expression. Chapter 26, Paragraph 8 of the 1689 Confession states that the continuing officers are "Bishops or Elders and Deacons", while the corresponding Article IX of the Savoy Platform states that the continuing officers are "Pastors, Teachers, Elders, and Deacons". However, when compared with Article XI of the Savoy Platform, it is found that "the office of pastor, teacher or elder" is one. Furthermore, the word "peculiar" in the 1689 Confession should not be taken as meaning "specific". The Shorter Oxford English Dictionary (Onions, 1968) shows that, from the 15th and 16th century, the word "peculiar" meant "exclusive, particular, or special". It could mean "singular, strange, or odd" but this meaning has to be excluded here due to context. Owen has expounded this in detail in his writings. According to Owen (1976, Vol. 16: 31):

> The rule of the church is, in general, *the exercise of the power or authority of Jesus Christ, given unto it, according unto the laws and directions prescribed by himself, unto its edification.* This power in *actu primo*, or fundamentally, is in the church itself; in *actu secundo*, or its exercise, in them that are especially called thereunto. [Emphasis original.]

At the risk of labouring the point, another quote from Owen is repeated here (16: 42):

> The organizing of a church is the placing or implanting in it those officers which the Lord Jesus Christ hath appointed to act and exercise his authority therein. For the rule and government of the church are the exertion of the authority of Christ in the hands of them unto whom it is committed, that is, the officers of it; not that all officers are called to rule, but that none are called to rule that are not so.
>
> The officers of the church in general are of two sorts, "bishops and deacons," Phil. i. 1; and their work is distributed into "prophecy and ministry," Rom. xii. 6, 7.
>
> The bishops or elders are of two sorts: – 1. Such as have authority to *teach* and administer the sacraments, which is commonly called the *power of order*; and also of *ruling*, which is called a power of jurisdiction, corruptly: and, 2. Some have only *power for rule*; of which sort are some in all the churches in the world.
>
> Those of the first sort are distinguished into *pastors* and *teachers*.
>
> The distinction between the elders themselves is not like that between elders and deacons, which is as unto the whole kind or nature of the office, but only with respect unto work and order, whereof we shall treat distinctly. [Emphasis original.]

Another example of misinterpretation and selective quotation by Renihan may be noted (Renihan, 1998: 156-158). He claims that John Owen "seems to circumscribe the sphere in which elders rule". He supports this claim by quoting at length Owen's explication of the nature of church power and authority, which Owen said is circumscribed "by Christ himself in his word", it is vested in officers from Christ himself "by his word and Spirit, through the ministry of the church", and it is not to be exercised at the pleasure of the officers "in a lordly or despotical manner", but rather their authority is "organical and ministerial only". Here, Renihan has confused the nature of church power and authority with the extent of its exercise. Renihan then makes another claim, namely that Owen argued that the rule of elders "may be reduced to three heads". They are (1) the admission and exclusion of members; (2) the direction of the church, that is, encouragement to mutual love, holiness, and service to others; (3) the conduct of worship, business meetings and other special meetings (Owen, 16: 136-137). Owen, however, was not arguing that the authority of the elders is *limited* to these three areas. Rather, he was delineating the multifaceted work of the elders under the three headings which, in practice, are coextensive with the life of the church. Today, one would use the expression "to summarize" in the same way that Owen used "to reduce". Owen was *summarizing* the work of the rule of elders under three headings. Owen had expounded in the preceding chapters the office of pastors, the office of teachers, and the office of ruling elders. He had expounded on the duties belonging particularly to the pastors and the teachers in the respective chapters, but he did not expound on the duty particular to the ruling elders. Instead, he made it clear that all elders, both the teaching and the ruling ones, share in the responsibility of the whole rule of the church, encompassing the teaching and the ruling: "the whole work of the church, as unto authoritative teaching and rule, is committed unto the elders; for authoritative teaching and ruling is teaching and ruling by virtue of office, and this office whereunto they do belong is that of elders" (Owen, 1976, Vol. 16: 111). The present writer has called this the principle of "the unity of the eldership" (Poh, 2000: 165-181). Owen's intention was to show that there is a category of rulers distinguished from the teaching elders who share in the responsibility of the overall rule of the church. In the chapter following, which is of immediate concern here, Owen began to expound on the rule of the church, shared by both the teaching and ruling elders.

This he explicated, under the three heads wrongly taken by Renihan as a limitation of the scope of rule imposed upon the elders. Owen ended the explication of these three heads by adding that these are in addition to the duty of "the pastoral office, or the duty of teaching elders". To these he added that the ruling elders, apart from sharing with the teaching elders rule in general, which had just been considered under the three heads, have the additional duty "to attend unto all things wherein *the rule or discipline* of the church is concerned". Twelve examples of the work and duty of ruling elders follow. Owen closed the chapter by saying (Owen, 16: 143):

> It is therefore evident, that neither the purity, nor the order, nor the beauty or glory of the churches of Christ, nor the representation of his own majesty and authority in the government of them, can be long preserved without the multiplication of elders in them, according to the proportion of their respective members, for their rule and guidance.

In summary, Owen was pleading for a plurality of elders, consisting of one or more pastors and a number of ruling elders, to rule the church well. The duties of rule are multifarious, and "reduced unto three heads" by Owen for ease of explication. Owen was not limiting the sphere of authority of the elders to less than the locus of the church, nor was he limiting the authority of the elders to less than is allowed by the Bible.

Other examples of misinterpretation are found in Renihan's attempt to prove, from the Church Minute Books, that decisions were arrived at by "unquestionably a form of democratic congregationalism", that there was "a high level of congregational participation in the decision making process", and that "no evidence can be found to support the notion that the elders of the church brought decisions to the churches for their consent" (Renihan, 1998: 160, 170, 174). The meetings of five churches, and an Association of churches (!), are referred to. However, none of these references proved what Renihan claims. The meetings only showed that the members met to consider church business, but did not show the process by which decisions were arrived at. Instead, they supported, and even proved, that "elders rule, with congregational consent". Renihan acknowledges that "Perhaps the most explicit statement of congregationalism is found in the Bagnio/Cripplegate church book", kept by Robert Steed, who was co-pastor and successor to Hanserd Knollys. The manuscript noted that (Bagnio/Cripplegate CMB):

> The church being assembled did unanimously agree that for the better carrying on of the work of God in it. That division might be prevented and peace preserved and purity and love maintained. That ten or twelve Brethren be desired to meet together to prepare matters for this church soe as that no materiall affaire be presented of transacted in the church till they have considered and agreed about it.

This was consented to with these limitations:

> 1. That none of the Brethren be excluded who shall be willing to be with them when they meet & to help in theire consultations.
> 2. That they shall determine nothing but only present their consultations and agreement to the church for their consideration, whose consent shall be the determination of it.
> 3. That when theire time or season of meeting is come any 5 or 7 of them shall be sufficient number to consider of such things as might be presented to them if the rest be absent.

It has been noted in Chapter 4 of this thesis that it was not unusual for churches to have some men meeting with the elders to deliberate over matters meant to be presented to the members' meeting for consent. Knollys's church was a large one, with close to a thousand coming regularly (Tolmie, 1977: 60). Although no elders were mentioned in the meeting of the ten or twelve brethren, is it not reasonable to assume that they were present? Can it possibly be conceived that a meeting of members of the church was convened, to discuss church matters, in which the elders were not present? Unlike Renihan, who draws wrong inferences from silence, one should draw right ones. The "office-bearers' meeting", or the "court of elders", as it might be called today, was made up of 5 or 7 members forming a quorum. Point 2 above should be noted. These brethren were to "present their consultations and agreement to the church for their consideration", meaning that the decision and reasons for it were presented to the members' meeting "for theire consideration". The gathered church did not raise issues, debate the issues they had raised, and make decisions on the issues. Instead, after hearing the issue presented to them, together with the factors taken into account for the decision made, and possibly allowing for questions and comments, the congregation was asked to give its consent. Naturally, the questions and comments would occasionally lead to differences of opinion such that it constituted "debate" of some kind, but certainly not of the kind found in the democratic Congregationalism of today.

Ten years later, this decision was reaffirmed and expanded, including the following points (Bagnio/Cripplegate CMB, 12):

> 5 That no stranger be present when any declare ye dealing of God with their Soules: or any other matter in ye church but members only (unless allowed by ye pastor)
> 6 That all those members yt frequently are absent from their communion wth the church, be carefully and constantly observed, and our Elders acquainted therewith; that they may be visited, & admonished according to rule.
> 9 That in all debates in ye church, there be observed a sober orderly behaviour as becometh saints: and but one speaking at a time.
> 12 That all matters & things that are finally concluded in & by the church, be recorded in the Church Booke.
> 13 That ye power of determining & concluding all matters & things be in & by th Church: The actuall exercise of all power (ministerially) &c. be by ye Elders or those the Church shall appoint, According to ye rule of our Lord and Law-giver Christ Jesus in ye Holy Scriptures.

This entry of the Church Minute Book has been referred to in Chapter 4 of the present thesis. It is pointed out that Knollys's church clearly had a pastor and ruling elders, a point ignored by Renihan. Renihan draws the following conclusions from this entry, which shall be listed consecutively for ease of discussion (Renihan, 1998: 165):

1 For this church, final authority was vested in the gathered congregation.

2 All "matters & things" were to be determined and concluded upon by the church.

3 These conclusions would then be enacted by the elders of the church.

4 The power of the elder is ministerial. He alone has the right to make the pronouncement of the church, but he does so on the basis of the decision of the church.

That final authority was vested in the gathered congregation no one will question. The decision of the elders' court could never be considered the decision of the church unless consented to by the latter. After all, the gathered church has been given

> all that power and authority, which is any way needfull, for their carrying on that order in worship, and discipline, which he [Christ] hath instituted for them to observe; with commands, and rules, for the due and right exerting, and executing of that power" (1689 Confession, Chapter 26, Article 7.)

Renihan begins to go wrong with the second conclusion. He claims that all "matters & things" were to be determined and concluded upon by the church, whereas the entry of the Church Minute Book says, "all matters & things that are *finally* concluded in & by the church" [emphasis added]. The gathered church only made conclusions on the "matters & things" brought to it by the elders' court which, as has been noted, included the twelve chosen brethren. Furthermore, if the "*all* matters & things" [emphasis added] were those initiated or proposed by the gathered church, the elders would have been left with nothing over which they had authority.

Renihan goes farther astray when he claims that the elders then enact the conclusions of the church. The elders are now reduced to being servants of the church when, according to the Independency of John Owen, upheld by Knollys's church, "the actuall exercise of all power" is by the "Elders or those the Church shall appoint". The 1689 Confession states this as follows (Article 8):

> And the Officers appointed by *Christ* to be chosen and set apart by the Church (so called and gathered) for the peculiar Administration of Ordinances, and Execution of Power, or Duty, which he instructs them with, or calls them to, to be continued to the end of the World are Bishops or Elders and Deacons.

Elders are to exercise all power "ministerially", that is, as servants of Christ, or, in service to Christ according to His law. (See Point 13 of the Bagnio/Cripplegate minutes above.) Two related matters need to be clarified, namely, from whom the authority to execute rule in the church is derived, and the meaning of the word "ministerially" as used in execution of the authority to rule. In the English Bible, the words "ministers" or "deacons" (e.g., 2 Cor. 3:6; 6:4; 1 Tim. 3:8, 12) and "ministry" (2 Tim. 4:5, 11) are translated from the Greek words διαχονοσ (diakonos) and διαχονια (diakonia). Since deacons serve in the mundane tasks of the church, and there is constant emphasis in the Bible to do all things for the edification of the church (e.g., 1 Cor. 14:3, 5), it is often assumed wrongly that a minister is one who serves the church. However, the correct meaning is that a minister is a servant of Christ, serving in the church. The execution of the power and authority entrusted to him is "ministerial", that is, in accordance to Christ's law. The Shorter Oxford English Dictionary shows that the word "ministerial" as used in the 16th century, meant "pertaining to, or entrusted with, the execution of the law, or of the commands of a superior". Not a single entry of its meaning in this dictionary includes the idea of service. John Owen, in his explication of the nature of rule in the church, used the word in the same way (Owen, 1976, Vol. 16: 131):

> This authority in the rulers of the church is neither *auto-cratical* or sovereign, nor *nomothetical* or legislative, nor *despotical* or absolute, but *organical* and **ministerial** only. The endless controversies which have sprung out of the mystery of iniquity [a reference to the Roman Catholic Church, cf. 1689 Confession, 26: 4] about an auto-cratical and monarchial government in the church, about power to make laws to bind the consciences of men, yea, to kill and destroy them, with the whole manner of the execution of this power, we are not concerned in. A pre-tence of any such power in the church is destructive of the kingly office of Christ, contrary to express commands of Scripture, and condemned by the apostles ... [Italics original. Emphasis in bold added.]

An earlier passage by Owen actually defines what is meant by the word "ministerial", which is the same as what has been determined from the Shorter Oxford English Dictionary, and which should be taken as the meaning of the word as used in the entry in the Bagnio/Cripplegate Church Minute Book (Owen, 16: 31, 33):

> The rule of the church is, in general, *the exercise of the power or authority of Jesus Christ, given unto it, according unto the laws and directions prescribed by himself, unto its edification.* This power in *actu primo*, or fundamentally, is in the church itself; in *actu secundo*, or its exercise, in them that are especially called thereunto... This is the especial nature and especial end of all power granted by Jesus Christ unto the church, namely, *a ministry unto edification*... Wherefore there is no rule of the church but what is **ministerial, consisting in an *authoritative declaration* and application of the commands and will of Christ unto the souls of men**; wherein those who exercise it are servants unto the church for its edification, for Jesus' sake, 2 Cor. iv. 5.
> [Italics original. Emphasis in bold added.]

Renihan is wrong in drawing the conclusion from the Church Minute Book that the elders' authority is limited to enacting the conclusions of the church. He is wrong in limiting the extent of their authority to the pronouncement of the church, on the basis of the decision of the church. One would have to ask, "Do all church meetings deal with issues that require a pronouncement?" Renihan would like us to think that this pronouncement was in connection with excommunication, as he claimed elsewhere in his thesis, whereas the entry says nothing of excommunication. If it is about the pronouncement of excommunication, as Renihan would like us to believe, which of the elders does it? Renihan conveniently overlooks the plural elders, the twelve appointed brethren, and the pastor referred to in the Church Minute Book.

Renihan's conclusion that "Church government in the Independent ecclesiological system was a carefully balanced interaction between elder rule and congregational democracy" could very well have been used to describe the system of church government delineated in "The Keys of the Kingdom", which is that of John Owen (Renihan, 1998: 175). Renihan's type of Independent system, however, is not that of John Owen. His definitions of "elder rule" and "congregational democracy" are neither Owen's nor the present writer's.

To Renihan, elder rule is limited in application to the pronouncement of the decision of the church in connection with church discipline, specifically in admonition, admission to membership, and exclusion from membership (Renihan, 1998: 145, 152, 153, 154, 156).
Renihan claims that the meetings of the Particular Baptist churches
showed an unquestionable form of democratic congregationalism,
that there was a high level of congregational participation in the
decision-making process, and that they bear greater resemblance to
the Congregationalism of the Brownists than the Independency of
Owen (Renihan, 1998: 160, 170, 174). Renihan is claiming that the
practice of the Particular Baptists of the 17th century resembles the
Congregationalism of today, and not the Independency of the John
Owen variety. How far he has succeeded in making his claim is for
the intelligent reader to judge.

7.3   RECOMMENDATIONS

The study of history gives one the satisfaction of knowing the past,
the ability to better understand the present, and the possibility of
working towards the future. The study of history for its own sake
will not be satisfying to one who claims the reality of the spiritual
realm, for which he lives. Now that the fact has been established
that the Particular Baptists of the 17th and 18th centuries practised
a form of church government similar to what was taught by John
Owen, infant baptism excepted, how should this impact ecclesiological praxis today? There are three areas with which Reformed Baptists
seem unsettled about, which will be addressed in turn.

7.3.1   Clarity on Ecclesiology Needed

The Reformers of the 16th century and their spiritual children held
to the principle of *sola scriptura*, from which arose the Regulative
Principle of Worship, which is expressed in the 1689 Confession as
follows (Chapter 1: 6):

> The whole Councel of God concerning all things (i) nec-
> essary for his own Glory, Mans Salvation, Faith and Life,
> is either expressely set down or necessarily contained in
> the *Holy Scripture*; unto which nothing at any time is to

be added, whether by new Revelation of the *spirit*, or traditions of men.

Nevertheless we acknowledge the (k) inward illumination of the Spirit of God, to be necessary for the saving understanding of such things as are revealed in the Word, and that there are some circumstances concerning the worship of God, and government of the Church common to humane actions and societies; which are to be (l) ordered by the light of nature, and Christian prudence according to the general rules of the Word, which are always to be observed.

(i) 2 Tim. 3. 15, 16, 17; Gal. 1. 8, 9.
(k) John 6. 45; 1 Cor. 2. 9, 10, 11, 12.
(l) 1 Cor. 11. 13, 14; 1 Cor. 14. 26 & 40.

The development of the Regulative Principle from the Reformation onwards, and the problems posed by the *adiaphora* (things indifferent), have been studied by others (Brooks, 2006: 80-98; Murray, 1965; Reisinger & Allen, 2001). By and large, those of the Reformed, Puritan, and Separatist tradition believe that the Scripture teaches a *jus divinum* form of church government. Surprisingly, the Reformed Baptists, who regard themselves as standing in the same tradition, are generally mute in claiming a *jus divinum* form of church government. Uncertainty as to which constitutes the biblical form of church government seems to hold sway, to the extent that one cannot be faulted for suspecting that, among many of them, the latitudinarian attitude described by the Scottish theologian John Dick lies latent (Murray, 1965: 37):

Some have supposed that the government of the Church is ambulatory; by which they mean, that no precise form has been prescribed, and that it is left to the wisdom of men to vary the form according to circumstances; to adapt it to the genius, and habits, and civil constitution of different nations. This is a summary mode of terminating all disputes about the subject.

A consistent stand on *sola scriptura* and the Regulative Principle would require that one believes in the possibility of determining the *jus divinum* form of church government from Scripture. The Particular Baptists had worked hard on this and come to the position of

Baptist Independency, which the Reformed Baptists of today would do well to adopt, and to do so unequivocally. Baptist Independency is different from modern Congregationalism, in which congregational democracy holds sway. In Baptist Independency, the elders are the rulers of the church. Neither the congregation, nor the deacons, share in the authority to rule. The locus of the elders' rule extends to all areas of the life of the church, be it the teaching, the outreach, the finance, the Youth Fellowship, the Women's Fellowship, etc. The elders rule with congregational consent, meaning that the decision of the elders does not become the decision of the church until the latter gives its consent to it. That is the basic meaning of "to rule", προιστημι, *proistemi* (1 Tim. 3:5 and 5:17): to stand before in rank, to preside. That is the basic meaning of "to have the rule", 'ηγεομαι, *hegeomai* (Heb. 13:7, 17): to lead or command with official authority. That is the basic meaning of "to consent", an expression used much in the writings of the Independents, including John Owen and Hanserd Knollys (e.g., Owen, 1976, Vol. 15: 501; Knollys, 1645: 17; 1681: 69). That is the basic meaning of "common suffrage", used in the writings of the Particular Baptists and in the 1689 Confession of Faith (e.g., Coxe, 1681: 6; Knollys, 1681:69; Confession, 1689: 26: 9). The meanings of "to rule" and "to consent" may not be reversed, perverted, or diluted at will.

Baptist Independency rejects the single-pastor-and-multiple-deacons system of rule. It also rejects the Absolute Equality view of the eldership, in which "all pastors are elders, and all elders are pastors". Benjamin Keach was not the father of the Absolute Equality view, for it was encountered earlier among the Presbyterians of the Westminster Assembly. Keach, however, must be regarded as the chief promulgator of this view among the Particular Baptists, for by his book, "The Glory of a True Church", others were influenced, including the influential John Gill, until it became prevalent in the 19th century. By having a plurality of elders who are equal in authority, with no provision made for the priority of the minister of God's Word, the traditional Reformed understanding of the call to the ministry is obviated. John Owen discussed the doctrine of the call to the ministry, which is similar to that taught by William Carr. It consists of two principal aspects: the call from God, and the call from the church. On the call from God, there is the enabling of the Spirit for ministry and the endowment of the necessary gifts to carry out the work of the ministry. On the call from the church, there are two basic steps, namely election and ordination (Owen, 1976, Vol. 16: 49-54; Copson, 1991: 98-101). Hercules Collins similarly spoke of the call of a person to the pastoral office, saying, "Tho it is most true that the Holy Ghost makes Men Overseers of the Church, and that Gifts and Graces are from Christ (which is his internal Call) yet he ought to have an external Call by the Church, to ordain him to Office" (Collins, 1702: 58). Collins further said, "That Unction and Divine Anointing which may make a Person a true Believer, may not be sufficient to make him a Minister. The Holy Ghost ... [needs] to make them Ministers, by a *Divine Power from on high*" (Collins, 1702: 53). [Emphasis original.] By denying the validity of ruling elders, and upholding a high view of the ministry at the same time (Dever, 2001: 87), Keach's view inevitably led to the single pastor situation. With the influence from the General Baptists in the 19th century, congregational democracy was adopted. The system of rule found among Particular Baptists from the 19th century onwards was one of the single-pastor-and-multiple-deacons, practising congregational democracy. Today, any attempt to recover a plurality and equality of elders in the church should ensure that it is of the Baptist Independent type, in which is upheld the priority of the ministry of God's Word, the validity of ruling elders, the unity of the eldership, and rule by elders with congregational consent. Together with the principles of autonomy of the local church and the headship of Christ, the Independency of the Particular Baptists is sufficiently defined. This understanding of Independency has been advanced in the book, "The Keys of the Kingdom", in greater detail (Poh, 2000).

7.3.2   Flexibility in Associationalism Needed

The biblical warrant for, and value of, regional associations of churches have been much debated in recent years (Kingdon, 1993; Renihan, 2001). As more churches are persuaded to associate together, others have become more entrenched in the belief of having only loose fellowship between churches. Strong words are beginning to be used to advocate associationalism: we are not to make the "sophomoric mistake" of understanding how words are used; we must be cautious of "linguistic imperialism"; Independency which believes in the competency of every distinct church to manage, without appeal, its own affairs displays its "most repulsive feature"; a church that is "not accountable to other churches" cannot be regarded as holding to the Confession of Faith and that is reason enough to leave it, etc. (Renihan, 2001: 104, 124, 154). However, to demand accountability of one church to others is to contradict the autonomy of the local church, as expressed in the 1689 Confession of Faith, Chapter 26: 7. A church is complete in Christ, without the need to associate. The communion of churches is not of the essence of church government but, rather, partakes of the nature of fellowship. Expressing frustration towards others in caustic rhetoric for their failure to agree with one on associationalism will only antagonize them. It is an expression of lack of charity towards one's brethren.

In Chapter 6 of this thesis, the achievements and failures of the General Assemblies of churches in the late 17th century are shown. Whatever the achievements had been, the fact was that they failed. Whatever had been the contributory factors, the lessons to be learned are many. The chief lesson must surely be that the theoretical basis for regional associations of churches may not be extended to a higher, or national level. Any attempt to associate on a national scale should be treated with caution. The sheer number of churches of, say, above fifty, in such an association would be too many to handle administratively so that much time, energy, manpower, and finance would be expended, at the expense of the health of the local churches.

It has been shown that the changes among the Particular Baptists after 1689 were in two directions. The mainstream, closed communion, churches were becoming tolerant of differences on issues such as the laying on of hands, congregational hymn-singing, and relationship with open communion churches. The open communion churches, like that at Broadmead, Bristol, were tightening on their theology and ecclesiology by adopting the 1689 Confession of Faith and moving towards closed membership while maintaining open communion. The lesson to learn is that a strong regional association of churches would accomplish much good, as happened with the Western Baptist Association. Strength would be defined by the adoption of a clear doctrinal basis, namely the 1689 Confession of Faith, the exclusion of those who could not comply with the Confession, and the ability to accept differences on lesser matters. Today, the less important matters would be whether a church practises open or closed communion, the version of Bible used, how the Lord's Day is kept, and the like. A group of churches founded by an individual, or by a church, would naturally gravitate together to form an association, the number of which would be modest – seldom more than twenty. A few other churches might request membership with them. The geographical spread of the member churches would be a factor in determining membership. A rules-based association would be necessary in the long run as the number of churches grows and more work is done. The rules should be kept basic, and the number of churches kept optimum to accomplish the ends of mutual help and missions effort.

It has been noted also that many Particular Baptist churches were not associated, both before and after the 1689 General Assembly in London. Not all the churches were convinced of the biblical warrant for structured, or fixed, associations. Today, there are many Reformed Baptist churches that hold to the same view of non-associationalism. It is unfair and untrue to label such churches "isolationist" for they do have fellowship with other churches. Often, just three to five churches in close fellowship, without being in fixed association, have been able to accomplish much in gospel work. Furthermore, with the advent of the internet, the improvement of communications, and the affordability of transportation, such a fellowship of churches need not be limited to a geographical region. Shared interests, personal friendships, and common concerns would bring churches together by interaction through the internet and occasional gatherings of church representatives.

7.3.3 The 1689 Confession and Missions

The 1689 Confession of Faith was accepted by virtually all the Calvinistic Baptist churches after the first General Assembly of churches in London, regardless of whether they were in fixed associations. The Confession of Faith was the strength of the Western Baptist Association, from the time Bernard Foskett introduced it. At the same time, a healthy mission-mindedness was maintained from the early 17th century to the end of the 18th century. The founding of local churches in other parts of the country was extended to Ireland, America, and then to India and beyond. In the early 19th century, the departure of the Particular Baptists in ecclesiology corresponded with their departure from evangelical Calvinism. As high Calvinism was adopted by some, others sought union with the General Baptists. R. W. Oliver observed that (Oliver, 2006: 336):

In all of the attempts to promote union among the churches
from the 1830s onwards, no attempt was made to bring
the churches back to the original basis of Particular Baptist unity as expressed in the *1689 Confession of Faith*.
The various discussions took place as though that *Confession* had never existed.

Around this time, in 1826, a Circular Letter of the Berks West and
London Association was issued, written by John Howard Hinton of
Reading. Hinton recounted the history of the church in Reading, and
claimed that the church in the 17th century operated according to
the congregational democracy of his time, saying (Hinton, 1826):

The constitution of the church was plainly in the strictest sense congregational. The whole authority invested
in the body collectively, without any distinction of one
class of members from another; and to the body was the
executive responsible, as appointed by it. Great freedom,
with some warmth and disorder of discussion, appears
also to have existed.

This was a mere conjecture on his part, as the last sentence above
shows. The entry of the Church Minute Book attached to the Circular
Letter did not show such "Great freedom, with some warmth and
disorder of discussion". This was an anachronism of a hundred years
later. That congregational democracy had set in by Hinton's time is
seen in the later part of the Circular Letter, which says:

Now the congregational system is strictly and essentially
popular. Its first principle is that the interests of the
church are to be promoted, and its duties to be fulfilled,
by the members as a body, and by each member as an
individual. This constitutes its vitality, the best and only
pledge of its stability. Let us beware therefore of a departure from this principle. It is not one that any portion of
church should wish to become dormant on the one hand,
or should suffer to become so on the other.

The Particular Baptists of the 17th and 18th centuries were characterized by a hearty adoption of the 1689 Confession of Faith which
was married to a healthy mission-mindedness. Once the Confession
was disregarded, the two doctrinal extremes of high Calvinism and

Arminianism came in, accompanied by the two practical manifestations of man-centredness – in the local church, as congregational democracy, and outside the church, in ecumenism. While this is not an attempt to paint all who practise congregational democracy with the same brush, especially with reference to the Reformed Baptist brethren, it should be acknowledged that the common understanding of that system of church government is man-centred, as can be seen in Hinton's description above.

The lesson to be learned is clear. Reformed Baptists today must combine a healthy interest in doctrinal purity with a healthy interest in missions. A healthy interest in doctrinal purity is shown by the adoption, and a heart-felt appreciation, of the 1689 Confession of Faith.

7.4 SUMMARY

The aim of this thesis has been to conduct a historical study and evaluation of the form of church government practised by the Particular Baptists of the 17th and 18th centuries, from the years 1650 to 1750. Under the principle of the Autonomy of the local church, it has been shown that the Particular Baptists of the 17th and 18th centuries practised believer's baptism and explicit church membership, and upheld covenant theology. Under the principle of the Headship of Christ, it has been shown that they practised the separation of church and state, upheld the divine right of the magistrate, and also believed in the liberty of conscience. Under the principle of Rule by Elders, it has been shown that the majority of the Particular Baptists practised a plurality of elders in which there was a distinction made between the roles of the pastor or minister and the ruling elders, although they occupy the same basic office of rule. Under the chapter entitled "The Byways", it has been shown how deviation from a plural eldership took place, leading to the single-pastor-and-multiple-deacons situation, accompanied by the disappearance of ruling elders and the practice of congregational democracy in governance. The single-pastor-and-multiple-deacons situation together with congregational democracy are actually characteristics of modern Congregationalism. Under the principle of the Communion of Churches, it has been shown that the regional associations of churches accomplished much good, while a number of issues remained unresolved – including open and closed communion, congregational hymn-singing, the training of ministers, etc. In this final chapter, an attempt is made to resolve the three ecclesiological issues controverted among Reformed Baptists today by applying the lessons learned from the Particular Baptists. First, it is shown that Reformed Baptists must return to, and adopt unequivocally, the Independency practised by the Particular Baptists. Second, Reformed Baptists must adopt a flexible attitude on the practice of the association of churches. Much good can be accomplished by having regional associations of churches, but national associations should be avoided, while those who practise a looser form of fellowship between churches should not be castigated. Third, Reformed Baptists must combine an appreciation of doctrine, shown by adherence to the 1689 Confession of Faith, with a strong mission-mindedness.

To the Particular Baptists, Independency was the divinely ordained form of church government used by God as the vehicle to carry out the Great Commission. The Great Commission was carried out with the view of establishing biblically ordered churches, which upheld the 1689 Confession of Faith. These three components of church life – mission-mindedness, biblical church order, and the 1689 Confession of Faith – arose from the thorough biblicism of the Particular Baptists. Reformed Baptists should work towards a recovery of these, while guarding against inflexibility towards those who differ on associationalism, the Bible versions used, open or closed communion, the manner of keeping the Lord's Day, etc. Let differences in these "lesser matters" be debated without rancour and with the view of drawing one another to closer conformity to the Bible. Comparatively, the recovery of the biblical form of church government seems to be of greater urgency.

Good gospel-order in the church was described by Hanserd Knollys as "a great Beauty and Ornament to the Church" (Knollys, 1681:52). Nehemiah Coxe regarded the order of the church to be for her "Edification and Beauty" (Coxe, 1681: 5). Benjamin Keach said that "The Glory and Beauty of a Congregation, is the most manifest, when the Authority of the Church, and the Dignity of the Pastoral Office is maintained" (Dever, 2001:87). To the Particular Baptists, the orderliness of the church does not exist for its own sake but for service to God. The well-ordered church is not static but dynamic, it is not merely beautiful but also full of vitality. The orderliness and vitality of the church was captured in the 1644 Confession, Article XXXIV

(Lumpkin, 1969: 165-166):

> To this Church he hath made his promises, and given the
> signes of his Covenant, presence, love, blessing, and pro-
> tection: here are the fountains and springs of his heav-
> enly grace continually flowing forth; thither ought all
> men to come, of all estates, that acknowledge him to be
> their Prophet, Priest, and King, to be inrolled amongst
> his household servants, to be under his heavenly conduct
> and government, to lead their lives in his walled sheep-
> fold, and watered garden, to have communion here with
> the Saints, that they may be made to be partakers of their
> inheritance in the Kingdome of God.

The "fountains and springs" and "walled sheep-fold and watered
garden" are derived from Song of Solomon 4:12 & 16, "A garden enclosed *is* my sister, *my* spouse, a spring shut up, a fountain sealed ...
Awake, O north *wind*, and come, O south! Blow upon my garden,
That its spices may flow out. Let my beloved come to his garden and
eat its pleasant fruits." This picture of the church, also expressed as
"a garden enclosed, and a fountain sealed", was commonly used by
the Particular Baptists in the 17th and 18th centuries (Keach, 1974:
333, 335; Brooks, 1861: 19; Hayden, 2006: 33; 217). When high
Calvinism affected the churches, John Gill was to describe the garden enclosed as "so closely surrounded, that it is not to be seen nor
known by the world; and indeed is not accessible to any but believers
in Christ" (Gill, 1810: IV: 662). Such seclusion, of course, was not
intended by the Particular Baptists when they used the picture of the
enclosed garden. While there were those who had forgotten, others had not, "that in the Canticles the invigorating wind would blow
upon the garden so that fragrant spices could 'flow out' " (Brown,
1986: 12).

✳ ✳ ✳ ✳ ✳

BIBLIOGRAPHY

1. Ainsworth, H. 1609. *A Defence of the Holy Scriptures, Worship, and Ministrie, used in the Christian Churches separated from Antichrist: Against the challenges, cavils and contradictions of M. Smyth: in his book intituled The differences of the Churches of the Separation.* Amsterdam: Imprinted by Giles Thorp.

2. *An Appendix.* 1677. In *A Confession of Faith put forth by the Elders and Brethren of many Congregations of Christians, (baptized upon Profession of their Faith) in London and the Country.* Facsimile Edition, 2000. Auburn, MA: B&R Press. 142 pp.

3. Anderson, PJ. 1979. Letters of Henry Jessey and John Tombes to the Churches of New England, 1645. *Baptist Quarterly.* Pp. 30-40.

4. Angus, J. 1895. *Baptist Authors and History, 1527-1800.* As found in Baptist Union of Great Britain and Ireland. 1895. *The Baptist Handbook for 1896.* Montana: Kessinger Publishing. 518 pp.

5. Anonymous. 1642. *A Short History of the Anabaptists of High and Low Germany.* London: Robert Austin, 56 pp.

6. *Bagnio/Cripplegate Church Minute Book 1695-1723.* The Angus Library, Regent's Park College, Oxford.

7. Bagshaw, E. 1671. *The Life and Death of Mr. Vavasor Powell, that Faithful Minister and Confessor of Jesus Christ.* London.

8. *Bampton Church Book 1690-1825.* The Angus Library, Regent's Park College, Oxford.

9. *Baptist History Homepage*: https://baptisthistoryhomepage.com/phila.query.answers.html .

10. Baylor, MG (ed.). 1991. *The Radical Reformation.* Cambridge University Press. 295 pp.

11. Bearman, A. 2005. *The Atlas of Independency: the ideas of John Owen (1616-1683) in the North Atlantic Christian world.* PhD thesis: Kansas State University.

12. Bell, MR. 2000. *Apocalypse How? Baptist Movements during the English Revolution.* Macon, Georgia: Mercer University Press. 299 pp.

13. Belyea, GL. 2007. Origins of the Particular Baptists. *Themelios* 32, No. 3. pp. 40-67.

14. Berkhof, L, 1949. *Systematic Theology.* London: The Banner of Truth Trust. 784 pp.

15. Berkhof, L. 1990. *Principles of Biblical Interpretation.* United States of America: Baker. 176 pp.

16. Birch, T. 1742. 'State Papers, 1653: December (1 of 4)', *A collection of the State Papers of John Thurloe, volume 1: 1638-1653* (1742), pp. 620-629.
    http://www.british-history.ac.uk/report.aspx?compid=55286
    Date accessed: 03 April 2010. John Thurloe (1616-1668) was trained as a lawyer, joined Oliver Cromwell's government as a secretary for state in 1652, and became head of intelligence in 1653. His spies intercepted mail and reported to Cromwell. Thurloe later became chancellor of the University of Glasgow.

17. Blauvelt, MT. 1937. *Oliver Cromwell: A Dictator's Tragedy.* New York: G. P. Putnam's Sons. 325pp.

18. Brand, CO, & Norman, RS (eds.). 2004. *Perspectives on Church Government: Five Views of Church Polity.* Nasville, Tennessee: Broadman & Holman.

19. Briggs, J. March 2004. *The Influence of Calvinism on seven-teenth-century English Baptists.* Baptist History and Heritage.
    http://findarticles.com/p/articles/mi_m0NXG/?tag=
    content;col1.
    Last accessed: February 2012.

20. Broadbent, EH. 1981. *The Pilgrim Church.* London: Pickering & Inglis. 452 pp.

21. Bromsgrove Baptist Church, *Church Record Book, Volume 1 (1670-1715).* Transcribed by Peter Wortley. Available from National Library of Australia.

22. Brooks, J. C. 2006. *Benjamin Keach and the Baptist Singing Controversy: Mediating Scripture, Confessional Heritage, and Christian Unity.* PhD Thesis, Florida State University. 166 pp.

23. Brooks, T. 1861. *Pictures of the Past: The History of the Baptist Church, Bourton-on-the-Water.* London: Judd & Glass. 118 pp.

24. *Broughton Church Book 1 1657-1684.* The Angus Library, Regent's Park College, Oxford.

25. *Broughton Church Book 2 1699-1730.* The Angus Library, Regent's Park College, Oxford.

26. Brown, R. 1986. *The English Baptists of the 18th Century.* London: The Baptist Historical Society. 187 pp.

27. Bunyan, J. 1672. *A Confession of My Faith and A Reason for My Practice in Worship.* London: John Wilkins.

28. Bunyan, J. 1673. *Differences In Judgment About Water Baptism No Bar To Communion.* London: John Wilkins.

29. Bunyan, J. 1685. *Questions About the Nature and Perpetuity of the Seventh-Day-Sabbath. And Proof, that the First Day of the Week is the True Christian-Sabbath.* London: John Wilkins. The page numbering is from The Works of that Eminent Servant of Christ, John Bunyan, Minister of the Gospel, and formerly Pastor of a Congregation at Bedford. Vol. 2. Philadelphia: Clark, LB (1836).

30. Bunyan Meeting. 1928. *The Church Book of Bunyan Meeting, 1650-1821.* London: J. M. Dent. 260 pp. Facsimile of the original folio in the possession of the trustees of Bunyan meeting at Bedford entitled A Booke Containing a Record of the Acts of a Congregation of Christ in and about Bedford and A Brief Account of their first Gathering, with an introduction by G. B. Harrison. London: J. M. Dent. 260 pp. The old style of dating is followed in which 25th March was regarded as New Year's Day. Officially the change to 1st January began in England about the year 1580, but in legal documents and in much of common usage the old form persisted until 1752.

31. Burnet, GV. 1833 (Routh, M. Ed.). *The History of my Own Times.* Six volumes. Oxford: Oxford University Press.

32. Burrage C. 1912. *The Early English Dissenters in the Light of Recent Research (1550-1641).* Cambridge: Cambridge University Press.

33. Campbell, D. 1892. *The Puritans in Holland, England, and America, Vol. 1 of two vols.* New York: Harper & Brothers. 509 pp.

34. Carroll, JM. 1931. *The Trail of Blood.* Lexington, KY: Ashland Avenue Baptist Church. 75 pp. This booklet promotes the Landmarkist view of Baptist origin.

35. Collier, T. 1645. *Certaine Queries: Or Points Now in Controvercy Examined, and answered by Scripture.* London.

36. Collier, T. 1647. *A Discovery of a New Creation.* London.

37. Collier, T. 1658. *The Seventh Day Sabbath Opened and Discovered, As it is Brought Forth, and to Be Observed Now in the Days of the Gospel: And the First Day of the Week, the Time of Publique Worship.* London.

38. Collins, H. 1680. *An Orthodox Catechism: Being the Sum of Christian Religion, Contained in the Law and Gospel.* London.

39. Collins, H. 1682. *Some Reasons for Separation from the Communion of the Church of England.* London: John How. London: John How. 24 pp.

40. Collins, H. 1702. *The Temple Repair'd.* London: William and Joseph Marshal. As available at http://www.mountzion pbc.org/books/HC_The%20Temple%20Repair%27d.htm. Last accessed: February, 2012.

41. Confession, 1646 (First published in 1644). *The Confession of Faith of those Churches which are commonly (though falsly) called Anabaptists.* This Confession was republished in 1646 with slight verbal modifications, and had an Appendix attached, which was written by Benjamin Cox, one of the original signatories. Reference will be made to the 1646 edition throughout, and referred to as the 1646 Confession, unless otherwise indicated. Three more editions followed, in 1651, 1652 and 1652, and an edition was also printed by a small company of Baptists in Scotland in 1653(Underhill, 1854: x; Lumpkin,1969: 152).

42. Confession, 1689 (First published in 1677). *A Confession of Faith put forth by the Elders and Brethren of many Congregations of Christians, (baptized upon Profession of their Faith) in London and the Country.* Facsimile Edition, 2000. Auburn, MA: B&R Press. 142 pp. This was adopted by the 1689 Assembly of Particular Baptist Churches meeting in London, with the Appendix on baptism left out. Reference will be made to the 1677 edition throughout, and referred to as the 1689 Confession, unless otherwise indicated.

43. Copeland, D. 2001. *Benjamin Keach and the Development of Baptist Traditions in Seventeenth-Century England.* New York: Edwin Mellen Press. 204 pp.

44. Copson, SL. 1991. *Association Life of the Particular Baptists of Northern England, 1699-1732.* London: The Baptist Historical Society. 153 pp.

45. Cotton, J. 1644. *The Keys of the Kingdom of Heaven, and Power Therefore According to the Word of God.* London: Matthew Simmons, for Thomas Goodwin & Philip Nye. 75 pp.

46. Cotton, J. 1645. *The Way of the Churches of Christ in New England.* London: Matthew Simmons. 116 pp.

47. Cox, B. 1646. *An Appendix to A Confession of Faith or A more full Declaration of the Faith and Judgment of Baptized Believers.* London. http://victorian.fortunecity.com/dadd/464/appendix.html. Accessed June 2010.

48. Coxe, N. 1677. *Vindiciae Veritatis, or a Confutation of the Heresies and Gross Errours asserted By Thomas Collier in his Additional Word to his Body of Divinity.* London: Nath. Ponder. 136 pp.

49. Coxe, N. 1681. *A Discourse of the Covenants that God made with men before the Law.* As found in Miller, Renihan and Orozo.

50. Coxe, N. 1681. *A Sermon Preached at the Ordination of an Elder and Deacons in a Baptized Congregation in London.* London: Tho. Fabian. 46 pp.

51. Cragg. R. 1957. *Puritanism in the Period of the Great Persecution 1660-1688.* Cambridge: University Press. 325 pp.

52. Cramp, JM. 1868. *Baptists History: Foundation of the Christian Church to the Close of the Eighteenth Century.* London: Elliot Stock. 559 pp.

53. Crosby, T. 1738-1740. *History of the Baptists. 4 vols.* London: Printed for the Editor. 2241 pp.

54. Cross, AR and Wood, NJ (eds.). 2010. *Exploring Baptist Origins.* Nottingham: Regent's Park College. 163 pp.

55. Danvers, H. 1674. *A Treatise of Laying on of Hands with the History Thereof, Both from the Scripture and Antiquity.* London: Francis Smith. 68 pp. Reprinted by BiblioBazaar, 2011. A copy of the second edition to this book, much expanded, was found recently.
http://gaspereaupress.blogspot.com/2010/01/regicide-baby-dunking-finger-pointing.html.
Accessed in April 2011.

56. Declaration. 1659. *A Declaration of several of the people called Anabaptists, in and about the city of London.* London.

57. Dever, M. E. (Ed.) 2001. *Polity: A Collection of Historic Baptist Documents.* United States of America: IX Marks Ministry. 586 pp.

58. Dever, ME. 2004. *Nine Marks of a Healthy Church.* Wheaton, Illinois: Crossway Books. 287 pp.

59. Dever, ME, and Alexander, P. 2005. *The Deliberate Church.* Wheaton, Illinois: Crossway Books. 287 pp.

60. *Devonshire Square Church Members Book 1702-1707* (Ms 20228/1A). The Petty France congregation merged with this church in 1727, meeting at Devonshire Square. London Metro-politan Archives.

61. Deweese, CW. 1990. *Baptist Church Covenants.* Nashville, TN: Broadman Press. 226 pp.
http://www.google.com.my/#hl=en&cp=41&gs_id=7g&xhr=t&q=Charles+deweese %2C+Baptist+church+covenants& pf=p&sclient=psy-ab&source=hp&pbx=1&oq=Charles+ deweese,+Baptist+church+covenants&aq=f&aqi=&aql= &gs_sm=&gs_upl=&bav=on.2,or.r_gc.r_pw.,cf.osb&fp= ef8f522059f100ff&biw=1206&bih=589.

62. Doddridge, P. 1745. *Charge preached at the Ordination of the Rev. Abraham Tozer.* London: Printed and sold by J. Waugh.

63. Du Plooy, A. le R. Undated. *Reformed Church Polity: Essays and Topics.* North-West University, Potchefstroom Campus. 129 pp.

64. Du Plooy, A. le R. 1982. Quoted in p. 50 of Du Plooy, A. le R. Undated. *Reformed Church Polity: Essays and Topics.* North-West University, Potchefstroom Campus. 129 pp.

65. Eccles, J. 1699. *The Funeral Sermon of John Spilsbury Together With His Personal Confession of Faith.* Microfilm No. 204, Reel 44, British Baptist Materials, Historical Commission of the Southern Baptist Convention. This source is reported in Old Faith Baptist Library.
http://victorian.fortunecity.com/dadd/464/funeral.html.
Accessed on 15 June 2010.

66. Edwards, T. 1646. *Gangraena: or a Catalogue and Discovery of many of the Errours, Heresies, Blasphemies and pernicious Practices of the Sectaries of this time, vented and acted in England in these four last years.* Third Edition Enlarged. London: Ralph Smith. 410pp. Edwards was out to discredit those who disagreed with him. His voluminous work should, therefore, be read with this in mind.
http://www.archive.org/stream/gangraena1and200dupeuoft
#page/n5/mode/2up.
Accessed in April, 2011.

67. Estep, WR. 1968. *Anabaptists and the Rise of the English Baptists.* The Quarterly Review 28, No. 4. pp. 43-53.

68. Estep, WR. 1969. *Anabaptists and the Rise of the English Baptists.* The Quarterly Review 29, No. 1. pp. 50-62.

69. Featley, D. 1645. *The Dippers Dipt, or the Anabaptists duck'ed and plung'd over Head and Eares.* London: Nicholas Bourne.

70. Fiddes, PS. 2010. *Church and Sect: Cross-Currents in Early Baptist Life.* See Cross, AR and Wood, NJ. 2010.

71. Firth, CH. 1934. *Oliver Cromwell and the Rule of the Puritans in England.* Elibron Classics 2004: Adamant Media Corp. 584 pp.

72. Fountain, DG. 1874. *Isaac Watts Remembered.* Oxford: Vivian Ridler. 111 pp.

73. Friend to the Coole Conference, 1644. *The Covenanter vindicated from perjurie.* London: T. Paine. 90 pp.

74. George, T. & D. (eds.) 1996. *Baptist Confessions, Covenants, and Catechisms.* Nashville, Tennessee: Broadman & Holman Publishers. 282 pp.

75. Gill, J. 1810. *An Exposition of the Old Testament, Nine volumes.* London: Matthews and Leigh.

76. Goodwin, T, Nye, P, Simpson, S, Burroughes, J, & Bridge, W. 1643. *An Apologicall Narration, Humbly Submitted to the Honourable Houses of Parliament.* London: Robert Dawlman. 31 pp.

77. Grantham, T. 1678. *Christianismus Primitivus: or, the Ancient Christian Religion, in its Nature, Certainty, Excellency, and Beauty, (Internal and External) particularly Considered, Asserted, and Vindicated, from The many Abuses which have Invaded that Sacred Profession, by Humane Innovation, or pretended Revelation.* London: Printed for Francis Smith.

78. Greaves, RL, and Zaller, R (eds.). *Biographical Dictionary of British Radicals in the Seventeenth Century.* 3 vols. Brighton: The Harvester Press. 371 pp.

79. Grell, OP, Israel, JI, & Tyacke, N. 1991. *From Persecution to Toleration. The Glorious Revolution and Religion in England.* Oxford: Clarendon Press. 456 pp.

80. Harris, T. 1987. *London Crowds in the Reign of Charles II: Propaganda and Politics from the Restoration until the Exclusion Crisis.* Cambridge: Cambridge Univeristy Press. 265 pp.

81. Harrison, F. M. 1964. *John Bunyan.* Edinburgh: Banner of Truth Trust. 213 pp.

82. Hayden, R (ed). 1974. *The Records of a Church of Christ in Bristol, 1640-1687.* Bristol: The Bristol Record Society.

83. Hayden, R. 2006. *Continuity and Change. Evangelical Calvinism among eighteenth-century Baptist ministers trained at Bristol Academy, 1690-1791.* Oxford: For the author and the Baptist Historical Society. 273 pp.

84. Haykin, MAG. 1994. *One Heart and One Soul: John Sutcliff of Olney, his friends and his times.* Darlington, England: Evangelical Press. 431 pp.

85. Haykin, MAG. 1996. *Kiffin, Knollys And Keach - Rediscovering Our English Baptist Heritage.* Leeds: Reformation Today Trust. 125 pp.

86. Heatherington, WM. 1853. *History of the Westminster Assembly of Divines.* New York: Robert Carter & Brothers. 311 pp. This is an account of the Westminster Assembly from the perspective of a Presbyterian.

87. Hill, C. 1972. *World Turned Upside Down.* London: Penguin Books. 431 pp.

88. Hinton, JH. 1826. *The Circular Letter from the Ministers and Messenger of the Particular Baptist Churches, Constituting the Berks West and London Association; Assembled at Newbury, September 12 and 13, 1826.* http://baptisthistoryhomepage.com/1826hist_bwlba.html. Last accessed, February 2012.

89. Hiscox, ET. 1978. *The New Directory for Baptist Churches.* Kregel. 598 pp.

90. Howard, K. W. H. 1976. *After the Puritans: The Axminster Ecclesiastica 1660-1698*. Great Britain: Gospel Tidings Publications. 281pp.

91. Hulse, E. 1993. *Our Baptist Heritage*. Leeds: Reformation Today Trust. 117 pp.

92. Humble Petition, 1649. *The Humble Petition and Representation of Several Churches of God in London, Commonly (though Falsly) called Anabaptists*. London.

93. Ivimey, J. 1811-1830. *A History of the English Baptists*. Four volumes. London: For the author, sold by Burditt, Button, Hamilton, Baynes, and Gale and Curtis.

94. Johnson, WB. 1846. *The Gospel Developed through the Government and Order of the Churches of Jesus Christ*. Richmond: H. K. Ellyson. Found in Dever, ME. 2001.

95. Jones, HG. 1869. *Historical Sketch of the Lower Dublin (or Pennepek) Baptist Church*. Morrisania, NY: By Author. 39 pp.
http://www.archive.org/stream/historicalsketch00jone#page/36/mode/2up.
Accessed in June 2010.

96. Jones, HM. 1995. *Transatlantic Brethren: Rev. Samuel Jones (1735-1814) and his friends: Baptists in Wales, Pennsylvania, and beyond*. Cranbury, NJ: Associated University Press, Inc. 373 pp.

97. Katz, DS. 1988. *Sabbath and Sectarianism in Seventeenth-Century England*. Leiden, The Netherlands: Brill, EJ. 224 pp.

98. Kaye, W. 1654. *A Plain Answer to the Eighteen Quaeries of John Whitehead, Commonly called Quaker*. London: Printed for N. E.

99. Keach, B. 1682. *Sion in distress, or The groans of the Protestant church*. London: Printed by George Larkin, for Enoch Prosser.

100. Keach, 1689. *Distressed Sion Relieved, or, The Garment of Praise for the Spirit of Heaviness*. London: Printed for Nath. Crouch.

101. Keach, B. 1689. *Gold Refin'd; Or, Baptism in its Primitive Purity. Proving Baptism in Water an Holy Institution of Jesus Christ, and to continue in the Church to the End of the World*. London: Printed for the Author, and are to be sold by Nathaniel Couch, at the sign of the Bell in the Poultry.

102. Keach, B. 1689. *The Gospel Minister's Maintenance Vindicated*. London: John Harris.

103. Keach, B. 1692. *To All the Baptized Churches and Faithful Brethren in England and Wales*. See Brooks, JC. 2006. Appendix A.

104. Keach, B. 1693. *The Ax Laid to the Root, or, One blow more at the foundation of infant baptism, and church membership.* London: For the author.

105. Keach, B. 1697. *The Glory of a True Church and its Discipline Display'd.* In Dever, ME. 2001.

106. Keach, B. 1974. *Exposition of the Parables in the Bible.* Grand Rapids. Michigan: Kregel Publications. 904 pp.

107. Kevan, EF. 1933. *London's Oldest Baptist Church: Wapping 1663-Walthamstow 1933.* London and Bedford: Kingsgate Press.192 pp.

108. Kiffin, W. 1641. *Epistle to Christian Mans Triall, by John Lilburne.* London.

109. Kiffin, W. 1681. *A Sober Discourse of Right to Church-Communion.* London: George Larkin for Enoch Prosser.

110. *Kiffin Manuscript.* 1641.
http://baptiststudiesonline.com/wp-content/uploads/2007/08/.PDF.
Accessed in March 2011.

111. Kiffin, W, Barrett, G, Steed, R, & Man, E. 1692. *A Serious Answer to a Late Book, Stiled, A Reply to Mr. Robert Stedd's Epistle Concerning Singing.* London: n. p. 64 pp.

112. Kiffin, W, Barrette, G, Steed, R, & Man, E. 1692. *To the Baptized Churches, their Elders, Ministers, and Members.* See Brooks, JC. 2006. Appendix B.

113. King, D. 1656. *A Way to Sion, Sought Out, and Found, for Believers to Walk in, Pts. I & II.* London, Edinburgh: Christopher Higgins.
http://victorian.fortunecity.com/dadd/464/WayToZion.html.
Last accessed, October 2011.

114. King, D. 1656. *A Postscript to my Book, Entitled, A Way to Zion.* Edinburgh: Christopher Higgins.

115. King, D. 1656. *Stumbling Blocks Removed Out of the Way.* Edinburgh.
http://victorian.fortunecity.com/dadd/464/stumbling.html.
Last accessed, October, 2011.

116. King, D. 1656. *Some Beams of Light for the Further Clearing of the Way.* London & Edinburgh: Christopher Higgins.
http://victorian.fortunecity.com/dadd/464/beams.html.
Last accessed, October 2011.

117. Kingdon, D. 1993. *Independency and Interdependency.* In Hulse, E. 1993. *Our Baptist Heritage.* Leeds: Reformation Today Trust. 117 pp.

118. Knollys, H. 1645. *A Moderate Answer unto Dr. Bastwicks Book, Called, Independency not God's Ordinance.* London: Jane Coe.

119. Knollys, H. 1646. *The Shining of a Flaming fire in Zion. Or, A Clear Answer unto 13 Exceptions against the Grounds of New Baptism.* London: Jane Coe. http://victorian.fortunecity.com/dadd/464/shinning.html. Accessed in June 2010.

120. Knollys, H. 1679. *Mystical Babylon Unvailed... Also A call to all the people of God to come out of Babylon.* London.

121. Knollys, H. 1681. *The World that Now is; and the World that is to Come: or the First and Second Coming of Jesus Christ.* London: Tho. Snowden. (a) 104 pp. (b) 48 pp.

122. Knollys, H. 1689. *An Exposition of the Whole Book of Revelation.* London. http://www.mountzionpbc.org/books/HK_Revelation.htm Date accessed: 19 July 2011. Also at: http://www.archive.org/details/expositionrevela 00knoluoft. Date accessed: 1 February, 2012.

123. Knollys, H. 1812. (Written in 1672, published by Kiffin in 1692.) *The Life and Death of that Old Disciple of Jesus Christ, and Eminent Minister of the Gospel, Mr. Hanserd Knollys, who died in the Ninety-third year of His Age.* Together with *Last Legacy to the Church.* London: E. Huntington. 67 pp. http://bereanbibleheritage.org/extraordinary/knollys_ hanserd.php Last accessed: December, 2010.

124. Kreitzer, LJ. 2010. *William Kiffin and His World.* Vol. 1. Oxford: Centre for Baptist History and Heritage Studies. 466 pp.

125. Lovegrove, DW. 2004. *Established Church, Sectarian People: Itinerancy and the Transformation of English Dissent, 1780-1830.* Cambridge: Cambridge University Press. 268 pp.

126. Lumpkin, WJ. ed. 1959, revised 1969. *Baptist Confessions of Faith.* Valley Forge: Judson Press. 444 pp.

127. MacDonald, MD. 1982. *London Calvinistic Baptists 1689-1727: Tensions Within a Dissenting Community under Toleration.* Unpublished D. Phil. Thesis, Regents's Park College, University of Oxford.

128. Manley, KR. 1987. *Origins of the Baptists: The Case for Development from Puritanism-Separatism.* Baptist History and Heritage. 22 Oct. pp. 38-43.

129. *Maze Pond Church Book 1691-1708.* The Angus Library, Regent's Park College, Oxford.

130. McGoldrick, JE. 1994. *Baptist Successionism: A Crucial Question in Baptist History.* Philadelphia: Scarecrow Press. 181 pp.

131. Miller, RD, Renihan, JM, and Orozo, F. (Eds.) 2005. *Covenant Theology From Adam to Christ.* Palmdale, CA: Reformed Academic Press. 376 pp.

132. Milner, T. 1845. *The Life, Times, And Correspondence Of The Rev. Isaac Watts, D.D.* London: Thomas Richardson & Son. 734 pp.

133. Milton, J. 1823. *Paradise Regained.* Chiswick: C. Whittingham. 220 pp. This is the companion volume to *Paradise Lost.* 290 pp.

134. Murray, IH. 1965. *The Reformation of the Church: A Collection of Reformed and Puritan Documents on Church Issues.* Edinburgh: Banner of Truth Trust. 414 pp.

135. Murray, I. 1973. *The Full Harvest 1860-1892: CH Spurgeon Autobiography, Vol. 2.* Edinburgh: The Banner of Truth Trust. 520 pp.

136. Murray, IH. 1983. *Ruling Elders – The Sketch of a Controversy.* The Banner of Truth 235. pp. 1-9.

137. A Narrative of the Proceedings of the General Assembly of Divers Pastors, Messengers and Ministring-Brethren of the Baptized Churches, met together in London, from Septemb. 3. To 12. 1689, from divers parts of England and Wales: Owning the Doctrine of Personal Election, and Final Perseverance. The Angus Library, Regent's Park College, Oxford.

138. A Nararative of the Proceedings of the General Assembly of the Elders and Messengers of the Baptized Churches sent from divers parts of England and Wales, which began in London the 9th of June, and ended the 16th of the same, 1690. The Angus Library, Regent's Park College, Oxford.

139. A Nararative of the Proceedings of the General Assembly of the Elders and Messengers of the Baptized Churches sent from divers parts of England and Wales, which began in London the 2d of June, and ended the 8th of the same, 1691. The Angus Library, Regent's Park College, Oxford.

140. A Narrative of the Proceedings of the General Assembly, Consisting of Elders, Ministers and Messengers, met together in London, from several Parts of England and Wales, on the 17th Day of the 3d Month, 1692, and continued unto the 24th of the same. The Angus Library, Regent's Park College, Oxford.

141. Neal, D. 1755. *The History of the Puritans, or Protestant Nonconformists, From the Death of King Charles I to the Act of Toleration by King William and Queen Mary, in the Year 1689. Vol. IV.* Dublin: Brice Edmond. 548 pp. Neal records the history from the perspective of an Independent.

142. Neal, D. 1822. *The History of the Puritans, or Protestant Nonconformists, From the Reformation in 1517 to the Revolution in 1688. Vol. III.* London: William Baynes and Son. 468 pp.

143. Newton, PA. 2005. *Elders In Congregational Life.* Grand Rapids: Kregel. 175 pp.

144. Nuttall, GF. 1957. *Visible Saints: the Congregational Way, 1640-1660.* Oxford: Basil Blackwell. 178 pp.

145. Oliver, RW. 2006. *History of the English Calvinistic Baptists 1771-1892.* Edinburgh: The Banner of Truth Trust. 410 pp.

146. Onions, CT. (Ed.) 1968. *The Shorter Oxford English Dictionary On Historical Principles*, Third Edition.

147. Owen, J. 1643. *The Duty Of Pastors And People Distinguished.* Works, Vol. 13. Goold, WH (ed), London: Banner of Truth Trust.

148. Owen, J. 1667. *A Brief Instruction In The Worship Of God And Discipline Of The Churches Of The New Testament.* Works, Vol. 15. Goold, WH (ed), London: Banner of Truth Trust.

149. Owen, J. 1669. *Truth and Innocence Vindicated.* Works, Vol. 13. Goold, WH (ed), London: Banner of Truth Trust.

150. Owen, J. 1689. *The True Nature Of A Gospel Church And Its Government.* Works, Vol. 16. Goold, WH (ed.), London: Banner of Truth Trust.

151. Owen, J. 1976. *The Works of John Owen.* 16 volumes. Goold, WH (ed.), London: Banner of Truth Trust.

152. Parratt, JK. 1966-1967. An Early Baptist on the Laying on of Hands. *Baptist Quarterly*, 21, pp. 325-327.

153. Patterson, WM. 1969. *Baptist Successionism: A Critical View.* Valley Forge: Judson Press. 80 pp.

154. Paul, T. 1673. *Some Serious Reflections on the Part of Mr. Bunions.* London: Francis Smith.

155. Payne, EA. 1956. Who were the Baptists? *The Baptist Quarterly* 16. pp. 339-342.

156. *Petty France Church Book (1675-1727)*, London Metropolitan Archives, 40 Northampton Road, London, EC1R 0HB. Formerly housed in the Guildhall Library, London.

157. Piggott, J. 1702. *A Sermon Preached at the Funeral of The Reverend Mr. Hercules Collins, Late Minister of the Gospel.* London: Bell, A. and Baker, J.

158. Piggott, J. 1714. *Eleven Sermons Preach'd Upon Special Occasions.* London: John Darby

159. Poh, BS. 2000 (First published, 1995). *The Keys Of The Kingdom: A Study On The Biblical Form Of Church Government.* Good News Enterprise. 417 pp. This book presents a biblical and comparative study of Independency, as interpreted from the 1689 Confession and the writings of John Owen. It was written before the advent of advanced internet facility so that there was no recourse to the primary sources of the Particular Baptists short of being a residential research student in some institution.

160. Poh, BS. 2006. *Against Parity*. Kuala Lumpur: Good News Enterprise. 74 pp.

161. Ramsbottom, B. A. 1989. *Stranger Than Fiction: The Life of William Kiffin*. United Kingdom: Gospel Standard Trust. 117 pp.

162. *Reading Church Books 1656-1894 (D/N2/1/1/1)*. These are the Kings Road Baptist Church Records, kept at Berkshire Record Office, 9 Coley Avenue, Reading, Berkshire RG1 6AF, United Kingdom. www.berkshirerecordoffice.org.uk

163. Reid, J. 1983 (reprint of 1811 & 1815). *Memoirs Of The Westminster Divines*. Edinburgh: The Banner of Truth Trust. 390 pp. A brief account of each person is given with the aim that "we may learn to be sincerely active, and resolutely passive, for Christ, and for his cause". The Preface also gives a useful account of the historical background of the seventeenth century.

164. Reisinger, EC and Allen, DM. 2001. *Worship: The Regulative Principle and the Biblical Practice of Accommodation*. Cape Coral, Florida: Founders Press.

165. Renihan, JM. 1996. An Examination of the Possible Influence of Menno Simons' "Foundation Book" upon the Particular Baptist Confession of 1644. *American Baptist Quarterly*, 15. No. 3. pp. 190-207.

166. Renihan, JM. 1998. *The Practical Ecclesiology of the English Particular Baptists, 1675-1705: The Doctrine of the Church in the Second London Baptist Confession as Implemented in the Subscribing Churches*. PhD Thesis. Trinity Evangelical Divinity School, Deerfield, Illinois. Ann Arbor: UMI Company. 428 pp. Published as *Edification and Beauty: The Practical Ecclesiology of the English Particular Baptists, 1675-1705*. Wipf & Stock Publishers on January 31 2009, 252 pp.

167. Renihan, JM (Ed.). 2001. *Denominations or Associations? Essays on Reformed Baptist Associations*. Amityville, New York: Calvary Press Publishing. 180 pp.

168. Renihan, M. 2001. *Antipaedobaptism in the Thought of John Tombes*. Auburn, MA: B & R Press. 261 pp.

169. Renihan, JM (Ed.). 2004. *True Confessions: Baptist Documents in the Reformed Family*. Owensboro, KY: RBAP. 291 pp.

170. Richardson, S. 1645. *Some Brief Considerations on Doctor Featley's Book, entitled, The Dipper Dipt*. London. Many writings of the period are available online at
http://baptisthistoryhomepage.com/1.google.books.links.html,
http://www.mountzionpbc.org/index/Articles_books_author.htm, and
http://pbl.oldfaithbaptist.org/.
Copies of the original mss. and microfilms are available from the National Library of Australia and Angus Library, Regent's Park College, Oxford.

171. Riker, DB. 2009. *A Catholic Reformed Theologian: Federalism and Baptism in the Thought of Benjamin Keach, 1640-1704*. Eugene, Oregon: Wipf & Stock Publishers. 257 pp.

172. Robinson, HW. 1922. Robert Steed of Bagnio Court, "Baptist Church Discipline 1689-1699". *Baptist Quarterly* 1.3 (July 1922). pp. 112-128.

173. Smit, CJ. 1985. Quoted in pp. 50-51 of Du Plooy, A. le R. Undated. *Reformed Church Polity: Essays and Topics*. North-West University, Potchefstroom Campus. 129 pp.

174. Spilsbury, J. 1652. *A Treatise Concerning the Lawful Subject of Baptism*. London: Henry Hills.
http://pbl.oldfaithbaptist.org/Ecclesiolog.html.
Accessed in June 2010.

175. Stassen, GH. 1962. Anabaptist Influence in the Origin of the Particular Baptists. *The Mennonite Quarterly Review* 36, No. 4. pp. 322-348.

176. Sutton, K. 1663. *A Christian Woman's Experiences of the glorious working of God's free grace*. Rotterdam: Henry Goddaeus.

177. Taylor, J. 1897. *History of College Street Church, Northampton*. Northampton: Taylor & Son. 178 pp.

178. Taylor, JA. 1641. *A Swarme of Sectaries, and Schismatiques*. Quoted in Bell, p. 61.

179. Tibbutt, H. G. 1972. *Some Early Nonconformist Church Books*. United Kingdom: The Publications of the Bedfordshire Historical Record Society, Vol. 51. 88 pp.

180. Tolmie, M. 1977. *The Triumph of the the Saints: The Separate Churches of London 1616-1649*. Cambridge: Cambridge University Press. 240 pp.

181. Tombes, J. 1641. *Fermentum Phariseorum, or, The Leaven of Pharisaicall Wil-Worship*. London: Richard Cotes.

182. Tombes, J. 1645. *Two Treatises and an Appendix to them Concerning Infant-Baptisme*. London: George Whittington.

183. Tombes, J. 1652. *An Addition to the Apology for the Two Treatises concerning Infant-Baptisme Published December 15, 1645*. London: Hen. Hills.

184. Tombes, J. 1652. *Praecursor: or A Forerunner To a large Review of the Dispute concerning Infant Baptism*. London: H. Hills.

185. Tombes, J. 1659. *Felo de Se. or, Mr. Richard Baxters Self-destroying*. London: Henry Hills.

186. Toon, P. 1971. *God's Statesman: The Life and Work of John Owen*. Exeter: Paternoster. 200 pp.

187. Toon, P. 1973. *Puritans and Calvinism*. Pennsylvania: Reiner Publications. 110 pp.

188. *Tottlebank Church Book 1669-1854*. The Angus Library, Regent's Park College, Oxford.

189. Troeltsch, E. 1931. Reprinted 1992. *The Social Teaching of the Christian Churches. Vols. I & II*. Louisville, Kentucky: Westminster John Knox Press. 1019 pp.

190. Underhill, EB. (Ed.). 1846. *Tracts on Liberty of Conscience*.

191. Underhill, EB. 1847. *The Records of a Church of Christ meeting at Broadmead, Bristol, 1640-1687*. Hanserd Knollys Society. London: J. Haddon. 526 pp. Underhill has been followed instead of a later edition by Hayden, R, 1947, which reproduces the original spelling and punctuations.

192. Underhill, EB. 1854. *Confessions of faith and other public documents illustrative of the history of the Baptist Churches of England in the 17th century*. Hanserd Knollys Society, London: Haddon Brothers & Co. 360 pp.

193. Underwood, AC. 1947. *A History of the English Baptists*. London: The Carey Kingsgate Press Ltd. 286 pp.

194. Vaughn, J. B. 1989. *Public Worship and Practical Theology in the Works of Benjamin Keach (1640-1704)*. PhD thesis. Published in 1990. United Kingdom: University of St. Andrews. 383 pp.

195. Waldron, S. E., Nichols, G. G., Hufstetler, J. A., Chanski, D. J. 1997. *In Defense of Parity: A Presentation of the Parity or Equality of Elders in the New Testament*. Grand Rapids: Truth For Eternity Ministries. 138 pp.

196. Walker, A. 2004. *The Excellent Benjamin Keach*. Ontario: Joshua Press. 423 pp.

197. Walton, RC. 1946. *The Gathered Community*. London: Carey Press. 184 pp.

198. Wamble, GH. 1955. *The Concept and Practice of Christian Fellowship: The Connectional and Inter-denominational Aspects Thereof, Among Seventeenth Century English Baptists*. DTh Thesis. Kentucky: Southern Baptist Theological Seminary. 541 pp.

199. Wardlaw, R. 1864. *Congregational Independency: The Church Polity of the New Testament*. Glasgow: James Maclehose. 354 pp. The Independency advocated in this book and practised by many churches of the time was one in which no ruling elders was countenanced.

200. Williams, W. 1874. *Apostolical Church Polity*. Philadelphia: American Baptist Publications Society. Found in Dever, ME. 2001.

201. White, BR. 1966a. The Organization Of The Particular Baptists, 1644-1660. *Journal of Ecclesiastical History*. Vol. XVII, No. 2.

202. White, BR. 1966b. Who Really Wrote the 'Manuscript'? *Baptist History and Heritage* 1. pp. 3-10.

203. White, BR. 1967. Baptist Beginnings and the Kiffin Manuscript. *Baptist History and Heritage* 2, pp. 29-34.

204. White, BR. 1968a. The Baptists of Reading 1652-1715. *The Baptist Quarterly*, Vol. 22, Issue 5. Baptist Historical Society. London.

205. White, BR. 1968b. The Doctrine Of The Church in the Particular Baptist Confession of 1644. *Journal of Theological Studies*. NS. Vol. XIX, Pt. 2. pp. 570-590.

206. White, BR. 1971. *The English Separatist Tradition: From the Marian Martyrs to the Pilgrim Fathers.* London: Oxford University Press. 179 pp.

207. White, BR (ed). 1971-77. *Association Records of the Particular Baptists of England, Wales and Ireland to 1660.* 3 vols. Index compiled by Howard, KWH. Consecutive pagination. London: The Baptist Historical Society.

208. White, BR. 1982-84. In Greaves, RL, and Zaller, R (eds.). *Biographical Dictionary of British Radicals in the Seventeenth Century.* 3 vols. Brighton: The Harvester Press. 371 pp.

209. White, BR. 1991. *The Twilight of Puritanism in the Years before and after 1688.* In Grell, OP, Israel, J, and Tyacke, N. (eds.), 1991.

210. White, BR. 1996 (revised edition of 1983). *The English Baptist of the 17th Century.* London: Baptist Historical Society. 176 pp.

211. Whitley, WT (Ed). 1915. *The Works of John Smyth, Fellow of Christ's College, 1594-8.* Two vols. Cambridge: Cambridge University Press. 474 pp.

212. Whitley, WT. 1923. *A History of British Baptists.* London: Charles Griffin and Company. 381pp.

213. Whitley, WT. 1924. Continental Anabaptists and Early English Baptists. *The Baptist Quarterly* 2. pp. 24-30.

214. Whittock, MJ. 1985. Baptist Roots: The Use of Models in Tracing Baptist Origins. *Evangelical Quarterly* 57.

215. Williams, W. 1874. *Apostolical Church Polity.* Philadelphia: American Baptist Publications Society. Found in Dever, ME. 2001.

216. Wolfe, D. (Ed.) 1944. *Leveller Manifestoes.* New York: Nelson and Sons. 440 pp.

217. Wood, A & Bliss, P (ed.). 1967. *Athenae oxonienses, an exact history of all the writers and bishops who have had their education in the University of Oxford; to which are added the Fasti; or, Annals of the said university.* New York: Johnson Reprint Corp. 519 pp.

218. Woodhouse, ASP. 1938. *Puritanism and Liberty.* London: Dent, JM, and Sons Limited. 506 pp.

219. Wortley, P. (Transcriber) 1974. *Bromsgrove Baptist Church: Church Record Book Volume One 1670-1715*. London: The Baptist Historical Society.

220. Wright, S. 2006. *The Early English Baptists, 1603-49*. Suffolk: Boydell Press. 288 pp.

SUBJECT INDEX

NAME INDEX

www.ingramcontent.com/pod-product-compliance
Lightning Source LLC
Chambersburg PA
CBHW062149080426
42734CB00010B/1624